PATTERNS IN POLITICS

READINGS IN AMERICAN GOVERNMENT

EDITED BY PETER W. WIELHOUWER

WESTERN MICHIGAN UNIVERSITY

cognella™

San Diego, CA

Bassim Hamadeh, CEO and Publisher
Christopher Foster, General Vice President
Michael Simpson, Vice President of Acquisitions
Jessica Knott, Managing Editor
Kevin Fahey, Cognella Marketing Manager
Jess Busch, Senior Graphic Designer
Jamie Giganti, Project Editor
Luiz Ferreira, Licensing Associate

First published in the United States of America in 2013 by Cognella, Inc.

Trademark Notice: Product or corporate names may be trademarks or registered trademarks, and are used only for identification and explanation without intent to infringe.

Printed in the United States of America

ISBN: 978-1-60927-177-0 (pbk)/ 978-1-60927-424-5 (br)

www.cognella.com   800.200.3908

Contents

POLITICAL CULTURE

CIVIL LIBERTIES

CIVIL RIGHTS

PUBLIC OPINION

POLITICAL PARTICIPATION

POLITICAL PARTIES

ELECTIONS & CAMPAIGNS

INTEREST GROUPS

THE MEDIA

CONGRESS

THE PRESIDENCY

THE JUDICIARY

PUBLIC POLICY

Purpose

The purpose of this reading is to introduce you to questions of "Human Governance."

Context

These questions relate to the kinds of human behaviors that society wants to be managed, and who in society should manage those behaviors. As you read this article, consider the kinds of "bad" behaviors of other people you want controlled or managed. This might range from rambunctious children in restaurants, property crimes, conflicts between neighbors or church members. What kinds of institutions in society ought to be the key players in managing and resolving these problems?

Thought Exercises

1. The article suggests that there is a difference between 'government' as a noun and 'government' as a verb. Do you find this distinction helpful?
2. What kinds behaviors are best managed by individuals, managed by families, managed by social groups, and which are best managed by civil governments?
3. While some people may be tempted to assign to the government the responsibility for most problems, to do so runs the risk of infringing on people's liberty. What do you think is the minimum level of government needed in a society? At what point does the government become too dominating?

1. Human Governance

By Dr. Peter W. Wielhouwer

I. What is Government?
- "Government" has two meanings; as a verb, it refers to the exercise of power to manage human behavior (it's similar to 'influence'); as a noun, it refers to an organization or agency authorized to exercise that power over some group of people.

What is governance?
- "Governance" is related to the verb form of the word government. Governance is the general process by which human behavior (individual or collective) is controlled or managed.
- Thus, when parents train their children about what behaviors are acceptable or unacceptable, they are exercising governance over their family. When you decide whether to work out in a gym, you are exercising governance over yourself. When a professor requires certain readings for a course, he or she is exercising governance over the class's students. When a government requires or proscribes certain behaviors (such as paying taxes or limiting the speed at which citizens can drive) it is exercising governance.
- Governance is inherent in the nature of humanity. In order to coexist (that is, to live together as a community and resolve the inevitable social conflicts that result from that coexistence), governance occurs at a wide range of levels in society, occurs in every society, and always has.

II. What is "legitimate authority"?
- A core question about governance is *Who has legitimate authority to exercise governance over whom?*
  - Legitimate is the idea of something that is rightful or lawful, while authority is the idea of legal power.
- So, **legitimate authority** is the rightful or lawful power to govern (ie, manage others' behavior). Legitimate authority comes from different places, depending on one's worldview.
  - It may be inherent in the nature of the relationship (eg, parents raising children)
  - It may be delegated by one party to another, (eg, when parents delegate the authority for providing education to the public schools)
  - It may be awarded (such as when a candidate wins an election, and gets to make laws for the community)
  - It may be assigned (such as when a constitution assigns law-making and law-executing authority to a legislature and a chief executive)

III. How does Governance occur?

- There are several questions that must be addressed when thinking about the problems of human governance.
- What human behaviors need to be controlled?
- What methods can be used to control behavior?
- What actors, entities, organizations or agencies have legitimate authority to manage behavior? And which groups will they have authority over?

IV. Institutions in every society exercise governance. … What are those institutions?

- Table 1 summarizes those kinds of institutions (understand, however, that what these look like specifically varies widely across societies).
- It's also helpful to observe that these institutions frequently come into conflict over the scope of their legitimate authority, and over which institutions/actors/agencies have primary authority over which people and behaviors. Such as …
  - Individual vs. Family
    » Must the children in a family obey the parents' rules? Do the parents' rules apply once a child is a legal "adult"?
  - Family vs. Civil government
    » Do parents retain the right to exercise choice and control over directing the education of their children? Do they retain the right to exercise corporal punishment, such as spanking? Who is best positioned to understand a child and determine what is in a child's best interest?
  - Civil government vs. Churches
    » Do governments exercise taxation power over church organizations? Are churches and church leaders permitted to publicly oppose government policies or endorse candidates for public office?
  - Local governments vs national governments vs international law
    » Should international governmental organizations dictate domestic policies to local governments? Which level of government shall have the power to determine which policies are selected and enacted (such as national defense, educational content, and traffic laws)?
- Political scientists are sometimes accused of being the "high priests of government" because we seem to focus on the role of civil governments as the sole means of managing governance problems.
  - It is important to realize that it is not the case that the civil government is necessarily the only or best institution to manage every kind of human behavior. While the civil government has very broad authority over very large groups and very broad swaths of behaviors, we ought to be cautious about the idea that the civil government is always the best, most appropriate institution for any given problem.
  - Because of the intimate character of human relationships, and because institutions closer to particular problems may have a more accurate understanding of situations, those institutions are often better situated to address the situations. Moreover, the application of the force of government (its primary method of enforcing behavior about rules) must always be balanced against the importance of individual liberty.
  - For example, when it comes to training children about what is acceptable behavior, as a father I would suggest that I am better equipped, by virtue of consanguinity and proximity, to make the most important decisions in that area than is an agent of the civil government (such as a public school teacher or a social worker) who doesn't have a comparable interest in my child as a unique individual. But, if, as a parent, my decisions demonstrate that I am bringing a substantial degree of harm to my chil-

dren, the civil government's involvement (through a social worker's intervention, for example) may be legitimated. Even then, however, government intervention may not be even the second best solution; perhaps intervention from a voluntary association, such as my church friends or church leadership (a voluntary association) will provide an adequate solution, thus preventing the need for government action altogether.

- Therefore, there are important governance roles to be played by each social institution. Sometimes parents are the most legitimate institution to handle certain problems; sometimes voluntary associations are; and sometimes the civil government is. A core question we thus need to address is which

institutions are in fact, best positioned to address which governance situations, and which methods are available to address those situations most effectively? The answers to these, and related questions, are usually strongly informed by one's worldview about the nature of nature, power, law, and authority in society.

V. What gives each institution the legitimate authority to govern?

In terms of American political history and society there are two primary traditions (sets of beliefs) that profoundly influenced the development of the US Constitution.

- The Judeo-Christian tradition, which asserts that …

Table 1

Kind of Institution	Authority over:	Examples of the institution	Methods of Governance
Individual	Self		self-discipline
Family	Family members	Nuclear family Extended family	social pressure, moral authority, corporal punishment
Voluntary Organizations	Group members	Churches, synagogues, mosques Fraternities, social clubs (like Lions, Elks, Rotary, country clubs) Employers & businesses	membership rules, social pressure, moral authority, employment policies
Civil Government	Residents, Citizens	Local, state, and national governments Government agencies (public schools, social service agencies, police departments) International governments (United Nations, International Criminal Court)	Imprisonment Death property confiscation (fines, taxes)

- God established specific kinds of institutions in society with distinct "jurisdictions" over specific kinds of behaviors.
- In the Western enlightenment tradition, which asserts that …
  - Individuals have inherent and inalienable rights, and governments derive their powers from the consent of the governed.
- Different societies and cultures have different solutions to human governance questions. (For example, Asian and Muslim traditions think about them differently.)

VI. Drawing on both of these traditions, the American political tradition produced the beliefs that led to the American Revolution, the declaration of rights in the Declaration of Independence, and the two US Constitutions. The purposes of civil government in general are

- To shape human behavior through collective agreements (laws) …
  - *Securing* basic individual rights and liberty
  - *Regulating* antisocial personal and group behavior
  - *Providing* public goods that would not be provided by individuals cooperatively
  - *Preventing* or *remedying* negative public outcomes
- To enforce collective agreements (laws) …
  - By *punishing* violations of laws
  - By *financing* public goods
  - By *enforcing* personal contracts

VII. How is Civil Governance implemented by governments?

- *Formal Institutions* (agencies or organizations), to which responsibility for civil governance is assigned.
  - Law making (legislatures)
  - Law implementation and enforcement (executives)
  - Law interpretation and application (courts)
- *Procedural Institutions* (rules) that the civil government must follow.
  - How selection to public office occurs (such as through elections)

- The degree of consensus needed to pass laws and manage conflict (such as majority rule)
- Mechanisms for appeal and law changing

VIII. How does governance relate to "politics"?

1. *Politics* is the management of conflict over who rules and what policies shall be made.
   - These reflect conflict over the key governance questions—what behaviors, what institutions, what methods.
   - Politics reflects struggles between institutions for governance authority.
2. "Successful" politics almost always requires bargaining and compromise.
   - *Bargaining* is a prolonged exchange of proposals and counterproposals.
   - *Compromise* involves conflict settlement in which each side concedes some of its preferences in order to secure others.

IX. Looking Forward

- As you engage with the textbook and the other readings in this course, keep in mind the questions about human governance, legitimate authority, and the nature of politics.
- For example, American Government textbooks often reprint lists of "Government's Greatest Achievements" (see the full list and discussion at www.brookings.edu/ papers/2000/11governance_light.aspx). As you review that list, note that many of these policy initiatives were controversial, and many emerged from a sometimes bruising political process because people have genuine differences about whether it was appropriate for the federal government to address them.
- There continues to be significant conflict over whether the government should promote (and fund) financial security in retirement, or whether that is something individuals should be responsible for themselves. Other conflicts seem to belong very appropriately in the realm of government's legitimate authority (such as expanding and defining the right to vote), but political conflicts were over which level of government (state or fed-

eral) ought to address those questions; the original version of the Constitution assigns this power to states, but some states did not treat their citizens equally, which prompted the federal government to exercise oversight over state election laws.

- Thus, the policies we'll read about inherently involve conflict about who ought to be managing whose behaviors, using what methods; resolution to those conflicts involve different political beliefs, people and groups, and social and governmental institutions.

Purpose

The purpose of this reading is to get you to think about what freedom means, and what makes a nation free.

Context

What is freedom? In what areas of social and political life do we value freedom? What kinds of rules are needed to facilitate (or secure) freedom? Do you think that freedom occurs naturally, or do societies need some mechanism of human governance in order to secure freedom? Think about the irony that, in order to protect freedom, societies need rules (that is, restrictions on freedom).

Thought Exercises

1. What regions of the world are generally "free" and which are generally "not free"?
2. What does Freedom House say makes a nation free?
3. What freedoms of importance to you would you be giving up to move from the United States to a nation that is only partly free or not free?

Web Links

1. Freedom House, Freedom in the World
    http://www.freedomhouse.org/uploads/fiw09/MOF09.pdf
2. Methodology excerpt
    http://www.freedomhouse.org/template.cfm?page=351&ana_page=362&year=2010

2. Map of Freedom

Freedom House

Survey Findings

Freedom Status	Country Breakdown	Population Breakdown
FREE	89 (46%)	3,055,885,000 (46%)
PARTLY FREE	62 (32%)	1,351,014,000 (20%)
NOT FREE	42 (22%)	2,276,292,000 (34%)
TOTAL	193	6,683,191,000

The Map of Freedom reflects the findings of Freedom House's Freedom in the World 2009 survey, which rates the level of political rights and civil liberties in 193 countries and 16 related and disputed territories during 2008. Based on these ratings, countries are divided into three categories: Free, Partly Free, and Not Free.

A Free country is one where there is broad scope for open political competition, a climate of respect for civil liberties, significant independent civic life, and independent media.

Partly Free countries are characterized by some restrictions on political rights and civil liberties, often in a context of corruption, weak rule of law, ethnic strife, or civil war.

A Not Free country is one where basic political rights are absent, and basic civil liberties are widely and systematically denied. Freedom House is an independent nongovernmental organization that supports the expansion of freedom worldwide.

Source: www.freedomhouse.org

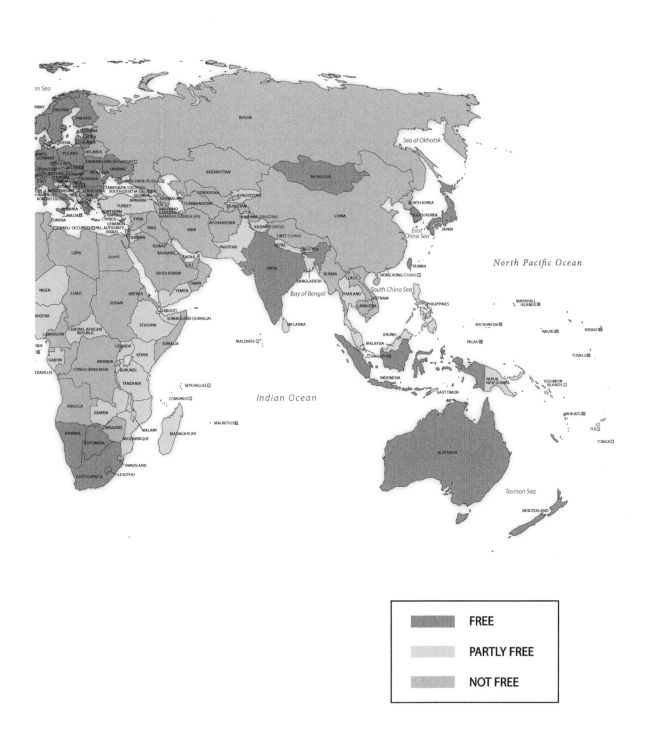

	FREE
	PARTLY FREE
	NOT FREE

3.Methodology

Freedom House

Introduction

The *Freedom in the World* survey provides an annual evaluation of the state of global freedom as experienced by individuals. The survey measures freedom—the opportunity to act spontaneously in a variety of fields outside the control of the government and other centers of potential domination—according to two broad categories: political rights and civil liberties. Political rights enable people to participate freely in the political process, including the right to vote freely for distinct alternatives in legitimate elections, compete for public office, join political parties and organizations, and elect representatives who have a decisive impact on public policies and are accountable to the electorate. Civil liberties allow for the freedoms of expression and belief, associational and organizational rights, rule of law, and personal autonomy without interference from the state.

The survey does not rate governments or government performance per se, but rather the real-world rights and freedoms enjoyed by individuals. Thus, while Freedom House considers the presence of legal rights, it places a greater emphasis on whether these rights are implemented in practice. Furthermore, freedoms can be affected by government officials, as well as by nonstate actors, including insurgents and other armed groups.

Freedom House does not maintain a culture-bound view of freedom. The methodology of the survey is grounded in basic standards of political rights and civil liberties, derived in large measure from relevant portions of the Universal Declaration of Human Rights. These standards apply to all countries and territories, irrespective of geographical location, ethnic or religious composition, or level of economic development. The survey operates from the assumption that freedom for all peoples is best achieved in liberal democratic societies.

The survey includes both analytical reports and numerical ratings for 194 countries and 14 select territories.[1] Each country and territory report

---

[1]These territories are selected based on their political significance and size. Freedom House divides territories into two categories: related territories and disputed territories. Related territories consist mostly of colonies, protectorates, and island dependencies of sovereign states that are in some relation of dependency to that state, and whose relationship is not currently in serious legal or political dispute. Disputed territories are areas within internationally recognized sovereign states whose status is in serious political or violent dispute, and whose conditions differ substantially from those of the relevant sovereign states. They are often outside of central government control and

includes an overview section, which provides historical background and a brief description of the year's major developments, as well as a section summarizing the current state of political rights and civil liberties. In addition, each country and territory is assigned a numerical rating—on a scale of 1 to 7—for political rights and an analogous rating for civil liberties; a rating of 1 indicates the highest degree of freedom and 7 the lowest level of freedom. These ratings, which are calculated based on the methodological process described below, determine whether a country is classified as Free, Partly Free, or Not Free by the survey.

The survey findings are reached after a multilayered process of analysis and evaluation by a team of regional experts and scholars. Although there is an element of subjectivity inherent in the survey findings, the ratings process emphasizes intellectual rigor and balanced and unbiased judgments.

History of the Survey

Freedom House's first year-end reviews of freedom began in the 1950s as the Balance Sheet of Freedom. This modest report provided assessments of political trends and their implications for individual freedom. In 1972, Freedom House launched a new, more comprehensive annual study called *The Comparative Study of Freedom.* Raymond Gastil, a Harvard-trained specialist in regional studies from the University of Washington in Seattle, developed the survey's methodology, which assigned political rights and civil liberties ratings to 151 countries and 45 territories and—based on these ratings—categorized them as Free, Partly Free, or Not Free. The findings appeared each year in Freedom House's *Freedom at Issue* bimonthly journal (later titled *Freedom Review*). The survey first appeared in

characterized by intense, longtime, and widespread insurgency or independence movements that enjoy popular support. Generally, the dispute faced by a territory is between independence for the territory or domination by an established state.

book form in 1978 under the title *Freedom in the World* and included short, explanatory narratives for each country and territory rated in the study, as well as a series of essays by leading scholars on related issues. *Freedom in the World* continued to be produced by Gastil until 1989, when a larger team of in-house survey analysts was established. In the mid-1990s, the expansion of *Freedom in the World's* country and territory narratives demanded the hiring of outside analysts—a group of regional experts from the academic, media, and human rights communities. The survey has continued to grow in size and scope; the 2010 edition is the most exhaustive in its history.

Research and Ratings Review Process

This year's survey covers developments from January 1, 2009, through December 31, 2009, in 194 countries and 14 territories. The research and ratings process involved 50 analysts and 18 senior-level academic advisers—the largest number to date. The analysts used a broad range of sources of information—including foreign and domestic news reports, academic analyses, nongovernmental organizations, think tanks, individual professional contacts, and visits to the region-in preparing the country and territory reports and ratings.

The country and territory ratings were proposed by the analyst responsible for each related report. The ratings were reviewed individually and on a comparative basis in a series of six regional meetings—Asia-Pacific, Central and Eastern Europe and the Former Soviet Union, Latin America and the Caribbean, Middle East and North Africa, sub-Saharan Africa, and Western Europe—involving the analysts, academic advisors with expertise in each region, and Freedom House staff. The ratings were compared to the previous year's findings, and any major proposed numerical shifts or category changes were subjected to more intensive scrutiny. These reviews were followed by cross-regional assessments in which efforts were made to ensure comparability and consistency in the findings. Many of the key country reports were also reviewed by the academic advisors.

Changes to the 2010 Edition of Freedom in the World

The survey's methodology is reviewed periodically by an advisory committee of political scientists with expertise in methodological issues. Over the years, the committee has made a number of modest methodological changes to adapt to evolving ideas about political rights and civil liberties. At the same time, the time series data are not revised retroactively, and any changes to the methodology are introduced incrementally in order to ensure the comparability of the ratings from year to year.

The following changes were made to the 2010 edition of the survey:

- **Territories**—Entities designated as related and disputed territories are no longer being identified with any particular country in order to avoid potential misunderstandings about the sometimes unclear relationship between the territory and the principal country or countries relating to them.
- **Kosovo**—Kosovo was removed from the list of territories and added as an independent country due to the handover of governance functions from the international community to domestic authorities, and as a result of its recognition by a significant number of states, most of which are classified by Freedom House as Free or Partly Free.
- **Chechnya**—Chechnya was dropped as a separate territory, and developments in this jurisdiction are now being addressed in the Russia report, due to the consolidation of power by pro-Kremlin forces, which have effectively eliminated any viable, active independence movement.

(NOTE: the complete checklist questions and keys to political rights and civil liberties ratings and status are listed in a separate document called "Checklist Questions and Guidelines".)

Scores—The ratings process is based on a checklist of 10 political rights questions and 15 civil liberties questions. The political rights questions are grouped into three subcategories: Electoral Process (3 questions), Political Pluralism and Participation (4), and Functioning of Government (3). The civil liberties questions are grouped into four subcategories: Freedom of Expression and Belief (4 questions), Associational and Organizational Rights (3), Rule of Law (4), and Personal Autonomy and Individual Rights (4). Scores are awarded to each of these questions on a scale of 0 to 4, where a score of 0 represents the smallest degree and 4 the greatest degree of rights or liberties present. The political rights section also contains two additional discretionary questions: question A (For traditional monarchies that have no parties or electoral process, does the system provide for genuine, meaningful consultation with the people, encourage public discussion of policy choices, and allow the right to petition the ruler?) and question B (Is the government or occupying power deliberately changing the ethnic composition of a country or territory so as to destroy a culture or tip the political balance in favor of another group?). For additional discretionary question A, a score of 1 to 4 may be added, as applicable, while for discretionary question B, a score of 1 to 4 may be subtracted (the worse the situation, the more that may be subtracted). The highest score that can be awarded to the political rights checklist is 40 (or a total score of 4 for each of the 10 questions). The highest score that can be awarded to the civil liberties checklist is 60 (or a total score of 4 for each of the 15 questions).

The scores from the previous survey edition are used as a benchmark for the current year under review. In general, a score is changed only if there has been a real-world development during the year that warrants a change (e.g., a crackdown on the media, the country's first free and fair elections) and is reflected accordingly in the narrative.

In answering both the political rights and civil liberties questions, Freedom House does not equate constitutional or other legal guarantees of rights with the on-the-ground fulfillment of these rights. While both laws and actual practices are factored into the ratings decisions, greater emphasis is placed on the latter.

For states and territories with small populations, the absence of pluralism in the political system or civil society is not necessarily viewed as a negative situation unless the government or other centers of domination are deliberately blocking its operation. For example, a small country without diverse political parties or media outlets or significant trade unions is not penalized if these limitations are determined to be a function of size and not overt restrictions.

Political Rights and Civil Liberties Ratings— The total score awarded to the political rights and civil liberties checklist determines the political rights and civil liberties rating. Each rating of 1 through 7, with 1 representing the highest and 7 the lowest level of freedom, corresponds to a range of total scores (see tables 1 and 2).

Status of Free, Partly Free, Not Free—Each pair of political rights and civil liberties ratings is averaged to determine an overall status of "Free," "Partly Free," or "Not Free." Those whose ratings average 1.0 to 2.5 are considered Free, 3.0 to 5.0 Partly Free, and 5.5 to 7.0 Not Free (see table 3). The designations of Free, Partly Free, and Not Free each cover a broad third of the available scores. Therefore, countries and territories within any one category, especially those at either end of the category, can have quite different human rights situations. In order to see the distinctions within each category, a country or territory's political rights and civil liberties ratings should be examined. For example, countries at the lowest end of the Free category (2 in political rights and 3 in civil liberties, or 3 in political rights and 2 in civil liberties) differ from those at the upper end of the Free group (1 for both political rights and civil liberties). Also, a designation of Free does not mean that a country enjoys perfect freedom

or lacks serious problems, only that it enjoys comparably more freedom than Partly Free or Not Free (or some other Free) countries.

Indications of Ratings and/or Status Changes—Each country or territory's political rights rating, civil liberties rating, and status is included in a statistics section that precedes each country or territory report. A change in a political rights or civil liberties rating since the previous survey edition is indicated with a symbol next to the rating that has changed. A brief ratings change explanation is included in the statistics section.

Trend Arrows—Positive or negative developments in a country or territory may also be reflected in the use of upward or downward trend arrows. A trend arrow is based on a particular development (such as an improvement in a country's state of religious freedom), which must be linked to a score change in the corresponding checklist question (in this case, an increase in the score for checklist question D2, which covers religious freedom). However, not all score increases or decreases warrant trend arrows. Whether a positive or negative development is significant enough to warrant a trend arrow is determined through consultations among the report writer, the regional academic advisers, and Freedom House staff. Also, trend arrows are assigned only in cases where score increases or decreases are not sufficient to warrant a ratings change; thus, a country cannot receive both a ratings change and a trend arrow during the same year. A trend arrow is indicated with an arrow next to the name of the country or territory that appears before the statistics section at the top of each country or territory report. A brief trend arrow explanation is included in the statistics section.

General Characteristics of Each Political Rights and Civil Liberties Rating

Political Rights

Rating of 1—Countries and territories with a rating of 1 enjoy a wide range of political rights, including free and fair elections. Candidates who are elected actually rule, political parties are competitive, the opposition plays an important role and enjoys real power, and minority groups have reasonable self-government or can participate in the government through informal consensus.

Rating of 2—Countries and territories with a rating of 2 have slightly weaker political rights than those with a rating of 1 because of such factors as some political corruption, limits on the functioning of political parties and opposition groups, and foreign or military influence on politics.

Ratings of 3, 4, 5—Countries and territories with a rating of 3, 4, or 5 include those that moderately protect almost all political rights to those that more strongly protect some political rights while less strongly protecting others. The same factors that undermine freedom in countries with a rating of 2 may also weaken political rights in those with a rating of 3, 4, or 5, but to an increasingly greater extent at each successive rating.

Rating of 6—Countries and territories with a rating of 6 have very restricted political rights. They are ruled by one-party or military dictatorships, religious hierarchies, or autocrats. They may allow a few political rights, such as some representation or autonomy for minority groups, and a few are traditional monarchies that tolerate political discussion and accept public petitions.

Rating of 7—Countries and territories with a rating of 7 have few or no political rights because of severe government oppression, sometimes in combination with civil war. They may also lack an authoritative and functioning central government and suffer from extreme violence or warlord rule that dominates political power.

Civil Liberties

Rating of 1—Countries and territories with a rating of 1 enjoy a wide range of civil liberties, including freedom of expression, assembly, association, education, and religion. They have an established and generally fair system of the rule of law (including an independent judiciary), allow free economic activity, and tend to strive for equality of opportunity for everyone, including women and minority groups.

Rating of 2—Countries and territories with a rating of 2 have slightly weaker civil liberties than those with a rating of 1 because of such factors as some limits on media independence, restrictions on trade union activities, and discrimination against minority groups and women.

Ratings of 3, 4, 5—Countries and territories with a rating of 3, 4, or 5 include those that moderately protect almost all civil liberties to those that more strongly protect some civil liberties while less strongly protecting others. The same factors that undermine freedom in countries with a rating of 2 may also weaken civil liberties in those with a rating of 3, 4, or 5, but to an increasingly greater extent at each successive rating.

Rating of 6—Countries and territories with a rating of 6 have very restricted civil liberties. They strongly limit the rights of expression and association and frequently hold political prisoners. They may allow a few civil liberties, such as some religious and social freedoms, some highly restricted private business activity, and some open and free private discussion.

Rating of 7—Countries and territories with a rating of 7 have few or no civil liberties. They allow virtually no freedom of expression or association, do not protect the rights of detainees and prisoners, and often control or dominate most economic activity.

Countries and territories generally have ratings in political rights and civil liberties that are within two ratings numbers of each other. For example, without a well-developed civil society, it is difficult, if not impossible, to have an atmosphere supportive of political rights. Consequently, there is no country in the survey with a rating of 6 or 7 for civil liberties and, at the same time, a rating of 1 or 2 for political rights.

Electoral Democracy Designation

In addition to providing numerical ratings, the survey assigns the designation "electoral democracy" to countries that have met certain minimum standards. In determining whether a country is an electoral democracy, Freedom House examines several key factors concerning the last major national election or elections.

To qualify as an electoral democracy, a state must have satisfied the following criteria:
1. A competitive, multiparty political system;
2. Universal adult suffrage for all citizens (with exceptions for restrictions that states may legitimately place on citizens as sanctions for criminal offenses);
3. Regularly contested elections conducted in conditions of ballot secrecy, reasonable ballot security, and in the absence of massive voter fraud, and that yield results that are representative of the public will;
4. Significant public access of major political parties to the electorate through the media and through generally open political campaigning.

The numerical benchmark for a country to be listed as an electoral democracy is a subtotal score of 7 or better (out of a possible total score of 12) for the political rights checklist subcategory A (the three questions on Electoral Process) and an overall political rights score of 20 or better (out of a possible total score of 40). In the case of presidential/parliamentary systems, both elections must have been free and fair on the basis of the above criteria; in parliamentary systems, the last nationwide elections for the national legislature must have been free and fair. The presence of certain irregularities during the electoral process does not automatically disqualify a country from being designated an electoral democracy. A country cannot be an electoral democracy if significant authority for national decisions resides in the hands of an unelected power, whether a monarch or a foreign international authority. A country is removed from the ranks of electoral democracies if its last national election failed to meet the criteria listed above, or if changes in law significantly eroded the public's possibility for electoral choice.

Freedom House's term "electoral democracy" differs from "liberal democracy" in that the latter also implies the presence of a substantial array of civil liberties. In the survey, all Free countries qualify as both electoral and liberal democracies. By contrast, some Partly Free countries qualify as electoral, but not liberal, democracies.

Purpose

The purpose of these readings is to get you think about the Declaration in its historical context.

Context

The Declaration of Independence is one of the most important documents in America's history. But there are some aspects of it that are not well known today, and these readings help to illuminate some of them. It is useful for us to look at both the final version of the Declaration (DOI) and Thomas Jefferson's original rough draft of the DOI

There are four parts to the Declaration:

I.   Preamble [First paragraph, through "impel them to the separation."

II.   Philosophical Justification [Second paragraph, "We hold these truths" through "let facts be submitted to a candid world."]

III. Grievances against the King [Through the second-to-last paragraph; "He has refused" through "in peace friends."

IV. Conclusion [Last paragraph; "We, therefore" through "our sacred honor."

This document is important because it contains the legal theory behind, and evidence supporting, the rebellion against England. It is considered to be one of the most important documents in support of liberty in world history, not just American history, because it lays out the basic purposes of government, the basis for where civil government gets its legitimate authority, and the rationale for altering or abolishing tyrannical forms of government. The DOI contains both legal and theological elements to it, and is interesting in the way it did (and did not) deal with the contentious issue of slavery in the new nation.

Thought Exercises

1. Read the Preamble and Philosophical Justification. Note the theological references (that is, where it mentions God, or synonyms for God). What do these references in this document suggest about the religious beliefs of the authors.
   - Read the same sections of Jefferson's rough draft. Aside from some minor wording changes, what significant changes do you observe between the draft and the final version? What do these changes suggest to you about the influence of Christianity on Jefferson's thinking, compared with its influence on the rest of men responsible for the document?
2. Compare the final version of the Declaration with Thomas Jefferson's original rough draft in another way. Note the long paragraph about slavery in the rough draft (there is a scan of this manuscript page in the reader). What does that paragraph tell you about Jefferson's attitude toward the issue?

- Why do you think the paragraph was not included in the final version of the Declaration? How can you reconcile the idea that Jefferson would leave out theological references, but include a criticism of the slave trade, alongside the other contributors adding in theological references, but taking out the slave trade criticism? What do these changes suggest to you about what the politics of that time required in order to generate broad agreement for the Declaration?

3. Consider what people nowadays might think when they read in the Declaration that all people are endowed by their creator with the inalienable right to the pursuit of happiness? How do we define happiness today? How do we pursue happiness?
   - Read the article by Carol V. Hamilton. How did she go about finding what the "pursuit of happiness" meant to the founding generation? What did she find that the phrase probably meant? How is that different from what people today would say about pursuing happiness?

Web Links

1. Declaration of Independence Original Draft text
   http://www.loc.gov/exhibits/declara/ruffdrft.html
2. Declaration of Independence images
   http://www.loc.gov/exhibits/treasures/trt001.html

4. Thomas Jefferson's 'original Rough draught' of the Declaration of Independence

By Thomas Jefferson

This is Professor Julian Boyd's reconstruction of Thomas Jefferson's "original Rough draught" of the Declaration of Independence before it was revised by the other members of the Committee of Five and by Congress.

A Declaration of the Representatives of the UNITED STATES OF AMERICA, in General Congress assembled.

When in the course of human events it becomes necessary for a people to advance from that subordination in which they have hitherto remained, & to assume among the powers of the earth the equal & independant station to which the laws of nature & of nature's god entitle them, a decent respect to the opinions of mankind requires that they should declare the causes which impel them to the change.

We hold these truths to be sacred & undeniable; that all men are created equal & independant, that from that equal creation they derive rights inherent & inalienable, among which are the preservation of life, & liberty, & the pursuit of happiness; that to secure these ends, governments are instituted among men, deriving their just powers from the consent of the governed; that whenever any form of government shall become destructive of these ends, it is the right of the people to alter or to abolish it, & to institute new government, laying it's foundation on such principles & organising it's powers in such

form, as to them shall seem most likely to effect their safety & happiness. prudence indeed will dictate that governments long established should not be changed for light & transient causes: and accordingly all experience hath shewn that mankind are more disposed to suffer while evils are sufferable, than to right themselves by abolishing the forms to which they are accustomed. but when a long train of abuses & usurpations, begun at a distinguished period, & pursuing invariably the same object, evinces a design to subject them to arbitrary power, it is their right, it is their duty, to throw off such government & to provide new guards for their future security. such has been the patient sufferance of these colonies; & such is now the necessity which constrains them to expunge their former systems of government. the history of his present majesty, is a history of unremitting injuries and usurpations, among which no one fact stands single or solitary to contradict the uniform tenor of the rest, all of which have in direct object the establishment of an absolute tyranny over these states. to prove this, let facts be submitted to a candid world, for the truth of which we pledge a faith yet unsullied by falsehood.

he has refused his assent to laws the most wholesome and necessary for the public good:

he has forbidden his governors to pass laws of immediate & pressing importance, unless suspended in their operation till his assent should be obtained;

and when so suspended, he has neglected utterly to attend to them.

he has refused to pass other laws for the accomodation of large districts of people unless those people would relinquish the right of representation, a right inestimable to them, formidable to tyrants alone:

he has dissolved Representative houses repeatedly & continually, for opposing with manly firmness his invasions on the rights of the people:

he has refused for a long space of time to cause others to be elected, whereby the legislative powers, incapable of annihilation, have returned to the people at large for their exercise, the state remaining in the mean time exposed to all the dangers of invasion from without, & convulsions within:

he has endeavored to prevent the population of these states; for that purpose obstructing the laws for naturalization of foreigners; refusing to pass others to encourage their migrations hither; & raising the conditions of new appropriations of lands:

he has suffered the administration of justice totally to cease in some of these colonies, refusing his assent to laws for establishing judiciary powers:

he has made our judges dependant on his will alone, for the tenure of their offices, and amount of their salaries:

he has erected a multitude of new offices by a self-assumed power, & sent hither swarms of officers to harrass our people & eat out their substance:

he has kept among us in times of peace standing armies & ships of war:

he has affected to render the military, independant of & superior to the civil power:

he has combined with others to subject us to a jurisdiction foreign to our constitutions and unacknoleged by our laws; giving his assent to their pretended acts of legislation, for quartering large bodies of armed troops among us;

for protecting them by a mock-trial from punishment for any murders they should commit on the inhabitants of these states;

for cutting off our trade with all parts of the world; for imposing taxes on us without our consent;

for depriving us of the benefits of trial by jury;

for transporting us beyond seas to be tried for pretended offences: for taking away our

charters, & altering fundamentally the forms of our governments;

for suspending our own legislatures & declaring themselves invested with power to legislate for us in all cases whatsoever:

he has abdicated government here, withdrawing his governors, & declaring us out of his allegiance & protection:

he has plundered our seas, ravaged our coasts, burnt our towns & destroyed the lives of our people:

he is at this time transporting large armies of foreign mercenaries to compleat the works of death, desolation & tyranny, already begun with circumstances of cruelty & perfidy unworthy the head of a civilized nation:

he has endeavored to bring on the inhabitants of our frontiers the merciless Indian savages, whose known rule of warfare is an undistinguished destruction of all ages, sexes, & conditions of existence:

he has incited treasonable insurrections in our fellow-subjects, with the allurements of forfeiture & confiscation of our property:

he has waged cruel war against human nature itself, violating it's most sacred rights of life & liberty in the persons of a distant people who never offended him, captivating & carrying them into slavery in another hemisphere, or to incur miserable death in their transportation thither. this piratical warfare, the opprobrium of infidel powers, is the warfare of the CHRISTIAN king of Great Britain. determined to keep open a market where MEN should be bought & sold, he has prostituted his negative for suppressing every legislative attempt to prohibit or to restrain this execrable commerce: and that this assemblage of horrors might want no fact of distinguished die, he is now exciting those very people to rise in arms among us, and to purchase that liberty of which he has deprived them, & murdering the people upon whom he also obtruded them; thus paying off former crimes committed against the liberties of one people, with crimes which he urges them to commit against the lives of another.

in every stage of these oppressions we have petitioned for redress in the most humble terms; our repeated petitions have been answered by repeated injury. a prince whose character is thus marked by every act which may define a tyrant, is unfit to be the ruler of a people who mean to be free. future ages will scarce believe that the hardiness of one man, adventured within the short compass of 12 years only, on so many acts of tyranny without a mask, over a people fostered & fixed in principles of liberty.

Nor have we been wanting in attentions to our British brethren. we have warned them from time to time of attempts by their legislature to extend a jurisdiction over these our states. we have reminded them of the circumstances of our emigration & settlement here, no one of which could warrant so strange a pretension: that these were effected at the expence of our own blood & treasure, unassisted by the wealth or the strength of Great Britain: that in constituting indeed our several forms of government, we had adopted one common king, thereby laying a foundation for perpetual league & amity with them: but that submission to their parliament was no part of our constitution, nor ever in idea, if history may be credited: and we appealed to their native justice & magnanimity, as well as to the ties of our common kindred to disavow these usurpations which were likely to interrupt our correspondence & connection. they too have been deaf to the voice of justice & of consanguinity, & when occasions have been given them, by the regular course of their laws, of removing from their councils the disturbers of our harmony, they have by their free election re-established them in power. at this very time too they are permitting their chief magistrate to send over not only soldiers of our common blood, but Scotch

& foreign mercenaries to invade & deluge us in blood. these facts have given the last stab to agonizing affection, and manly spirit bids us to renounce for ever these unfeeling brethren. we must endeavor to forget our former love for them, and to hold them as we hold the rest of mankind, enemies in war, in peace friends. we might have been a free & great people together; but a communication of grandeur & of freedom it seems is below their dignity. be it so, since they will have it: the road to glory & happiness is open to us too; we will climb it in a separate state, and acquiesce in the necessity which pronounces our everlasting Adieu!

We therefore the representatives of the United States of America in General Congress assembled do, in the name & by authority of the good people of these states, reject and renounce all allegiance & subjection to the kings of Great Britain & all others who may hereafter claim by, through, or under them; we utterly dissolve & break off all political connection which may have heretofore subsisted between us & the people or parliament of Great Britain; and finally we do assert and declare these colonies to be free and independant states, and that as free & independant states they shall hereafter have power to levy war, conclude peace, contract alliances, establish commerce, & to do all other acts and things which independent states may of right do. And for the support of this declaration we mutually pledge to each other our lives, our fortunes, & our sacred honour.

"abolishing our most valuable laws

for taking away our charters & altering fundamentally the forms of our governments

for suspending our own legislatures & declaring themselves invested with power to legislate for us in all cases whatsoever:

he has abdicated government here, by declaring us out of his protection & waging war against us, withdrawing his governors, & declaring us out of his allegiance & protection:]

he has plundered our seas, ravaged our coasts, burnt our towns & destroyed the lives of our people:

he is at this time transporting large armies of foreign mercenaries to compleat the works of death, desolation & tyranny already begun with circumstances of cruelty & perfidy unworthy the head of a civilized nation:

he has endeavored to bring on the inhabitants of our frontiers the merciless Indian savages, whose known rule of warfare is an undistinguished destruction of all ages, sexes, & conditions [of existence:]

[he has incited treasonable insurrections of our fellow-citizens, with the allurements of forfeiture & confiscation of our property:

he has waged cruel war against human nature itself, violating it's most sacred rights of life & liberty in the persons of a distant people who never offended him, captivating & carrying them into slavery in another hemisphere, or to incur miserable death in their transportation thither. this piratical warfare, the opprobrium of infidel powers, is the warfare of the Christian king of Great Britain. determined to keep open a market where MEN should be bought & sold, he has prostituted his negative for suppressing every legislative attempt to prohibit or to restrain this execrable commerce: and that this assemblage of horrors might want no fact of distinguished die, he is now exciting those very people to rise in arms among us, and to purchase that liberty of which he has deprived them, by murdering the people upon whom he also obtruded them: thus paying off former crimes committed against the liberties of one people, with crimes which he urges them to commit against the lives of another.]

in every stage of these oppressions we have petitioned for redress in the most humble terms; our repeated petitions have been answered only by repeated injuries. a prince whose character is thus marked by every act which may define a tyrant, is unfit to be the ruler of a people who mean to be free. future ages will scarce believe that the hardiness of one man, adventured within the short compass of twelve years only, to lay a foundation so broad & undisguised, for tyranny over a people fostered & fixed in principles of freedom.]

6. The Surprising Origins and Meaning of the "Pursuit of Happiness"

By Carol V. Hamilton

"The pursuit of happiness" is the most famous phrase in the Declaration of Independence. Conventional history and popular wisdom attribute the phrase to the genius of Thomas Jefferson when in an imaginative leap, he replaced the third term of John Locke's trinity, "life, liberty, and property." It was a felicitous, even thrilling, substitution. Yet the true history and philosophical meaning of the famous phrase are apparently unknown.

In an article entitled "The Pursuit of Happiness," posted at the *Huffington Post* July 4, 2007, Daniel Brook summed up what most of us learned in school: "The eighteenth-century British political philosopher John Locke wrote that governments are instituted to secure people's rights to 'life, liberty, and property.' And in 1776, Thomas Jefferson begged to differ. When he penned the Declaration of Independence, ratified on the Fourth of July, he edited out Locke's right to 'property' and substituted his own more broadminded, distinctly American concept: the right to 'the pursuit of happiness.'"

Familiar as all this sounds, Brook is wrong on three points. John Locke lived from 1634 to 1704, making him a man of the seventeenth century, not the eighteenth. Jefferson did not substitute his "own" phrase. Nor is that concept "distinctly American." It is an import, and Jefferson borrowed it.

The phrase has meant different things to different people. To Europeans it has suggested the core claim—or delusion—of American exceptionalism. To cross-racial or gay couples bringing lawsuits in court, it has meant, or included, the right to marry. And sadly, for many Americans, Jefferson might just as well have left "property" in place. To them the pursuit of happiness means no more than the pursuit of wealth and status as embodied in a McMansion, a Lexus, and membership in a country club. Even more sadly, Jefferson's own "property" included about two hundred human beings whom he did not permit to pursue their own happiness.

The "pursuit of happiness" has led its own life in popular culture. It provided the title for a 1933–34 Broadway comedy written by Lawrence Langner and Armina Marshall. That comedy became a musical of the same title in the 1940s. In the 1980s it was the name of a Canadian rock group whose first big hit was the single, "I'm an Adult Now." In 1993 the phrase served as the title of a self-help book whose subtitle was "Discovering the Pathway to Fulfillment, Well-Being, and Enduring Personal Joy." The phrase, coyly misspelled, was appropriated for the title of a 2006 Will Smith movie about upward mobility, the acquisition of wealth, and the triumph of talent over adversity. Blogging on the subject on

November 8, 2007, Arianna Huffington lamented contemporary greed, our happy hours and Happy Meals, but concluded, "but the American idea, embedded deep in our cultural DNA, is inspiring us to pursue a much less shallow happiness." Most recently, in his new book Kids are Americans Too, Bill O'Reilly erroneously wrote, "the Constitution guarantees us life, liberty, and the pursuit of happiness." He was corrected by an American kid, Courtney Yong of San Francisco, a city O'Reilly often castigates.

If Thomas Jefferson did not coin the phrase, who did? Wikipedia (drawing on, I think, an old edition of the Encyclopedia Britannica) attributes its coinage to Dr. Samuel Johnson in his long fable *Rasselas, Prince of Abyssinia*, published in 1759. Rasselas is an Abyssinian prince who lives in the Happy Valley, a paradise in every respect imaginable. But the Prince is discontented. Accompanied by his sister Nekayah and a wise, well-traveled poet, he escapes from his utopia and travels around the known world. They visit the Great Pyramid, where a dear friend of Nekayah is kidnapped by Arabs. Wounded by this loss, the Princess laments: "what is to be expected from our pursuit of happiness when we find the state of life to be such, that happiness itself is the cause of misery?"

In 1770 Dr. Johnson used the phrase again in a political essay entitled "The False Alarm." He began by observing that the "improvement and diffusion of philosophy" among his contemporaries had led to a diminution of "false alarms" about events such as solar eclipses, which once aroused terror in the populace. He predicted that advances in "political knowledge" and the "theory of man" will further erode "causeless discontent and seditious violence." But while humans are neutral about scientific discoveries, they will never be neutral about politics. "The politician's improvements," he observed, in a statement that still resonates today, "are opposed by every passion that can exclude conviction or suppress it; by ambition, by avarice, by hope, and by terror, by public faction, and private animosity."

What Dr. Johnson called "civil wisdom" was, he wrote, lacking in the English public. Therefore,

in another resonant passage, he declared: "We are still so much unacquainted with our own state, and so unskillful in the *pursuit of happiness*, that we shudder without danger, complain without grievances, and suffer our quiet to be disturbed, and our commerce to be interrupted, by an opposition to the government, raised only by interest, and supported only by clamor, which yet has so far prevailed upon ignorance and timidity, that many favor it, as reasonable, and many dread it, as powerful."

It seems unlikely that Jefferson plucked "the pursuit of happiness" from the prose of a Tory like Dr. Johnson. Jefferson's intellectual heroes were Newton, Bacon, and Locke, and it was actually in Locke that he must have found the phrase. It appears not in the Two Treatises on Government but in the 1690 essay *Concerning Human Understanding*. There, in a long and thorny passage, Locke wrote:

The necessity of pursuing happiness [is] the foundation of liberty. As therefore the highest perfection of intellectual nature lies in a careful and constant pursuit of true and solid happiness; so the care of ourselves, that we mistake not imaginary for real happiness, is the necessary foundation of our liberty. The stronger ties we have to an unalterable pursuit of happiness in general, which is our greatest good, and which, as such, our desires always follow, the more are we free from any necessary determination of our will to any particular action, and from a necessary compliance with our desire, set upon any particular, and then appearing preferable good, till we have duly examined whether it has a tendency to, or be inconsistent with, our real happiness: and therefore, till we are as much informed upon this inquiry as the weight of the matter, and the nature of the case demands, we are, by the necessity of preferring and pursuing true happiness as our greatest good, obliged to suspend the satisfaction of our desires in particular cases.

Just the ideas that inspired our intellectual Founders were primarily European imports, so that defining American phrase, "the pursuit of happiness," is not native to our shores. Furthermore, as the quotation from Locke demonstrates, "the pursuit of happiness" is a complicated concept. It is not merely sensual or hedonistic, but engages the intellect, requiring the careful discrimination of imaginary happiness from "true and solid" happiness. It is the "foundation of liberty" because it frees us from enslavement to particular desires.

The Greek word for "happiness" is *eudaimonia*. In the passage above, Locke is invoking Greek and Roman ethics in which *eudaimonia* is linked to *arete*, the Greek word for "virtue" or "excellence." In the *Nicomachean Ethics*, Aristotle wrote, "the happy man lives well and does well; for we have practically defined happiness as a sort of good life and good action." Happiness is not, he argued, equivalent to wealth, honor, or pleasure. It is an end in itself, not the means to an end. The philosophical lineage of happiness can be traced from Socrates, Plato, and Aristotle through the Stoics, Skeptics, and Epicureans.

Jefferson admired Epicurus and owned eight copies of *De rerum Natura (On the Nature of Things)* by Lucretius, a Roman disciple of Epicurus. In a letter Jefferson wrote to William Short on October 13, 1819, he declared, "I too am an Epicurean. I consider the genuine doctrines of Epicurus as containing everything rational in moral philosophy which Greece and Rome have left us." At the end of the letter, Jefferson made a summary of the key points of Epicurean doctrine, including:

> Moral.—Happiness the aim of life.
> Virtue the foundation of happiness.
> Utility the test of virtue.

Properly understood, therefore, when John Locke, Samuel Johnson, and Thomas Jefferson wrote of "the pursuit of happiness," they were invoking the Greek and Roman philosophical tradition in which happiness is bound up with the civic virtues of courage, moderation, and justice. Because they are civic virtues, not just personal attributes, they implicate the social aspect of *eudaimonia*. The pursuit of happiness, therefore, is not merely a matter of achieving individual pleasure. That is why Alexander Hamilton and other founders referred to "social happiness." During this political season, as Americans are scrutinizing presidential candidates, we would do well to ponder that.

Web Link

1. The Surprising Origins and Meaning of the "Pursuit of Happiness," History News Network
   http://hnn.us/articles/46460.html

Purpose

The purpose of this reading is to help you see the connection between the Declaration of Independence and the Constitution.

Context

Political science professor Donald Lutz discusses the practice in the early years of our nation of producing state political documents in two stages: a charter of rights, followed by a document of forming the state governments. He then draws the conclusion that this practice was likely intentionally followed at the national level, in the creation of the Declaration in 1776, followed by the drafting of the first US Constitution, the "Articles of Confederation," in 1777 (it was ratified and went into effect in 1781). That having failed to secure the nation, in 1787 the Continental Congress then called for revisions to the Articles that resulted in the current US Constitution.

Thought Exercises

Consider the Declaration's main ideas about the nature of government, its source of authority, and the objections that it states about the King's abuse of his authority. The Constitution has four underlying principles for organizing the government: republicanism (representative democracy), federalism (division of power between the national and state governments, separation of powers (spreading out the tasks of the civil government across the three branches), and checks and balances (giving each branch the ability to limit the power of the other branches).

1. Summarize in your own words the connections that Lutz sees between the Declaration and the US Constitutions of 1777 and 1787.
2. What connections do you see between the ideas in the Declaration and the organizing ideas of the Constitution of 1787?
3. Read the preamble to the US Constitution (reprinted in most American Government textbooks). What connections do you see between the ideas in the Declaration and the purposes of the government in the Constitution's preamble?

7. Excerpt from The Origins of American Constitutionalism

The Declaration of Independence

By Donald Lutz

During the colonial years, Americans had evolved the practice of using a compact to organize themselves as a people, to create a government, to set forth their basic values, and to describe the institutions for collective decision making. By linking the last foundation element to the charter form, Americans created from the compact and the charter a new type of political document, which we now tend to call a constitution. However, during the last half of the eighteenth century, the term constitution referred primarily to that part of the foundation document containing the institutional description. The entire document, with all the foundation elements, was a compact.

The differentiation of a complete foundation document into two parts—one composed of a preamble and a bill of rights, the other describing the form of government—had a number of interesting and useful implications. For example, John Locke saw civil society as arising from a double agreement—the first a unanimous agreement to form a society and be bound by the majority in collective decisions, and the second a majority agreement on the form of government to have. The great strength of such a view was that the majority could alter or overthrow the government without forcing the people back into a state of nature. Since the first part of the agreement

was still in effect, and was self-executing, the majority would quickly build a new government. Replacing a government thereby became a riskless and relatively easy thing to do. The idea was not original with Locke, however; it was in earlier writings by Europeans and was implicit in many colonial documents. Indeed, the earliest political covenants often used unanimous consent, an important aspect of which was the agreement to be bound by the majority in designing government and passing laws.

Americans could likewise create themselves as a people and set forth their basic values and commitments in one part of a document, the preamble and bill of rights, with the expectation that changing the second part, which described the form of government, would not alter or endanger the first part. A distinction between a constitution and a bill of rights thus made sense from Locke's point of view, since the majority could easily and safely revise or replace a constitution and thus a form of government. It also made sense for Americans, since that is what they had been doing since long before Locke published his *Second Treatise*.

Separating the two parts of a compact in principle also meant they could be separated in fact. That is, the bill of rights and/or the document standing as a social compact could be approved independently and kept safe from any tampering while a constitution was being modified. For example, on the same day in 1776, Delaware passed its Declaration of Rights and its constitution but published them separately, even though the last article of the constitution (Article 30) states that neither the Declaration of Rights nor five sections of the constitution could be violated. Clearly, the two pieces, though separate, were firmly linked. In one way or another, all the first fourteen states except Georgia made the distinction by separating their documents into two parts or through other explicit means. The preamble to the New Jersey Constitution of 1776, for example, described itself as a compact composed of a "charter of rights and the form of a Constitution."[1]

Colonial Americans preferred as foundation documents compacts that contained constitutions. After independence, Americans used the same form to establish their state governments. It would be surprising if their national document was not similar. The Declaration of Independence together with the first national constitution, the Articles of Confederation, were the Americans' national compact. When the Articles proved inadequate, the Constitution was written in the summer of 1787. There was, however, no need to replace the Declaration of Independence, since the people it created still existed. Changing the government but leaving the social compact untouched was in line not only with Locke's theory but also with long-standing practice in America. If the social compact represented by the Declaration of Independence had not still been in effect, there would have been no basis for a new national constitution. Americans, then, still live under a national compact.

The Declaration of Independence and the preamble to the U.S. Constitution together create a people, define the kind of people they are or wish to become, and establish a government. The Constitution describes the institutions for collective decision making. Few Americans think about the documents in this fashion, at least in an explicit way, yet few seem to find it strange that the Bicentennial lasted from 1976 through 1987. Americans understand the connection between the Declaration and the Constitution almost intuitively.

---

[1] The Declaration of Rights is recorded in *Laws of the State of Delaware, 1770-1797* (2 vols.; Newcastle, 1797), II, 89-102; New Jersey's constitution is in Francis N. Thorpe (ed.), *The Federal and State Constitutions, Colonial Charters and Other Organic Laws of the United States* (7 vols.; Washington, D.C., 1907), V, 2594.

Purpose

The purpose of these readings is to see the importance that the founding generation placed upon the new Constitution's organizing principle of federalism as a means of preventing the influence of domestic "factions," the emergence of a tyranny of the majority, and the influence of factious political leaders.

Context

As we will see in a later reading, Montesquieu (1689-1755) was one of the most-frequently-cited European enlightenment authors cited in the founding era's political writings. The people opposed to the second US Constitution (the "Anti-Federalists") often cited Montesquieu as supporting their belief that the constitution created a republic that was unlikely to succeed because it was too big and that as a "confederacy" the nation would be too weak. Federalist #9 directly addresses this concern. Federalist #10 addresses the positive effects of the "confederal" system created by the constitution, by pointing out that its design would control several negative effects of majoritarian democracy (in which the majority always rules). This was and still is important, because majorities will often prefer government policies that benefit themselves at the expense of minorities (not just racial minorities, but social and economic minorities as well).

Thought Questions

1. The Anti-Federalists often cited Montesquieu as evidence that the kind of republic proposed in the second US Constitution could not work. How does Federalist #9 address this? How effective is the author's use of Montesquieu's writings in this debate?
2. Referring to Federalist #10, how does Madison define a faction? How is this kind of faction different from or similar to modern examples of interest groups?
3. Madison argues that some solutions to the problems of factions are infeasible? Which solutions are they? Why does he argue that they can not or should not be implemented?
4. Madison concludes that a "confederacy" is the best solution to the problem of majority rule. Why does majority rule need to be controlled or limited? How does the Constitution accomplish this?
5. How does Madison argue that the constitution controls the problem of factious leaders? Why do they need to be controlled or limited in the first place?

8. The Federalist No. 9 and No. 10 Excerpts

Federalist No. 9 Excerpt
The Utility of the Union as a Safeguard Against Domestic Faction and Insurrection

Independent Journal Wednesday, November 21, 1787
[Alexander Hamilton]

To the People of the State of New York:

A FIRM Union will be of the utmost moment to the peace and liberty of the States, as a barrier against domestic faction and insurrection. It is impossible to read the history of the petty republics of Greece and Italy without feeling sensations of horror and disgust at the distractions with which they were continually agitated, and at the rapid succession of revolutions by which they were kept in a state of perpetual vibration between the extremes of tyranny and anarchy. If they exhibit occasional calms, these only serve as short-lived contrast to the furious storms that are to succeed. If now and then intervals of felicity open to view, we behold them with a mixture of regret, arising from the reflection that the pleasing scenes before us are soon to be overwhelmed by the tempestuous waves of sedition and party rage. If momentary rays of glory break forth from the gloom, while they dazzle us with a transient and fleeting brilliancy, they at the same time admonish us to lament that the vices of government should pervert the direction and tarnish the lustre of those bright talents and exalted endowments for which the favored soils that produced them have been so justly celebrated.

From the disorders that disfigure the annals of those republics the advocates of despotism have drawn arguments, not only against the forms of republican government, but against the very principles of civil liberty. They have decried all free government as inconsistent with the order of society, and have indulged themselves in malicious exultation over its friends and partisans. Happily for mankind, stupendous fabrics reared on the basis of liberty, which have flourished for ages, have, in a few glorious instances, refuted their gloomy sophisms. And, I trust, America will be the broad and solid foundation of other edifices, not less magnificent, which will be equally permanent monuments of their errors … .

The science of politics, however, like most other sciences, has received great improvement [in its knowledge republican government]. The efficacy of various principles is now well understood, which were either not known at all, or imperfectly known to the ancients. The regular distribution of power into distinct departments; the introduction of legislative balances and checks; the institution of courts composed of judges holding their offices during good behavior; the representation of the people in the legislature by deputies of their own election: these are wholly new discoveries, or have made their principal progress towards perfection in modern times. They are means, and powerful means, by which the excellences of republican government may be retained and its imperfections lessened or avoided. To this catalogue of circumstances that tend to the amelioration of popular systems of civil government, I shall venture, however novel it may appear to some, to add one more, on a principle which has been made the foundation of an objection to the new Constitution; I mean the ENLARGEMENT of the ORBIT within which such systems are to revolve, either in respect to the dimensions of a single State or to the consolidation of several smaller States into one great Confederacy. ...

The utility of a Confederacy, as well to suppress faction and to guard the internal tranquility of States, as to increase their external force and security, is in reality not a new idea. It has been practiced upon in different countries and ages, and has received the sanction of the most approved writers on the subject of politics. The opponents of the plan proposed have, with great assiduity, cited and circulated the observations of Montesquieu on the necessity of a contracted territory for a republican government. But they seem not to have been apprised of the sentiments of that great man expressed in another part of his work.

When Montesquieu recommends a small extent for republics, the standards he had in view were of dimensions far short of the limits of almost every one of these States. Neither Virginia, Massachusetts, Pennsylvania, New York, North Carolina, nor Georgia can by any means be compared with the models from which he reasoned and to which the terms of his description apply. If we therefore take his ideas on this point as the criterion of truth, we shall be driven to the alternative either of taking refuge at once in the arms of monarchy, or of splitting ourselves into an infinity of little, jealous, clashing, tumultuous commonwealths, the wretched nurseries of unceasing discord, and the miserable objects of universal pity or contempt ...

So far are the suggestions of Montesquieu from standing in opposition to a general Union of the States, that he explicitly treats of a CONFEDERATE REPUBLIC as the expedient for extending the sphere of popular government, and reconciling the advantages of monarchy with those of republicanism.

"It is very probable," (says he[1]) "that mankind would have been obliged at length to live constantly under the government of a SINGLE PERSON, had they not contrived a kind of constitution that has all the internal advantages of a republican, together with the external force of a monarchical government. I mean a CONFEDERATE REPUBLIC.

"This form of government is a convention by which several smaller states agree to become members of a larger one, which they intend to form. It is a kind of assemblage of societies that constitute a new one, capable of increasing, by means of new associations, till they arrive to such a degree of power as to be able to provide for the security of the united body. ..."

[The] more immediate design of this paper [is] to illustrate the tendency of the Union to repress domestic faction and insurrection ...

The definition of a confederate republic seems simply to be "an assemblage of societies," or an association of two or more states into one state. The extent, modifications, and objects of the federal authority are mere matters of discretion. So long as the separate organization of the members be not abolished; so long as it exists, by a constitutional necessity, for local purposes; though it should be in perfect subordination to the general authority of the union, it would still be, in fact and in theory, an association of states, or a confederacy. The proposed Constitution, so far from implying an abolition of the State governments, makes them constituent parts of the national sovereignty, by allowing them a direct representation in the Senate, and leaves in their possession certain exclusive and very important portions of sovereign power. This fully corresponds, in every rational import of the terms, with the idea of a federal government. ...

PUBLIUS

1. *Spirit of Laws*, Vol. I., Book IX., Chap. I.

The Federalist No. 10 Excerpt
The Utility of the Union as a Safeguard Against Domestic Faction and Insurrection (continued)

Daily Advertiser
Thursday, November 22, 1787
[James Madison]

To the People of the State of New York:
AMONG the numerous advantages promised by a well constructed Union, none deserves to be more accurately developed than its tendency to break and control the violence of faction. The friend of popular governments never finds himself so much alarmed for their character and fate, as when he contemplates their propensity to this dangerous vice. He will not fail, therefore, to set a due value on any plan which, without violating the principles to which he is attached, provides a proper cure for it. The instability, injustice, and confusion introduced into the public councils, have, in truth, been the mortal diseases under which popular governments have everywhere perished; Complaints are everywhere heard from our most considerate and virtuous citizens, equally the friends of public and private faith, and of public and personal liberty, that our governments are too unstable, that the public good is disregarded in the conflicts of rival parties, and that measures are too often decided, not according to the rules of justice and the rights of the minor party, but by the superior force of an interested and overbearing majority. However anxiously we may wish that these complaints had no foundation, the evidence, of known facts will not permit us to deny that they are in some degree true. ... These must be chiefly, if not wholly, effects of the unsteadiness and injustice with which a factious spirit has tainted our public administrations.

By a faction, I understand a number of citizens, whether amounting to a majority or a minority of the whole, who are united and actuated by some common impulse of passion, or of interest, adverse to the rights of other citizens, or to the permanent and aggregate interests of the community.

There are two methods of curing the mischiefs of faction: the one, by removing its causes; the other, by controlling its effects.

There are again two methods of removing the causes of faction: the one, by destroying the liberty which is essential to its existence; the other, by giving to every citizen the same opinions, the same passions, and the same interests.

It could never be more truly said than of the first remedy, that it was worse than the disease. Liberty is to faction what air is to fire, an aliment without which it instantly expires. But it could not be less folly to abolish liberty, which is essential to political life, because it nourishes faction, than it would be to wish the annihilation of air, which is essential to animal life, because it imparts to fire its destructive agency.

The second expedient is as impracticable as the first would be unwise. As long as the reason of man continues fallible, and he is at liberty to exercise it, different opinions will be formed. As long as the connection subsists between his reason and his self-love, his opinions and his passions will have a reciprocal influence on each other; and the former will be objects to which the latter will attach themselves. The diversity in the faculties of men, from which the rights of property originate, is not less an insuperable obstacle to a uniformity of interests. The protection of these faculties is the first object of government. From the protection of different and unequal faculties of acquiring property, the possession of different degrees and kinds of property immediately results; and from the influence of these on the sentiments and views of the respective proprietors, ensues a division of the society into different interests and parties.

The latent causes of faction are thus sown in the nature of man; and we see them everywhere brought into different degrees of activity, according to the different circumstances of civil society. A zeal for different opinions concerning religion, concerning government, and many other points, as well of speculation as of practice; an attachment to different leaders ambitiously contending for pre-eminence and power; or to persons of other descriptions whose fortunes have been interesting to the human passions, have, in turn, divided mankind into parties, inflamed them with mutual animosity, and rendered them much more disposed to vex and oppress each other than to co-operate for their common good. So strong is this propensity of mankind to fall into mutual animosities, that where no substantial occasion presents itself, the most frivolous and fanciful distinctions have been sufficient to kindle their unfriendly passions and excite their most violent conflicts. But the most common and durable source of factions has been the various and unequal distribution of property. Those who hold and those who are without property have ever formed distinct interests in society. Those who are creditors, and those who are debtors, fall under a like discrimination. A landed interest, a manufacturing interest, a mercantile interest, a moneyed interest, with many lesser interests, grow up of necessity in civilized nations, and divide them into different classes, actuated by different sentiments and views. The regulation of these various and interfering interests forms the principal task of modern legislation, and involves the spirit of party and faction in the necessary and ordinary operations of the government.

No man is allowed to be a judge in his own cause, because his interest would certainly bias his judgment, and, not improbably, corrupt his integrity. With equal, nay with greater reason, a body of men are unfit to be both judges and parties at the same time; yet what are many of the most important acts of legislation, but so many judicial determinations, not indeed concerning the rights of single persons, but concerning the rights of large bodies of citizens? And what are the different classes of legislators but advocates and parties to the causes which they determine? …

It is in vain to say that enlightened statesmen will be able to adjust these clashing interests, and render them all subservient to the public good. Enlightened statesmen will not always be at the helm. …

The inference to which we are brought is, that the causes of faction cannot be removed, and that relief is only to be sought in the means of controlling its effects.

If a faction consists of less than a majority, relief is supplied by the republican principle, which enables the majority to defeat its sinister views by regular vote. … When a majority is included in a faction, the form of popular government, on the other hand, enables it to sacrifice to its ruling passion or interest both the public good and the rights of other citizens.

To secure the public good and private rights against the danger of such a faction, and at the same time to preserve the spirit and the form of popular government, is then the great object to which our inquiries are directed. …

By what means is this object attainable? Evidently by one of two only. Either the existence of the same passion or interest in a majority at the same time must be prevented, or the majority, having such coexistent passion or interest, must be rendered, by their number and local situation, unable to concert and carry into effect schemes of oppression. …

From this view of the subject it may be concluded that a pure democracy, by which I mean a society consisting of a small number of citizens, who assemble and administer the government in person, can admit of no cure for the mischiefs of faction. A common passion or interest will, in almost every case, be felt by a majority of the whole; a communication and concert result from the form of government itself; and there is nothing to check the inducements to sacrifice the weaker party or an obnoxious individual. Hence it is that such democracies have ever been spectacles of turbulence and contention; have ever been found incompatible with personal security or the rights of property; and have in general been as short in their lives as they have been violent in their deaths. Theoretic politicians, who have patronized this species of government, have erroneously supposed that by reducing mankind to a perfect equality in their political rights, they would, at the same time, be perfectly equalized and assimilated in their possessions, their opinions, and their passions.

A republic, by which I mean a government in which the scheme of representation takes place, opens a different prospect, and promises the cure for which we are seeking. Let us examine the points in which it varies from pure democracy, and we shall comprehend both the nature of the cure and the efficacy which it must derive from the Union.

The two great points of difference between a democracy and a republic are: first, the delegation of the government, in the latter, to a small number of citizens elected by the rest; secondly, the greater number of citizens, and greater sphere of country, over which the latter may be extended.

The effect of the first difference is, on the one hand, to refine and enlarge the public views, by passing them through the medium of a chosen body of citizens, whose wisdom may best discern the true interest of their country, and whose patriotism and love of justice will be least likely to sacrifice it to temporary or partial considerations. Under such a regulation, it may well happen that the public voice, pronounced by the representatives of the people, will be more consonant to the public good than if pronounced by the people themselves, convened for the purpose. On the other hand, the effect may be inverted. Men of factious tempers, of local prejudices, or of sinister designs, may, by intrigue, by corruption, or by other means, first obtain the suffrages, and then betray the interests, of the people. The question resulting is, whether small or extensive republics are more favorable to the election of proper guardians of the public weal; and it is clearly decided in favor of the latter by two obvious considerations:

In the first place, it is to be remarked that, however small the republic may be, the representatives must be raised to a certain number, in order to guard against the cabals of a few; and that, however large it may be, they must be limited to a certain number, in order to guard against the confusion of a multitude. Hence, the number of representatives in the two cases not being in proportion to that of the two constituents, and being proportionally greater in the small republic, it follows that, if the proportion of fit characters be not less in the large than in the small republic, the former will present a greater option, and consequently a greater probability of a fit choice.

In the next place, as each representative will be chosen by a greater number of citizens in the large than in the small republic, it will be more difficult for unworthy candidates to practice with success the vicious arts by which elections are too often carried; and the suffrages of the people being more free, will be more likely to centre in men who possess the most attractive merit and the most diffusive and established characters. …

The other point of difference is, the greater number of citizens and extent of territory which may be brought within the compass of republican than of democratic government; and it is this circumstance principally which renders factious combinations less to be dreaded in the former than in the latter. The smaller the society, the fewer probably will be the distinct parties and interests composing it; the fewer the distinct parties and interests, the more frequently will a majority be found of the same party; and the smaller the number of individuals composing a majority, and the smaller the compass within which they are placed, the more easily will they concert and execute their plans of oppression. Extend the sphere, and you take in a greater variety of parties and interests; you make it less probable that a majority of the whole will have a common motive to invade the rights of other citizens; or if such a common motive exists, it will be more difficult for all who feel it to discover their own strength, and to act in unison with each other. …

Hence, it clearly appears, that the same advantage which a republic has over a democracy, in controlling the effects of faction, is enjoyed by a large over a small republic,—is enjoyed by the Union over the States composing it. …

The influence of factious leaders may kindle a flame within their particular States, but will be unable to spread a general conflagration through the other States. A religious sect may degenerate into a political faction in a part of the Confederacy; but the variety of sects dispersed over the entire face of it must secure the national councils against any danger from that source. A rage for paper money, for an abolition of debts, for an equal division of property, or for any other improper or wicked project, will be less apt to pervade the whole body of the Union than a particular member of it; in the same proportion as such a malady is more likely to taint a particular county or district, than an entire State.

In the extent and proper structure of the Union, therefore, we behold a republican remedy for the diseases most incident to republican government. And according to the degree of pleasure and pride we feel in being republicans, ought to be our zeal in cherishing the spirit and supporting the character of Federalists.

PUBLIUS

Purpose

The purpose of this reading is to give you insight into the state of women's power and rights in the time of the American Revolution.

Context

John Adams was one of the key actors in the United States' founding period. He was on the committee that produced the Declaration of Independence, and he was our nation's second president under the second Constitution. This exchange of letters between him and his wife Abigail show the tensions that existed even then between the political power that men exercised and under which women lived. Until the twentieth century, the mindset of most men was not one of oppressing of women, but of patriarchy (male headship of family and society) and paternalism (an attitude of care for someone else who is weaker) (e.g., Wilson, DiIulio, and Bose 2011, 140-141). These ideas can be seen in the letters, as well as the frustration that at least some women felt. These letters were written during the weeks leading up to the drafting and signing of the Declaration of Independence.

Thought Exercises

Read the letters between John and Abigail Adams.
1. What are the social (as opposed to political) problems they discuss?
2. What kinds of requests does Abigail make of John with regard to women and politics? What is her rationale for her requests?
3. What is John's response to her requests? What is his rationale for denying her requests?
4. Do you perceive that John believes that women are really powerless? Does he seem to think they would be permanently left in their current political situation?
5. Consider their exchanges in the social and cultural context of that time. What evidence do you see of the ideas of paternalistic and patriarchal thinking? Some people today would call these ideas "oppression" of women. What do you think? Do you think it is fair to judge peoples' attitudes in 1776 with the values of the twenty-first century? Why or why not? Put yourself in their place. Imagine students in the year 2250 looking back at the way you think and act, on the things you write in your emails and social media postings. Would it be fair for them to stand in judgment of you based on the values of their time? Why or why not?

Web Links

1. *http://www.masshist.org/digitaladams/aea/cfm/doc.cfm?id=L17760331aa*
2. *http://www.masshist.org/digitaladams/aea/cfm/doc.cfm?id=L17760414ja&archive=&hi=&mod e=&noimages=&numrecs=&query=&queryid=&rec=&start=1&tag=*
3. *http://www.masshist.org/digitaladams/aea/cfm/doc.cfm?id=L17760507aa*

9. John and Abigail Adams Letters

Letter from Abigail Adams to John Adams, 31 March–5 April 1776

Braintree March 31, 1776

I wish you would ever write me a Letter half as long as I write you; and tell me if you may where your Fleet are gone? What sort of Defence Virginia can make against our common Enemy? Whether it is so situated as to make an able Defence? Are not the Gentery Lords and the common people vassals, are they not like the uncivilized Natives Brittain represents us to be? I hope their Riffel Men who have shewen themselves very savage and even Blood thirsty; are not a specimen of the Generality of the people.

I [*illegible*] am willing to allow the Colony great merit for having produced a Washington but they have been shamefully duped by a Dunmore.

I have sometimes been ready to think that the passion for Liberty cannot be Eaquelly Strong in the Breasts of those who have been accustomed to deprive their fellow Creatures of theirs. Of this I am certain that it is not founded upon that generous and christian principal of doing to others as we would that others should do unto us.

Do not you want to see Boston; I am fearfull of the small pox, or I should have been in before this time. I got Mr. Crane to go to our House and

see what state it was in. I find it has been occupied by one of the Doctors of a Regiment, very dirty, but no other damage has been done to it. The few things which were left in it are all gone. Cranch has the key which he never deliverd up. I have wrote to him for it and am determined to get it cleand as soon as possible and shut it up. I look upon it a new acquisition of property, a property which one month ago I did not value at a single Shilling, and could with pleasure have seen it in flames.

The Town in General is left in a better state than we expected, more oweing to a percipitate flight than any Regard to the inhabitants, tho some individuals discoverd a sense of honour and justice and have left the rent of the Houses in which they were, for the owners and the furniture unhurt, or if damaged sufficent to make it good.

Others have committed abominable Ravages. The Mansion House of your President is safe and the furniture unhurt whilst both the House and Furniture of the Solisiter General have fallen a prey to their own merciless party. Surely the very Fiends feel a Reverential awe for Virtue and patriotism, whilst they Detest the paricide and traitor.

I feel very differently at the approach of spring to what I did a month ago. We knew not then whether we could plant or sow with safety, whether when we had toild we could reap the fruits of our own industery, whether we could rest in our own Cottages, or whether we should not be driven from the sea coasts to seek shelter in the wilderness, but now we feel as if we might sit under our own vine and eat the good of the land.

I feel a gaieti de Coar to which before I was a stranger. I think the Sun looks brighter, the Birds sing more melodiously, and Nature puts on a more chearfull countanance. We feel a temporary peace, and the poor fugitives are returning to their deserted habitations.

Tho we felicitate ourselves, we sympathize with those who are trembling least the Lot of Boston should be theirs. But they cannot be in similar circumstances unless pusilanimity and cowardise should take possession of them. They have time and warning given them to see the Evil and shun it.—I long to hear that you have declared an independency—and by the way in the new Code of Laws which I suppose it will be necessary for you to make I desire you would Remember the Ladies, and be more generous and favourable to them than your ancestors. Do not put such unlimited power into the hands of the Husbands. Remember all Men would be tyrants if they could. If perticuliar care and attention is not paid to the Laidies we are determined to foment a Rebelion, and will not hold ourselves bound by any Laws in which we have no voice, or Representation.

That your Sex are Naturally Tyrannical is a Truth so thoroughly established as to admit of no dispute, but such of you as wish to be happy willingly give up the harsh title of Master for the more tender and endearing one of Friend. Why then, not put it out of the power of the vicious and the Lawless to use us with cruelty and indignity with impunity. Men of Sense in all Ages abhor those customs which treat us only as the vassals of your Sex. Regard us then as Beings placed by providence under your protection and in immitation of the Supreem Being make use of that power only for our happiness.

April 5

Not having an opportunity of sending this I shall add a few lines more; tho not with a heart so gay. I have been attending the sick chamber of our Neighbour Trot whose affliction I most sensibly feel but cannot discribe, striped of two lovely children in one week. Gorge the Eldest died on wedensday and Billy the youngest on fryday, with the Canker fever, a terible disorder so much like the throat distemper, that it differs but little from it. Betsy Cranch has been very bad, but upon the recovery. Becky Peck they do not expect will live out the day. Many grown persons are now sick with it, in this street 5. It rages much in other Towns. The Mumps too are very frequent. Isaac is now confined with it. Our own little flock are yet well. My Heart trembles with anxiety for them. God preserve them.

I want to hear much oftener from you than I do. March 8 [John to Abigail, 08 March 1776] was the last date of any that I have yet had.—You inquire of whether I am making Salt peter. I have not yet attempted it, but after Soap making believe I shall make the experiment. I find as much as I can do to manufacture cloathing for my family whowhich would else be Naked. I know of but one person in this part of the Town who has made any, that is Mr. Tertias Bass as he is calld who has got very near an hundred weight which has been found to be very good. I have heard of some others in the other parishes. Mr. Reed of Weymouth has been applied to, to go to Andover to the mills which are now at work, and has gone. I have lately seen a small Manuscrip describing the proportions for the various sorts of powder, such as fit for cannon, small arms and pistols [*illegible*] . If it would be of any Service your way I will get it transcribed and send it to you. -Every one of your Friends send their Regards, and all the little ones. Your Brothers youngest child lies bad with convulsion fitts. Adieu. I need not say how much I am Your ever faithfull Friend.

Adams Family Papers, Massachusetts Historical Society.

Source of transcription: Butterfield, L.H., ed. *Adams Family Correspondence*. Vol. 1. Cambridge, Mass. : Belknap Press of Harvard University Press, 1963.

Letter from John Adams to Abigail Adams, 14 April 1776

Ap. 14, 1776

You justly complain of my short Letters, but the critical State of Things and the Multiplicity of Avocations must plead my Excuse. You ask where the Fleet is. The inclosed Papers will inform you. You ask what Sort of Defence Virginia can make. I believe they will make an able Defence. Their Militia and minute Men have been some time employed in training them selves, and they have Nine Battallions of regulars as they call them, maintained among them, under good Officers, at the Continental Expence. They have set up a Number of Manufactories of Fire Arms, which are busily employed. They are tolerably supplied with Powder, and are successfull and assiduous, in making Salt Petre. Their neighbouring Sister or rather Daughter Colony of North Carolina, which is a warlike Colony, and has several Battallions at the Continental Expence, as well as a pretty good Militia, are ready to assist them, and they are in very good Spirits, and seem determined to make a brave Resistance.—The Gentry are very rich, and the common People very poor.

This Inequality of Property, gives an Aristocratical Turn to all their Proceedings, and occasions a strong Aversion in their Patricians, to Common Sense. But the Spirit of these Barons, is coming down, and it must submit.

It is very true, as you observe they have been duped by Dunmore. But this is a Common Case. All the Colonies are duped, more or less, at one Time and another. A more egregious Bubble was never blown up, than the Story of Commissioners coming to treat with the Congress. Yet it has gained Credit like a Charm, not only without but against the clearest Evidence. I never shall forget the Delusion, which seized our best and most sagacious Friends the dear Inhabitants of Boston, the Winter before last. Credulity and the Want of Foresight, are Imperfections in the human Character, that no Politician can sufficiently guard against.

You have given me some Pleasure, by your Account of a certain House in Queen Street. I had burned it, long ago, in Imagination. It rises now to my View like a Phoenix.—What shall I say of the Solicitor General? I pity his pretty Children, I pity his Father, and his sisters. I wish I could be clear that it is no moral Evil to pity him and his Lady. Upon Repentance they will certainly have a large Share in the Compassions of many. But [illegible] let Us take Warning and give it to our Children. Whenever Vanity, and Gaiety, a Love of Pomp and Dress, Furniture, Equipage, Buildings, great Company, expensive Diversions, and elegant Entertainments get the better of the Principles and Judgments of Men or Women there is no knowing where they will stop, nor into what Evils, natural, moral, or political, they will lead us.

Your Description of your own Gaiety de Coeur, charms me. Thanks be to God you have just Cause to rejoice—and may the bright Prospect be obscured by no Cloud.

As to Declarations of Independency, be patient. Read our Privateering Laws, and our Commercial Laws. What signifies a Word.

As to your extraordinary Code of Laws, I cannot but laugh. We have been told that our Struggle has loosened the bands of Government every where. That Children and Apprentices were disobedient—that schools and Colledges were grown turbulent—that Indians slighted their Guardians and Negroes grew insolent to their Masters.

But your Letter was the first Intimation that another Tribe more numerous and powerfull than all the rest were grown discontented.—This is rather too coarse a Compliment but you are so saucy, I wont blot it out.

Depend upon it, We know better than to repeal our Masculine systems. Altho they are in full Force, you know they are little more than Theory.

We dare not exert our Power in its full Latitude. We are obliged to go fair, and softly, and in Practice you know We are the subjects. We have only the Name of Masters, and rather than give up this, which would compleatly subject Us to the Despotism of the Peticoat, I hope General Washington, and all our brave Heroes would fight. I am sure every good Politician would plot, as long as he would against Despotism, Empire, Monarchy, Aristocracy, Oligarcy, or Ochlocracy.—A fine Story indeed. I begin to think the Ministry as deep as they are wicked. After stirring up Tories, Landjobbers, Trimmers, Bigots, Canadians, Indians, Negroes, Hanoverians, Hessians, Russians, Irish Roman Catholicks, Scotch Renegadoes, at last they have stimulated the to demand new Priviledges and threaten to rebell.

Cite web page as: Letter from John Adams to Abigail Adams, 14 April 1776 [electronic edition]. *Adams Family Papers: An Electronic Archive.* Massachusetts Historical Society. http://www.masshist.org/digitaladams/

Original manuscript: Adams, John. Letter from John Adams to Abigail Adams, 14 April 1776. 4 pages. Original manuscript from the Adams Family Papers, Massachusetts Historical Society.

Source of transcription: Butterfield, L.H., ed. *Adams Family Correspondence.* Vol. 1. Cambridge, Mass. : Belknap Press of Harvard University Press, 1963.

Letter from Abigail Adams to John Adams, 7–9 May 1776

[Braintree] May 7, 1776

How many are the solitary hours I spend, ruminating upon the past, and anticipating the future, whilst you overwhelmd with the cares of State, have but few moments you can devote to any individual. All domestick pleasures and injoyments are absorbed in the great and important duty you owe your Country "for our Country is as it were a secondary God, and the First and greatest parent. It is to be preferred to Parents, Wives, Children, Friends and all things the Gods only excepted. For if our Country perishes it is as imposible to save an Individual, as to preserve one of the fingers of a Mortified Hand." Thus do I supress every wish, and silence every Murmer, acquiesceing in a painfull Seperation from the companion of my youth, and the Friend of my Heart.

I believe tis near ten days since I wrote you a line. I have not felt in a humour to entertain you. If I had taken up my pen perhaps some unbecomeing invective might have fallen from it; the Eyes of our Rulers have been closed and a Lethargy has seazd almost every Member. I fear a fatal Security has taken possession of them. [illegible] Whilst the Building is on flame they tremble at the expence of water to quench it, in short two months has elapsed since the evacuation of Boston, and very little has been done in that time to secure it, or the Harbour from future invasion till the people are all in a flame; and no one among us that I have heard of even mentions expence, they think universally that there has been an amaizing neglect some where. Many have turnd out as volunteers to work upon Nodles Island, and many more would go upon Nantaskit if it was once set on foot. "Tis a Maxim of state That power and Liberty are like Heat and moisture; where they are well mixt every thing prospers, where they are single, they are destructive."

A Goverment of more Stability is much wanted in this colony, and they are ready to receive them it from the Hands of the Congress, and since I have begun with Maxims of State I will add an other viz. that a people may let a king fall, yet still remain a people, but if a king let his people slip from him, he is no longer a king. And as this is most certainly our case, why not proclaim to the World in decisive terms your own importance?

Shall we not be dispiced by foreign powers for hesitateing so long at a word?

I can not say that I think you very generous to the Ladies, for whilst you are proclaiming peace and good will to Men, Emancipating all Nations, you insist upon retaining an absolute power over Wives. But you must remember that

Arbitary power is like most other things which are very hard, very liable to be broken—and notwithstanding all your wise Laws and Maxims we have it in our power not only to free ourselves but to subdue our Masters, and without voilence throw both your natural and legal authority at our feet "Charm by accepting, by submitting sway Yet have our Humour most when we obey."

I thank you for several Letters which I have received since I wrote Last. They alleviate a tedious absence, and I long earnestly for a Saturday Evening, and experience a similar pleasure to that which I used to experience find in the return of my Friend upon that day after a weeks absence. The Idea of a year dissolves all my Phylosophy.

Our Little ones whom you so often recommend to my care and instruction shall not be deficient in virtue or probity if the precepts of a Mother have their desired Effect, but they would be doubly inforced could they be indulged with the example of a Father constantly before them; I often point them to their Sire

"engaged in a corrupted State
Wrestling with vice and faction."

May 9

I designd to have finished the sheet, but an opportunity offering I close only just inform you that May the 7 our privateers took two prises in the Bay in fair sight of the Man of war, one a Brig from Irland the other from fyall loaded with wine Brandy and the other Beaf &c. The wind was East and a flood tide, so that the tenders could not get out tho they tried several times, the Light house fired Signal guns, but all would not do, they took them in triumph and carried them into Lyn.

Johnny and Charls have the Mumps, a bad disorder, but they are not very bad. Pray be kind enough to remember me at all times and write as often as you possibly can to your Portia

Cite web page as: Letter from Abigail Adams to John Adams, 7–9 May 1776 [electronic edition]. *Adams Family Papers: An Electronic Archive.* Massachusetts Historical Society. http://www.masshist.org/digitaladams/

Original manuscript: Adams, Abigail. Letter from Abigail Adams to John Adams, 7–9 May 1776. 3 pages. Original manuscript from the Adams Family Papers, Massachusetts Historical Society.

Source of transcription: Butterfield, L.H., ed. *Adams Family Correspondence.* Vol. 1. Cambridge, Mass.: Belknap Press of Harvard University Press, 1963.

Purpose

The purpose of this reading is to help you understand the relative influence of different authors and writings on the political debates occurring during the founding period.

Context

Professor Lutz performed a systematic analysis of the writings being circulated during the founding era. He randomly selected one-third of the political writings of the period between 1760 and 1805 and looked at who those writings were quoting or citing in their political arguments. His sample included nearly 1000 political writings. He then counted those references in order to determine who and what writings were influential during that time period. This is the most thorough analysis of its kind, and his findings may surprise you.

Thought Exercises

Read the Lutz selection.

1. What document does he find is the most frequently cited by political writers of the founding era? What were the main ideas of that most-frequently-cited document? On the surface, what does this suggest about the ideas that most heavily influenced political thinking in that time?

2. Who were the most frequently cited authors outside of the Bible? What does Lutz conclude about the influence of these authors on American political writers, and how their influence changed over time?

3. In the second paragraph, Lutz lists the most frequent parts of the Bible that were quoted by founding-era political authors. These include the book of Romans, chapter 13 and the books of 1 Peter and the Gospel of John. Footnote #2 lists other biblical texts also frequently cited. Look up a few of these references and research what they say about politics, citizenship, and government. (If you don't happen to have a Bible you can find it online at www.biblegateway.com; I suggest that you begin with the version called New International Version (1984).) What ideas can you find in those passages that line up with ideas expressed in the Declaration of Independence and the Constitution?

10. Excerpt from The Origins of American Constitutionalism

By Donald Lutz

The relative influence of European thinkers on American political thought is a large and complex question not to be answered in any but a provisional way here. We can, however, identify the broad trends of influence and which European thinkers need to be especially considered. One means to this end is an examination of the citations in public political literature written between 1760 and 1805.[1] If we ask which book was most frequently cited in that literature, the answer is, the Bible. Table 1 shows that the biblical tradition accounted for roughly one-third of the citations in the sample. However, the sample includes about one-third of all significant secular publications, but only about one-tenth of the reprinted sermons. Even with this undercount, Saint Paul is cited about as frequently as Montesquieu and Blackstone, the two most-cited secular authors, and Deuteronomy is cited almost twice as often as all of Locke's writings put together. A strictly proportional sample with respect to secular and religious sources would have resulted in an abundance of religious references.

About three-fourths of all references to the Bible came from reprinted sermons. The other citations to the Bible came from secular works and, if taken alone, would represent 9 percent of all citations—about equal to the percentage for classical writers. Although the citations came from virtually every part of the Bible, Saint Paul was the favorite in the New Testament, especially the parts of his Epistle to the Romans in which he discusses the basis for and limits on obedience to political authorities. Saint Peter was next, and then John's Gospel. Deuteronomy was the most-cited Old Testament book, followed by Isaiah, Genesis, Exodus, and Leviticus. As one might expect, the authors referred most frequently to the sections about covenants and God's promises to Israel, as well as to similar passages in Joshua, I and II Samuel, I and II Kings, and Matthew's Gospel.[2]

---

[1] See Donald S. Lutz, "The Relative Influence of European Writers on Late Eighteenth-Century American Political Thought," *American Political Science Review*, LXXVIII (1984), 189–97.

---

[2] Other prominently cited books of the Bible were Psalms, Proverbs, Jeremiah, Chronicles, and Judges. In Deuteronomy, favorite sections included Chapters 1 (13-17), 4 (20, 23, 29-40), 5, 8, 9, 10, 27, 29, and 31. Other frequently used passages were Exodus 24 (3-8) and 25; Leviticus 24 (though all Leviticus was cited promiscuously); I Samuel 3 (11) and 20; II Samuel 7; I Kings 8 (22-66); II Kings 23 (1-3); and Joshua 4 and 5.

The prominence of ministers in the political literature of the period attests to the continuing influence of religion during the founding era. Table 1 shows, however, a peak period of biblical citation in the 1770s. The movement toward independence found the clergy out in front, and they were also most vigorous in maintaining morale during the war. Approximately 80 percent of the political pamphlets published during the 1770s were reprinted sermons. When reading comprehensively in the political literature of the war years, one cannot but be struck by the extent to which biblical sources used by ministers and traditional Whigs undergirded the justification for the break with Britain, the rationale for continuing the war, and the basic principles of Americans' writing their own constitutions.

References to writers identified with the European Enlightenment were fairly constant throughout the forty-five-year founding era. However, as Table 3 shows, the writers within this category changed significantly over the years. A writer's relative prominence usually varies over time. When discussing influence, we should, for example, distinguish the revolutionary years from the years surrounding the writing of the United States Constitution.

Montesquieu and Locke were most prominent during the 1760s—more than 60 percent of all references to Enlightenment thinkers. During the 1770s these two account for more than 75 percent of all Enlightenment references. It is of considerable interest that during the 1760s, references to Locke were primarily in pieces dealing with the relationship of the colonists in America to Britain. In the 1770s, references to Locke appeared most often in works justifying the break with England and the writing of new constitutions. On the other hand, writers on constitutional design cited Montesquieu heavily. As the framing of state and national constitutions continued in the 1780s, Montesquieu became so important that

Table 1. Distribution of Citations

Category	1760s	1770s	1780s	1790s	1800–1805	% of Total N
Bible	24%	44%	34%	29%	38%	34%
Enlightenment	32 (21)	18 (11)	24 (23)	21 (20)	18 (17)	22 (19)
Whig	10 (21)	20 (27)	19 (20)	17 (18)	15 (16)	18 (21)
Common Law	12	4	9	14	20	11
Classical	8	11	10	11	2	9
Other	14	3	4	8	7	6
	100%	100%	100%	100%	100%	100%
	n=216	n=544	n=1,306	n=674	n=414	N=3154

The categories are those developed by Bernard Bailyn (*The Ideological Origins of the American Revolution* [Cambridge, Mass., 1967]). No significant change results if we break Bailyn's Enlightenment category into the three subcategories described by D. Lundberg and H. F. May ("The Enlightened Reader in America," *American Quarterly*, XXVIII [special issue, 1976], 262–93). The First Enlightenment, dominated by Montesquieu, Locke, and Pufendorf, comprises 16 percent of all citations. The more radical writers of the Second Enlightenment, such as Voltaire, Diderot, and Helvetius, garner 2 percent. The Third Enlightenment, typified by Beccaria, Rousseau, Mably, and Raynal, receives 4 percent of the citations. The total is the 22 percent listed here for all Enlightenment writers. Bailyn's scheme is one of the most prominent, but still controversial. For example, shifting Locke to the category of Whigs, as many or most of the Founders perceived him, yields the percentages that are in parentheses.

he alone accounts for almost 60 percent of all Enlightenment references.

Locke's rate of citation, which during the 1760s and 1770s was the highest for any secular writer, fell off drastically and did not recover. After the writing of the Constitution, references to Montesquieu also declined, and during the 1790s those authors who cited him were mainly concerned with state constitutions. This overall pattern is not at all surprising. Locke is profound on establishing a civil society and on opposing tyranny, but has relatively little to say about institutional design. Therefore he was properly influential in Americans' justifying their resistance to the Stamp Act, their break with England, and their writing their own constitutions. His influence on the design of any constitution, state or national, is probably exaggerated, and finding him hidden in passages of the U.S. Constitution is an exercise that requires more evidence than has hitherto been provided.

Montesquieu was prominent during the period of constitution writing, as were two other Enlightenment writers—Beccaria and De Lolme. The period of state constitution writing also brought to the fore a host of English Whig writers. Cato (Trenchard and Gordon), Hoadley, Bolingbroke, Price, Burgh, Milton, Molesworth, Priestley, Macaulay, Sidney, Somers, Harrington, and Rapin were most heavily cited during the late 1770s and through the 1780s. There were also many other Enlightenment writers cited as well, including Robertson, Grotius, Rousseau, Pope, Raynai, Mably, Burlamaqui, and Vattel. All in all, during the period of constitution writing, Enlightenment and Whig authors were cited about equally as a group, though the Whigs were nearly three times as numerous.

Table 2. Frequency of Citation

1. Montesquieu	8.3%	19. Shakespeare	.8
2. Blackstone	7.9	20. Livy	.8
3. Locke	2.9	21. Pope	.7
4. Hume	2.7	22. Milton	.7
5. Plutarch	1.5	23. Tacitus	.6
6. Beccaria	1.5	24. Coxe	.6
7. Trenchard & Gordon (Cato)	1.4	25. Plato	.5
8. De Lolme	1.4	27. Mably	.5
9. Pufendorf	1.3	28. Machiavelli	.5
10. Coke	1.3	29. Vattel	.5
11. Cicero	1.2	30. Petyt	.5
12. Hobbes	1.0	31. Voltaire	.5
13. Robertson	.9	32. Robison	.5
14. Grotius	.9	33. Sidney	.5
15. Rousseau	.9	34. Somers	.5
16. Bolingbroke	.9	35. Harrington	.5
17. Bacon	.8	36. Rapin	.5
18. Price	.8		

These thirty-six writers together account for about half of all citations. Among those just below the cut-off for this table are: Burlamaqui, Godwin, Adam Smith, Voiney, Shaftesbury, Hooker, Burlingame, Hoadley, Molesworth, Ptiesdey, Macaulay, Goldsmith, Hutcheson, Burgh, Defoe, Paley, Fortescue, Virgil, Polybius, Aristotle, and Thucydides.

Table 3. Most-Cited Secular Thinkers

	1760s	1770s	1780s	1790s	1800–1805	% of Total N
Montesquieu	8%	7%	14%	4%	1%	8.3%
Blackstone	1	3	7	11	15	7.9
Locke	11	7	1	1	1	2.9
Hume	1	1	1	6	5	2.7
Plutarch	1	3	1	2	0	1.5
Beccaria	0	1	3	0	0	1.5
Cato*	1	1	3	0	0	1.4
De Lolme	0	0	3	1	0	1.4
Pufendorf	4	0	1	0	5	1.3
Coke	5	0	1	2	4	1.3
Cicero	1	1	1	2	1	1.2
Hobbes	0	1	1	0	0	1.0
Subtotal	33%	25%	37%	29%	32%	32.4%
Others	67	75	63	71	68	67.6
	100%	100%	100%	100%	100%	100.0%
	n = 216	n = 544	n = 1,306	n = 674	n = 414	N = 3,154

The list contains more than 180 names. The last column allows more precise recovery of the number of citations over the era, but all other percentages are rounded off to the nearest whole number. The use of 0% indicates less than .5% of the citations for a given decade rather than no citations whatsoever.

*"Cato" refers to a series of pamphlets together known as *Cato's Letters*, written by the English Whigs John Trenchard and Thomas Gordon.

Purpose

The purpose of these readings is to help you understand the context for Thomas Jefferson's famous statement about the U.S. Constitution erecting a "wall of separation between Church & State."

Context

The election of 1800 was one of the most contentious in U.S. history, even by today's standards. One of the major sets of accusations against candidate Thomas Jefferson is that his election would usher in a time of anti-religious persecutions along with a dramatic deterioration of civility and social stability. After Jefferson was elected, an association of Baptists in Connecticut wrote a letter to him expressing their concerns about his views regarding the relationship between the civil government and religious institutions. These concerns were not new to American politics; a vigorous debate had been taking place on this subject since the early colonial years in the 1630s and 1640s. Jefferson responded carefully to the Baptists' concerns (for a brief analysis of his overall response, see Dreisbach, link on p. 50).

Jefferson's letter remained largely unknown until a U.S. Supreme Court case in 1947 (Everson v. Board of Education). This case stated, for the first time in American history, that there was a doctrine of "separation of church and state" that was intended to protect the government from religious organizations. While the First Amendment to the Constitution does prohibit Congress from "establishing" an officially-sanctioned religion, the Everson decision's interpretation of Jefferson's letter led some groups and politicians to the argument that religious institutions had no role in influencing government leaders, policies, or institutions. But is that what Jefferson had in mind?

The letter from the Danbury Baptists Association asks no questions. Instead, it states a series of concerns about how people of faith will be treated under Jefferson's administration; about the ambiguity of the first amendment's establishment and free exercise clauses; and finally, about whether some politicians ("who seek after power and gain under the pretense of government and religion") might attempt to begin regulating the way churches governed themselves. These are essentially concerns over human governance—which institutions have the legitimate authority to govern the actions of what people?

Thought Exercises

1. Read the letter from the Danbury Baptists. As a religious body, do they seem to be challenging Jefferson (accused of being an atheist during the 1800 campaign) and his legitimacy as their president?
2. Can you find their concerns expressed in the second paragraph? What is the part that primarily expresses their concern over the civil government's potential power over churches?
3. Now read Jefferson's response. What does he say in response to their concerns?

4. You might be interested to know that Jefferson did not invent the metaphor of a "wall of separation" between church and state. Rather, the image was first used, as best as we can tell, in a sermon or religious tract written by the famous pastor Roger Williams in or around 1644. Williams argued that there was indeed a wall of separation between the church and the government, but the wall was there for the protection of the church from the power of the civil governments, and was designed to keep governments from imposing their own rules on "the kingdom of Christ." How does that match up with the concerns of the Danbury Baptists? How does it match up with Jefferson's response? How does it match up with the way the phrase "separation of church and state" was used in the 1947 Everson case?

11. Letters Between Thomas Jefferson and the Danbury Baptists

The address of the Danbury Baptists Association in the state of Connecticut, assembled October 7, 1801

To Thomas Jefferson, Esq., President of the United States of America

Sir,

Among the many million in America and Europe who rejoice in your election to office; we embrace the first opportunity which we have enjoyed in our collective capacity, since your inauguration, to express our great satisfaction, in your appointment to the chief magistracy in the United States: And though our mode of expression may be less courtly and pompous than what many others clothe their addresses with, we beg you, sir, to believe that none are more sincere.

Our sentiments are uniformly on the side of religious liberty—that religion is at all times and places a matter between God and individuals—that no man ought to suffer in name, person, or effects on account of his religious opinions—that the legitimate power of civil government extends no further than to punish the man who works ill to his neighbors; But, sir, our constitution of government is not specific. Our ancient charter together with the law made coincident therewith, were adopted as the basis of our government, at the time of our revolution; and such had been our laws and usages, and such still are; that religion is considered as the first object of legislation; and therefore what religious privileges we enjoy (as a minor part of the state) we enjoy as favors granted, and not as inalienable rights; and these favors we receive at the expense of such degrading acknowledgements as are inconsistent with the rights of freemen. It is not to be wondered at therefore; if those who seek after power and gain under the pretense of government and religion should reproach their fellow men—should reproach their order magistrate, as a enemy of religion, law, and good order, because he will not, dare not, assume the prerogatives of Jehovah and make laws to govern the kingdom of Christ.

Sir, we are sensible that the president of the United States is not the national legislator, and also sensible that the national government cannot destroy the laws of each state; but our hopes are strong that the sentiments of our beloved president, which have had such genial effect already, like the radiant beams of the sun, will shine and prevail through all these states and all the world, till hierarchy and tyranny be destroyed from the earth. Sir, when we reflect on your past services, and see a glow of philanthropy and good will shining forth in a course of more than thirty years we have reason to believe that America's God has raised you up to fill the chair of state out of that goodwill which he bears to the millions which you preside over. May God strengthen you for your arduous task which providence and the voice of the people have called you to sustain and support you enjoy administration against all the predetermined opposition of those who wish to raise to wealth and importance on the poverty and subjection of the people.

And may the Lord preserve you safe from every evil and bring you at last to his heavenly kingdom through Jesus Christ our Glorious Mediator.

Signed in behalf of the association, Nehemiah Dodge

Ephraim Robbins

Stephen S. Nelson

Thomas Jefferson's Letter to the Danbury Baptist Association

To messers. Nehemiah Dodge, Ephraim Robbins, & Stephen S. Nelson, a committee of the Danbury Baptist association in the state of Connecticut.

Gentlemen

The affectionate sentiments of esteem and approbation which you are so good as to express towards me, on behalf of the Danbury Baptist association, give me the highest satisfaction. My duties dictate a faithful and zealous pursuit of the interests of my constituents, & in proportion as they are persuaded of my fidelity to those duties, the discharge of them becomes more and more pleasing.

Believing with you that religion is a matter which lies solely between Man & his God, that he owes account to none other for his faith or his worship, that the legitimate powers of government reach actions only, & not opinions, I contemplate with sovereign reverence that act of the whole American people which declared that their legislature should "make no law respecting an establishment of religion, or prohibiting the free exercise thereof," thus building a wall of separation between Church & State. Adhering to this expression of the supreme will of the nation in behalf of the rights of conscience, I shall see with sincere satisfaction the progress of those sentiments which tend to restore to man all his natural rights, convinced he has no natural right in opposition to his social duties.

I reciprocate your kind prayers for the protection & blessing of the common father and creator of man, and tender you for yourselves & your religious association, assurances of my high respect & esteem.

Th Jefferson

Jan. 1. 1802

Web Link

1. Letters between the Danbury Baptists Association and Thomas Jefferson
   http://www.billofrightsinstitute.org/page.aspx?pid=517

Purpose

The purpose of these readings is to help you better understand what "Jim Crow" laws were that discriminated against African-Americans, and how leaders in the black community envisioned the most effective ways to bring about social and political change.

Context

The Pilgrim reading on Jim Crow laws describes the kinds of formal and informal laws that governed African-Americans in the United States, especially in the southern states, between the end of the Civil War (1861-1865) and the Voting Rights Act of 1964. As you will read, while most American government textbooks emphasize the political parts of Jim Crow, the philosophy of Jim Crow permeated all kinds of relations between racial groups.

In the late 1800s and early 1900s there were two main approaches African-American leaders took to addressing this situation; Booker T. Washington, a former slave, and W.E.B. DuBois epitomized these two approaches. As the Civil Rights Movement gained steam in the 1950s and 1960s other leaders picked up the mantle of the two approaches to change, with Martin Luther King, Jr. following, to some degree, in the footsteps of Booker T. Washington, and with Malcom X following in the path marked out by DuBois. While these readings draw upon the two earlier leaders, the speeches of Dr. King and Malcom X are readily available online.

Thought Exercises

1. Read the speech given by Booker T. Washington in 1895. Summarize in your own words how he frames the challenges facing the black community. What kinds of solutions and strategies does he suggest will be most effective in bringing about the economic, social, and political advancement of African-Americans?
2. Read the interview of W.E.B. Du Bois by journalist Ralph McGill. Summarize the approach that Du Bois advocated to deal with discrimination.
3. Compare and contrast Washington's and DuBois' approaches. How were their goals similar? How were they different? How did they come to perceive the struggle by the end of each of their lives?
4. Washington was born a slave, and DuBois was born free. How do you think their different personal experiences shaped their respective approaches to discrimination?
5. View Martin Luther King's "I have a dream" speech on Youtube http://youtu.be/iEMXaTk-tUfA. Then listen to the recording of Malcom X's "Ballots to Bullets" speech http://youtu.be/D9BVEnEsn6Y (warning: Malcom X curses several times in this speech).
   a. Compare these two civil rights leaders with their predecessors. How are the four similar, and how are they different?
6. What have you learned about the differences of opinion within the black American community as it pertains to the pursuit of civil rights in the USA?

12. What Was Jim Crow?

By David Pilgrim

Jim Crow was the name of the racial caste system which operated primarily, but not exclusively in southern and border states, between 1877 and the mid-1960s. Jim Crow was more than a series of rigid anti-Black laws. It was a way of life. Under Jim Crow, African Americans were relegated to the status of second class citizens. Jim Crow represented the legitimization of anti-Black racism. Many Christian ministers and theologians taught that Whites were the Chosen people, Blacks were cursed to be servants, and God supported racial segregation. Craniologists, eugenicists, phrenologists, and Social Darwinists, at every educational level, buttressed the belief that Blacks were innately intellectually and culturally inferior to Whites. Pro-segregation politicians gave eloquent speeches on the great danger of integration: the mongrelization of the White race. Newspaper and magazine writers routinely referred to Blacks as niggers, coons, and darkies; and worse, their articles reinforced anti-Black stereotypes. Even children's games portrayed Blacks as inferior beings (see "From Hostility to Reverence: 100 Years of African-American Imagery in Games"). All major societal institutions reflected and supported the oppression of Blacks.

The Jim Crow system was undergirded by the following beliefs or rationalizations: Whites were superior to Blacks in all important ways, including but not limited to intelligence, morality, and civilized behavior; sexual relations between Blacks and Whites would produce a mongrel race which would destroy America; treating Blacks as equals would encourage interracial sexual unions; any activity which suggested social equality encouraged interracial sexual relations; if necessary, violence must be used to keep Blacks at the bottom of the racial hierarchy. The following Jim Crow etiquette norms show how inclusive and pervasive these norms were:

a. Black male could not offer his hand (to shake hands) with a White male because it implied being socially equal. Obviously, a Black male could not offer his hand or any other part of his body to a White woman, because he risked being accused of rape.

b. Blacks and Whites were not supposed to eat together. If they did eat together, Whites were to be served first, and some sort of partition was to be placed between them.

c. Under no circumstance was a Black male to offer to light the cigarette of a White female—that gesture implied intimacy.

d. Blacks were not allowed to show public affection toward one another in public, especially kissing, because it offended Whites.

e. Jim Crow etiquette prescribed that Blacks were introduced to Whites, never Whites to Blacks. For example: "Mr. Peters (the White person), this is Charlie (the Black person), that I spoke to you about."

f. Whites did not use courtesy titles of respect when referring to Blacks, for example, Mr., Mrs., Miss., Sir, or Ma'am. Instead, Blacks were called by their first names. Blacks had to use courtesy titles when referring to Whites, and were not allowed to call them by their first names.

g. If a Black person rode in a car driven by a White person, the Black person sat in the back seat, or the back of a truck.

h. White motorists had the right-of-way at all intersections.

Stetson Kennedy, the author of *Jim Crow Guide*, offered these simple rules that Blacks were supposed to observe in conversing with Whites:

1. Never assert or even intimate that a White person is lying.
2. Never impute dishonorable intentions to a White person.
3. Never suggest that a White person is from an inferior class.
4. Never lay claim to, or overly demonstrate, superior knowledge or intelligence.
5. Never curse a White person.
6. Never laugh derisively at a White person.
7. Never comment upon the appearance of a White female.[1]

Jim Crow etiquette operated in conjunction with Jim Crow laws (black codes). When most people think of Jim Crow they think of laws (not the Jim Crow etiquette) which excluded Blacks from public transport and facilities, juries, jobs, and neighborhoods. The passage of the 13th, 14th, and 15th Amendments to the Constitution had granted Blacks the same legal protections as

---

[1]Kennedy, Stetson. *Jim Crow Guide: The Way It Was*. Boca Raton: Florida Atlantic University Press, 1959/1990, pp. 216-217.

Whites. However, after 1877, and the election of Republican Rutherford B. Hayes, southern and border states began restricting the liberties of Blacks. Unfortunately for Blacks, the Supreme Court helped undermine the Constitutional protections of Blacks with the infamous Plessy v. Ferguson (1896) case, which legitimized Jim Crow laws and the Jim Crow way of life.

In 1890, Louisiana passed the "Separate Car Law," which purported to aid passenger comfort by creating "equal but separate" cars for Blacks and Whites. This was a ruse. No public accommodations, including railway travel, provided Blacks with equal facilities. The Louisiana law made it illegal for Blacks to sit in coach seats reserved for Whites, and Whites could not sit in seats reserved for Blacks. In 1891, a group of Blacks decided to test the Jim Crow law. They had Homer A. Plessy, who was seven-eights White and one-eighth Black (therefore, Black), sit in the White-only railroad coach. He was arrested. Plessy's lawyer argued that Louisiana did not have the right to label one citizen as White and another Black for the purposes of restricting their rights and privileges. In Plessy, the Supreme Court stated that so long as state governments provided legal process and legal freedoms for Blacks, equal to those of Whites, they could maintain separate institutions to facilitate these rights. The Court, by a 7-2 vote, upheld the Louisiana law, declaring that racial separation did not necessarily mean an abrogation of equality. In practice, Plessy represented the legitimization of two societies: one White, and advantaged; the other, Black, disadvantaged and despised.

Blacks were denied the right to vote by grandfather clauses (laws that restricted the right to vote to people whose ancestors had voted before the Civil War), poll taxes (fees charged to poor Blacks), white primaries (only Democrats could vote, only Whites could be Democrats), and literacy tests ("Name all the Vice Presidents and Supreme Court Justices throughout America's history"). Plessy sent this message to southern and border states: Discrimination against Blacks is acceptable.

Jim Crow states passed statutes severely regulating social interactions between the races. Jim Crow signs were placed above water fountains, door entrances and exits, and in front of public facilities. There were separate hospitals for Blacks and Whites, separate prisons, separate public and private schools, separate churches, separate cemeteries, separate public restrooms, and separate public accommodations. In most instances, the Black facilities were grossly inferior—generally, older, less-well-kept. In other cases, there were no Black facilities—no Colored public restroom, no public beach, no place to sit or eat. Plessy gave Jim Crow states a legal way to ignore their constitutional obligations to their Black citizens.

Jim Crow laws touched every aspect of everyday life. For example, in 1935, Oklahoma prohibited Blacks and Whites from boating together. Boating implied social equality. In 1905, Georgia established separate parks for Blacks and Whites. In 1930, Birmingham, Alabama, made it illegal for Blacks and Whites to play checkers or dominoes together. Here are some of the typical Jim Crow laws, as compiled by the Martin Luther King, Jr., National Historic Site Interpretive Staff:

- Barbers. No colored barber shall serve as a barber (to) white girls or women (Georgia).
- Blind Wards. The board of trustees shall … maintain a separate building … on separate ground for the admission, care, instruction, and support of all blind persons of the colored or black race (Louisiana).
- Burial. The officer in charge shall not bury, or allow to be buried, any colored persons upon ground set apart or used for the burial of white persons (Georgia).
- Buses. All passenger stations in this state operated by any motor transportation company shall have separate waiting rooms or space and separate ticket windows for the white and colored races (Alabama).
- Child Custody. It shall be unlawful for any parent, relative, or other white person in this State, having the control or custody of any white child, by right of guardian-

ship, natural or acquired, or otherwise, to dispose of, give or surrender such white child permanently into the custody, control, maintenance, or support, of a negro (South Carolina).
- Education. The schools for white children and the schools for negro children shall be conducted separately (Florida).
- Libraries. The state librarian is directed to fit up and maintain a separate place for the use of the colored people who may come to the library for the purpose of reading books or periodicals (North Carolina).
- Mental Hospitals. The Board of Control shall see that proper and distinct apartments are arranged for said patients, so that in no case shall Negroes and white persons be together (Georgia).
- Militia. The white and colored militia shall be separately enrolled, and shall never be compelled to serve in the same organization. No organization of colored troops shall be permitted where white troops are available and where whites are permitted to be organized, colored troops shall be under the command of white officers (North Carolina).
- Nurses. No person or corporation shall require any White female nurse to nurse in wards or rooms in hospitals, either public or private, in which negro men are placed (Alabama).
- Prisons. The warden shall see that the white convicts shall have separate apartments for both eating and sleeping from the negro convicts (Mississippi).
- Reform Schools. The children of white and colored races committed to the houses of reform shall be kept entirely separate from each other (Kentucky).
- Teaching. Any instructor who shall teach in any school, college or institution where members of the white and colored race are received and enrolled as pupils for instruction shall be deemed guilty of a misdemeanor, and upon conviction thereof, shall be fined … (Oklahoma).

- Wine and Beer. All persons licensed to conduct the business of selling beer or wine … shall serve either white people exclusively or colored people exclusively and shall not sell to the two races within the same room at any time (Georgia).[2]

The Jim Crow laws and system of etiquette were undergirded by violence, real and threatened. Blacks who violated Jim Crow norms, for example, drinking from the White water fountain or trying to vote, risked their homes, their jobs, even their lives. Whites could physically beat Blacks with impunity. Blacks had little legal recourse against these assaults because the Jim Crow criminal justice system was all-White: police, prosecutors, judges, juries, and prison officials.

Violence was instrumental for Jim Crow. It was a method of social control. The most extreme forms of Jim Crow violence were lynchings.

Lynchings were public, often sadistic, murders carried out by mobs. Between 1882, when the first reliable data were collected, and 1968, when lynchings had become rare, there were 4,730 known lynchings, including 3,440 Black men and women. Most of the victims of Lynch-Law were hanged or shot, but some were burned at the stake, castrated, beaten with clubs, or dismembered. In the mid-1800s, Whites constituted the majority of victims (and perpetrators); however, by the period of Radical Reconstruction, Blacks became the most frequent lynching victims. This is an early indication that lynching was used as an intimidation tool to keep Blacks, in this case the newly-freedmen, "in their places." The great majority of lynchings occurred in southern and border states, where the resentment against Blacks ran deepest. According to the social economist Gunnar Myrdal: "The southern states account for nine-tenths of the lynchings. More than two thirds of the remaining one-tenth occurred in the six states which immediately border the South."[3]

Many Whites claimed that although lynchings were distasteful, they were necessary supplements to the criminal justice system because Blacks were prone to violent crimes, especially the rapes of White women. Arthur Raper investigated nearly a century of lynchings and concluded that approximately one-third of all the victims were falsely accused.[4]

Under Jim Crow any and all sexual interactions between Black men and White women was illegal, illicit, socially repugnant, and within the Jim Crow definition of rape. Although only 19.2 percent of the lynching victims between 1882 to 1951 were even accused of rape, Lynch law was often supported on the popular belief that lynchings were necessary to protect White women from Black rapists. Myrdal refutes this belief in this way: "There is much reason to believe that this figure (19.2) has been inflated by the fact that a mob which makes the accusation of rape is secure from any further investigation; by the broad Southern definition of rape to include all sexual relations between Negro men and white women; and by the psychopathic fears of white women in their contacts with Negro men."[5] Most Blacks were lynched for demanding civil rights, violating Jim Crow etiquette or laws, or in the aftermath of race riots.

Lynchings were most common in small and middle-sized towns where Blacks often were economic competitors to the local Whites. These Whites resented any economic and political gains made by Blacks. Lynchers were seldomly arrested, and if arrested, rarely convicted. Raper estimated that "at least one-half of the lynchings are carried out with police officers participating, and that in nine-tenths of the others the officers either condone or wink at the mob action."[6] Lynching served

---

[2]This list was derived from a larger list composed by the Martin Luther King, Jr., National Historic Site Interpretive Staff. Last Updated January 5, 1998. The web address is: http//www.nps.gov/malu/documents/jim crowlaws.htm.

[3]Gunnar Myrdal, *An American Dilemma.* New York: 1944, pp. 560-561.

[4]Myrdal, op. cit., .561.

[5]Ibid., pp. 561 -562.

[6]Arthur. A. Raper, *The Tragedy of Lynching.* Chapel Hill, 1933, pp. 13-14.

many purposes: it was cheap entertainment; it served as a rallying, uniting point for Whites; it functioned as an ego-massage for low-income, low-status Whites; it was a method of defending White domination and helped stop or retard the fledgling social equality movement.

Lynch mobs directed their hatred against one (sometimes several) victims. The victim was an example of what happened to a Black man who tried to vote, or who looked at a White woman, or who tried to get a White man's job. Unfortunately for Blacks, sometimes the mob was not satisfied to murder a single or several victims. Instead, in the spirit of pogroms, the mobs went into Black communities and destroyed additional lives and property. Their immediate goal was to drive out—through death or expulsion—all Blacks; the larger goal was to maintain, at all costs, White supremacy. These pogrom-like actions are often referred to as riots; however, Gunnar Myrdal was right when he described these "riots" as "a terrorization or massacre … a mass lynching."[7] Interestingly, these mass lynchings were primarily urban phenomena, whereas the lynching of single victims was primarily a rural phenomena.

James Weldon Johnson, the famous Black writer, labeled 1919 as "The Red Summer." It was red from racial tension; it was red from bloodletting. During the summer of 1919, there were race riots in Chicago, Illinois; Knoxville and Nashville, Tennessee; Charleston, South Carolina; Omaha, Nebraska; and two dozen other cities. W.E.B. DuBois, the Black social scientist and civil rights activist, wrote: "During that year seventy-seven Negroes were lynched, of whom one was a woman and eleven were soldiers; of these, fourteen were publicly burned, eleven of them being burned alive. That year there were race riots large and small in twenty-six American cities including thirty-eight killed in a Chicago riot of August; from twenty-five to fifty in Phillips County, Arkansas; and six killed in Washington."[8]

The riots of 1919 were not the first or last "mass lynchings" of Blacks, as evidenced by the race riots in Wilmington, North Carolina (1898); Atlanta, Georgia (1906); Springfield, Illinois (1908); East St. Louis, Illinois (1917); Tulsa, Oklahoma (1921); and Detroit, Michigan (1943). Joseph Boskin, author of *Urban Racial Violence*, claimed that the riots of the 1900s had the following traits:

1. In each of the race riots, with few exceptions, it was White people that sparked the incident by attacking Black people.
2. In the majority of the riots, some extraordinary social condition prevailed at the time of the riot: prewar social changes, wartime mobility, post-war adjustment, or economic depression.
3. The majority of the riots occurred during the hot summer months.
4. Rumor played an extremely important role in causing many riots. Rumors of some criminal activity by Blacks against Whites perpetuated the actions of the White mobs.
5. The police force, more than any other institution, was invariably involved as a precipitating cause or perpetuating factor in the riots. In almost every one of the riots, the police sided with the attackers, either by actually participating in, or by failing to quell the attack.
6. In almost every instance, the fighting occurred within the Black community.[9]

Boskin omitted the following: the mass media, especially newspapers often published inflammatory articles about "Black criminals" immediately before the riots; Blacks were not only killed, but their homes and businesses were looted, and many who did not flee were left homeless; and, the goal of the White rioters, as was true of White lynchers of single victims, was to instill fear and terror into Blacks, thereby buttressing White domination. The Jim Crow hierarchy could not work without

[7]Myrdal, op. cit., p. 566.
[8]W.E.B. Dubois, Originally in *Dust of Dawn*. Cited here from *DuBois: Writings*, Nathan Huggins (editor). New

York: Viking Press, 1986, p. 747.
[9]Joseph Boskin, *Urban Racial Violence*. Beverly Hills, 1976, pp. 14-15.

violence being used against those on the bottom rung. George Fredrickson, a historian, stated it this way: "Lynching represented … a way of using fear and terror to check 'dangerous' tendencies in a black community considered to be ineffectively regimented or supervised. As such it constituted a confession that the regular institutions of a segregated society provided an inadequate measure of day-to-day control."[10]

Many Blacks resisted the indignities of Jim Crow, and, far too often, they paid for their bravery with their lives.

Web Link

1. David Pilgrim, "What was Jim Crow?"
    http://www.ferris.edu/jimcrow/what.htm

---

[10]George M. Fredrickson, *The Black Image In The White Mind: The Debate on Afro-American Character and Destiny 1817-1914*. New York: Harper & Row, 1971, p. 272.

13. Booker T. Washington Delivers the 1895 Atlanta Compromise Speech

Mr. President and Gentlemen of the Board of Directors and Citizens:

One-third of the population of the South is of the Negro race. No enterprise seeking the material, civil, or moral welfare of this section can disregard this element of our population and reach the highest success. I but convey to you, Mr. President and Directors, the sentiment of the masses of my race when I say that in no way have the value and manhood of the American Negro been more fittingly and generously recognized than by the managers of this magnificent Exposition at every stage of its progress. It is a recognition that will do more to cement the friendship of the two races than any occurrence since the dawn of our freedom.

Not only this, but the opportunity here afforded will awaken among us a new era of industrial progress. Ignorant and inexperienced, it is not strange that in the first years of our new life we began at the top instead of at the bottom; that a seat in Congress or the state legislature was more sought than real estate or industrial skill; that the political convention or stump speaking had more attractions than starting a dairy farm or truck garden.

A ship lost at sea for many days suddenly sighted a friendly vessel. From the mast of the unfortunate vessel was seen a signal," Water, water; we die of thirst!" The answer from the friendly vessel at once came back, "Cast down your bucket where you are." A second time the signal, "Water, water; send us water!" ran up from the distressed vessel, and was answered, "Cast down your bucket where you are." And a third and fourth signal for water was answered, "Cast down your bucket where you are." The captain of the distressed vessel, at last heeding the injunction, cast down his bucket, and it came up full of fresh, sparkling water from the mouth of the Amazon River. To those of my race who depend on bettering their condition in a foreign land or who underestimate the importance of cultivating friendly relations with the Southern white man, who is their next-door neighbor, I would say: "Cast down your bucket where you are"—cast it down in making friends in every manly way of the people of all races by whom we are surrounded.

Cast it down in agriculture, mechanics, in commerce, in domestic service, and in the professions. And in this connection it is well to bear in mind that whatever other sins the South may be called to bear, when it comes to business, pure and simple, it is in the South that the Negro is given a man's chance in the commercial world, and in nothing is this Exposition more eloquent than in emphasizing this chance. Our greatest danger is that in the great leap from slavery to freedom we may overlook the fact that the masses of us are to live by the productions of our hands, and fail to keep in mind that we shall prosper in proportion as we learn to dignify and glorify common labour, and put brains and skill into the common occupations of life; shall prosper in proportion as we learn to draw the line between the superficial and the substantial, the ornamental gewgaws of life and the useful. No race can prosper till it learns that there is as much dignity in tilling a field as in writing a poem. It is at the bottom of life we must begin, and not at the top. Nor should we permit our grievances to overshadow our opportunities.

To those of the white race who look to the incoming of those of foreign birth and strange tongue and habits for the prosperity of the South, were I permitted I would repeat what I say to my own race," Cast down your bucket where you are." Cast it down among the eight millions of Negroes whose habits you know, whose fidelity and love you have tested in days when to have proved treacherous meant the ruin of your firesides. Cast down your bucket among these people who have, without strikes and labour wars, tilled your fields, cleared your forests, builded your railroads and cities, and brought forth treasures from the bowels of the earth, and helped make possible this magnificent representation of the progress of the South. Casting down your bucket among my people, helping and encouraging them as you are doing on these grounds, and to education of head, hand, and heart, you will find that they will buy your surplus land, make blossom the waste places in your fields, and run your factories. While doing this, you can be sure in the future, as in the past, that you and your families will be surrounded by the most patient, faithful, law-abiding, and unresentful people that the world has seen. As we have proved our loyalty to you in the past, in nursing your children, watching by the sick-bed of your mothers and fathers, and often following them with tear-dimmed eyes to their graves, so in the future, in our humble way, we shall stand by you with a devotion that no foreigner can approach, ready to lay down our lives, if need be, in defense of yours, interlacing our industrial, commercial, civil, and religious life with yours in a way that shall make the interests of both races one. In all things that are purely social we can be as separate as the fingers, yet one as the hand in all things essential to mutual progress.

There is no defense or security for any of us except in the highest intelligence and development of all. If anywhere there are efforts tending to curtail the fullest growth of the Negro, let these efforts be turned into stimulating, encouraging, and making him the most useful and intelligent citizen. Effort or means so invested will pay a thousand per cent interest. These efforts will be twice blessed—blessing him that gives and him that takes. There is no escape through law of man or God from the inevitable:

The laws of changeless justice bind Oppressor with oppressed;

And close as sin and suffering joined We march to fate abreast …

Nearly sixteen millions of hands will aid you in pulling the load upward, or they will pull against you the load downward. We shall constitute one-third and more of the ignorance and crime of the South, or one-third [of] its intelligence and progress; we shall contribute one-third to the business and industrial prosperity of the South, or we shall prove a veritable body of death, stagnating, depressing, retarding every effort to advance the body politic.

Gentlemen of the Exposition, as we present to you our humble effort at an exhibition of our progress, you must not expect overmuch. Starting thirty years ago with ownership here and there in a few quilts and pumpkins and chickens (gathered from miscellaneous sources), remember the path that has led from these to the inventions and production of agricultural implements, buggies, steam-engines, newspapers, books, statuary, carving, paintings, the management of drug stores and banks, has not been trodden without contact with thorns and thistles. While we take pride in what we exhibit as a result of our independent efforts, we do not for a moment forget that our part in this exhibition would fall far short of your expectations but for the constant help that has come to our educational life, not only from the Southern states, but especially from Northern philanthropists, who have made their gifts a constant stream of blessing and encouragement.

The wisest among my race understand that the agitation of questions of social equality is the extremest folly, and that progress in the enjoyment of all the privileges that will come to us must be the result of severe and constant struggle rather than of artificial forcing. No race that has anything to contribute to the markets of the world is long in any degree ostracized. It is important and right that all privileges of the law be ours, but it is vastly more important that we be prepared for the exercise of these privileges. The opportunity to earn a dollar in a factory just now is worth infinitely more than the opportunity to spend a dollar in an opera-house.

In conclusion, may I repeat that nothing in thirty years has given us more hope and encouragement, and drawn us so near to you of the white race, as this opportunity offered by the Exposition; and here bending, as it were, over the altar that represents the results of the struggles of your race and mine, both starting practically empty-handed three decades ago, I pledge that in your effort to work out the great and intricate problem which God has laid at the doors of the South, you shall have at all times the patient, sympathetic help of my race; only let this be constantly in mind, that, while from representations in these buildings of the product of field, of forest, of mine, of factory, letters, and art, much good will come, yet far above and beyond material benefits will be that higher good, that, let us pray God, will come, in a blotting out of sectional differences and racial animosities and suspicions, in a determination to administer absolute justice, in a willing obedience among all classes to the mandates of law. This, coupled with our material prosperity, will bring into our beloved South a new heaven and a new earth.

Web Link

1. Booker T. Washington, 1895 Atlanta Compromise Speech
    http://historymatters.gmu.edu/d/39/

14. W.E.B. Du Bois

By Ralph McGill

W.E.B. DuBois was a spokesman for the Negro's rights at a time when few were listening: he was highly intelligent, but toward the end of his career, he became embittered, a Communist, and finally left the United States and took refuge in Ghana. There shortly before his death, Ralph McGill sought him out for this talk

A Luncheon given in early 1963 by Conor Cruise O'Brien, vice-chancellor of the University of Ghana, beautiful on the gentle hills of Legon near Accra, made possible a subsequent talk with William Edward Burghardt DuBois. Until one met him he was myth grown out of some seventy-five years of the often turbulent and tragic history of the South's and the nation's trauma of race. I did not expect the first question, after greetings, to be concerned with the author of the Uncle Remus stories. But it was.

Did you know Joel Harris?

"No," I replied, "he died some years before I went to work on the Atlanta Constitution. After going there; I got to know three of his sons and a daughter. He wrote some of the Uncle Remus stories at the old double-rolltop desk I have in my office."

"I had a letter of introduction to him after I went to Atlanta," he said. "One day I decided to present it. Walking to his office, I passed by a grocery store that had on display out front the drying fingers of a recently lynched Negro."

He fell silent. No one else said anything. Outside the windows of his spacious house, provided by the government, in the old residential section of Ghana, there was a sound of children at play. A breath of air blew in past the flowering shrubs near the windows. We waited—his wife, his stepson, David, Mark Lewis, of the U.S. Information Agency office in Accra, a wide-eyed, solemn-faced young Ghanaian girl who was nurse to the aged and ailing man, and I.

The frail body of the ninety-five-year-old man lay stretched on a sofa. He wore trousers, a soft white shirt, and socks and slippers. His mustache and goatee were carefully trimmed. He had been asleep when we arrived. We had waited perhaps half an hour for him to awaken and then be dressed. Neither illness nor a prostate operation in a London hospital some months before, where Ghana's president, Kwame Nkrumah, had insisted he go, had reduced the fire of his mind, though he said his memory was not as quick as before.

There was a lot of history in the slender, sick, and slowly dying man. At ninety-four he had become a citizen of Ghana, where he had resided since 1960. Three years before, he had requested membership in the Communist Party, because he had ceased to believe, he stated, that any other system, would produce the sort of world he wanted. But in keeping with his controversial past, he denounced the U.S. Communist program to set up an all-Negro state somewhere in the South. The idea was repellent to him.

Always the fiercely independent, sensitive intellectual, he had been for more than fifty years a passionate fighter for full civil rights and equality of citizenship for the Negro. This placed him in opposition to Booker T. Washington well before the turn of the century. He had helped found the NAACP but had broken with it in 1948 because of its "timidity" and his own growing obsession with Communist causes and ideology.

As I waited for him to speak and studied his face, revealing that his mind was going backward in time and memory, he seemed to me somehow alien to the old colonial house that some long-departed English civil servant had occupied in the Gold Coast days. On its walls were richly and beautifully wrought red hangings of Chinese silk and a few paintings. There were busts of Marx, Lenin, and Mao Tse-tung. Save for the sculptured head of Marx, there was no evidence of Russian art, though DuBois had made a number of journeys to Moscow. One sensed that perhaps the Chinese intellectuals, with their polished manners, had more attraction for the man who for most of his life had himself been somewhat formal in manner and had often worn a pince-nez, carried a cane, and kept carefully trimmed both goatee and mustache. The Chinese had honored him in Peking on his ninety-first birthday with a dinner at which Premier Chou En-lai had been present. Ghana's President Nkrumah, as a student in the United States, had become an apostle of DuBois's Pan-Africa policy. Ghana honored him as a citizen-scholar. Yet the feeling persisted that although the DuBois concept of the Negro's proper status in America was coming into being, the old fighter seemed lonely and unrequited by life.

At last he spoke, his ivory-colored face changing from reflection to anger.

"I saw those fingers ... ! didn't go to see Joel Harris and present my letter. I never went!"

"I wish you had gone," I said. "Joel Chandler Harris was a good man, as were his closest associates."

"No," he replied, "it was no use. He and they had no question in their minds about the status of the Negro as a separated, lesser citizen. They perhaps were kind men, as you say. They unhesitatingly lived up to a paternalistic role, a sort of noblesse oblige. But that was all. The status slowly had become immutable insofar as the South's leaders of that time were concerned. Booker T. Washington had helped them rationalize it. I do not think that he meant to do so. But he did. In fact, he put a public stamp of acceptance on it there in your city when he spoke at the Atlanta Exposition."

"I've read that address many times," I said. "I also have talked with men who saw and heard him deliver it. They've told me of the tremendous drama of that day. They said that when he came to his key paragraph, he began it by holding up both arms, the fingers of each hand spread wide, and said, 'In all things that are purely social we can be as separate as the fingers, yet as the hand'—and here Washington quickly clinched each hand—'in all things essential to mutual progress.'"

DuBois nodded.

"I know," he said, "and in that same speech he implicitly abandoned all political and social rights."

There was a long pause.

"I never thought Washington was a bad man," he said. "I believed him to be sincere, though wrong. He and I came from different backgrounds. I was born free. Washington was born slave. He felt the lash of an overseer across his back. I was born in Massachusetts, he on a slave plantation in the South. My great-grandfather fought with the Colonial Army in New England in the American Revolution." (This earned the grandfather his freedom.) "I had a happy childhood and acceptance in the community. Washington's childhood was hard. I had many more advantages: Fisk University, Harvard, graduate years in Europe. Washington had little formal schooling. I admired much about him. Washington," he said, a smile softening the severe, gaunt lines of his face, "died in 1915. A lot of people think I died at the same time."

"Could you pinpoint the beginning of the controversy and break between him and you?"

"The controversy," he said, "developed more between our followers than between us. It is my opinion that Washington died a sad and disillusioned man who felt he had been betrayed by white America. I don't know that, but I believe it. In the early years I did not dissent entirely from Washington's program. I was sure that out of his own background he saw the Negro's problem from its lowest economic level. He never really repudiated the higher ends of justice which were then denied.

"As Washington began to attain stature as leader of his new, small, and struggling school at Tuskegee," DuBois continued, "he gave total emphasis to economic progress through industrial and vocational education. He believed that if the Negro could be taught skills and find jobs, and if others could become small landowners, a yeoman class would develop that would, in time, be recognized as worthy of what already was their civil rights, and that they would then be fully accepted as citizens. So he appealed to moderation, and he publicly postponed attainment of political rights and accepted the system of segregation.

"I know Washington believed in what Frederick Douglass had crusaded for from emancipation until his death in 1895. But he made a compromise.

"We talked about it. I went with him to see some of the Eastern philanthropists who were helping him with his school. Washington would promise them happy and contented labor for their new enterprises. He reminded them there would be no strikers. I remember once I went with him to call on Andrew Carnegie—with whom he had a warm and financially rewarding relationship. On the way there Washington said to me:

"'Have you read Mr. Carnegie's book?'"

"'No,' I replied, 'I haven't.'"

"'You ought to,' he said; 'Mr. Carnegie likes it.'"

DuBois chuckled softly. "When we got to Mr. Carnegie's office," he said, "he left me to wait downstairs. I never knew whether Mr. Carnegie

had expressed an opinion about me or whether Washington didn't trust me to be meek. It probably was the latter. I never read the book."

Washington came to national prominence by way of the Atlanta Exposition speech in 1895. It is possible that his decision toward acceptance of the political status quo was influenced by the frustrations and failures of Frederick Douglass. Douglass had been a crusading abolitionist, and he carried his fervor into the years from 1865 until his death, demanding full and equal citizenship. Washington had watched the party of Lincoln cast off the Negro in the historic compromise with Southern leaders that enabled Rutherford B. Hayes to be elected in 1876. The price of this steal of a national election was a removal of occupying federal troops and an end to the radical reconstruction that had been imposed after Lincoln's assassination. This deal had left the future of the newly freed, largely uneducated Negro to "states rights" decisions. By 1895 the several Southern states had about completed total disfranchisement of the Negro by way of constitutional amendments and legislative statutes. Washington's decision may have lacked a certain idealism, but it was born out of present reality. He may have died feeling a certain betrayal; he nonetheless had made a substantial contribution to preparing many thousands of Negroes for participation in the drive for long-denied rights that began after his death. It came to fruition in the late 1940s and culminated in the 1954 school decision and others that quickly grew out of it. There was a greatness about Washington.

"As I came to see it," said DuBois, "Washington bartered away much that was not his to barter. Certainly I did not believe that the skills of an artisan bricklayer, plasterer, or shoemaker, and the good farmer would cause the white South, grimly busy with disfranchisement and separation, to change the direction of things. I realized the need for what Washington was doing. Yet it seemed to me he was giving up essential ground that would be hard to win back. I don't think Washington saw this until the last years of his life. He kept hoping. But before he died he must have known that he and his hopes had been rejected and that he had, without so intending, helped make stronger—and more fiercely defended—a separation and rejection that made a mockery of all he had hoped and dreamed. I felt grief for him when I learned of his death because I believe he died in sorrow and a sense of betrayal."

There was time for one more question. Booker T. Washington's influence was supreme in racial leadership for twenty years. He was frequently attacked by Negro intellectuals. But he had so successfully appealed to what was a national mood that developed in the years after the Hayes-Tilden election of 1876 that he easily put down all opposition. He had the support and friendship of powerful figures in the industrial and political life of the nation. He was a guest in their homes and in their private cars. And always he came away with money to help educate greatly disadvantaged young Negroes. Many historians believe that Washington's postponement of a decision on Negro rights was largely influential in the U.S. Supreme Court's separate-but-equal decision of 1896, a year after Washington's separated fingers were upraised in the Atlanta Exposition address. Certain it was that Washington's appeasement view, however temporary he anticipated it to be, came to be accepted, North and South, as the view of the Negro himself. Washington was confronted with that conclusion on those occasions when his speeches called attention to the fact that the Negro must, one day, be admitted to the ballot and to full citizenship. Southern editors and leaders invariably took him sharply to task, demanding to know what he meant and why he had changed his mind after the Atlanta speech.

There was no doubt in DuBois's mind. He was sure, he said, that without Washington's position there would have been no Plessy-Ferguson decision in 1896.

There was a sense of unreality in talking about all that was past with DuBois, who after 1915 had been one of the stormy, and sometimes storm-tossed leaders in the struggle for civil rights. He was always a bit arrogant, or so those who worked most closely with him felt. Except for one summer early in his teaching career spent in the South's poorer plantation region, he had never been directly interested in the masses. W. E. B. DuBois

was an intellectual and a scholar. He dreamed, his associates and biographers say, of creating a "talented tenth" that would supply the leadership necessary to winning rights and full equality for the Negro.

He was most comfortable with small groups of intellectuals and good conversationalists. In the 1930s he proclaimed in The Crisis, the NAACP magazine which he edited, that he wrote his personal column for sophisticated persons, not for "fools and illiterates."

He was best at polemics. Delay and contradiction drove him to frustration and frequent outbursts of invective and criticism that revealed the storm within him. He once admitted that he, opposing racial prejudice, was "one of the greatest sinners" in the intensity of his prejudice against white persons. He was honest enough to say that he expected prejudice and therefore may have even caused it by anticipating it. In Darkwater, published in 1920, he concluded a section of verse which condemned "The White World's Vermin and Filth," with the lines:

I hate them, Oh!
I hate them well,
I hate them, Christ! As I hate hell!
If I were God I'd sound their knell
This day.

Oswald Garrison Villard, who admired DuBois very much and who had worked with him in the NAACP, wrote in 1920 of the personal bitterness "that so often mars his work." In the same year, in a letter to a friend, he said, "I think I pity Dr. DuBois more than any man in America."

The Crisis was founded in 1910 with encouragement from Villard and others who disagreed with Booker T. Washington's policies. The magazine legally was the property of the NAACP, but in making DuBois editor and promising him independence of action, they asked him only to agree not to make The Crisis a personal organ and to avoid personal rancor. This pledge was not well kept. But DuBois made The Crisis a dynamic and forceful voice for the major objectives of the association. In 1910, the magazine condemned the proposal to establish segregated public schools in Chicago, Philadelphia, Columbus, Ohio, and Atlantic City. In 1913, DuBois joined with Villard and others in a written protest to President Wilson against segregated practices in government employment. In 1917, DuBois launched an attack on the white primary system, which was the chief barrier to Negro participation in the ballot. Some of the white social reformers of his time who gave him consistent support, although occasionally they became dismayed by his polemic excesses, were Jane Addams, John Dewey, William Dean Howells, John H. Holmes, Lincoln Steffens, Stephen S. Wise, William H. Ward, and Lillian D. Wald.

By 1916 one NAACP board and many of DuBois's most ardent supporters were becoming increasingly embarrassed by his extremes of editorial expression. His race prejudice was more and more apparent. Typical of these editorial comments in The Crisis was one stating that "the most ordinary Negro is a distinct gentleman, but it takes extraordinary training and opportunity to make the average white man anything but a hog."

Slowly DuBois's bitterness narrowed his once piercing view. He broke with Walter White, executive secretary of the NAACP. Editors of Negro newspapers who dared criticize him were dismissed as "croaking toads." DuBois left The Crisis editorial chair in 1934 to go to Atlanta to teach, and the magazine ceased publication soon after. For a long time it had been mostly a personal organization for DuBois. and he was beyond question as Walter White said, "one of the chief molders of modern thought regarding the Negro," but he had to rule. The Negro in America, despite harsh discriminations and segregation, was making great advances and producing new

leaders for the changing times. DuBois could accept neither them nor the changing scene.

Ten years after his retirement from The Crisis, he was back with the NAACP, but his influence and position had lessened. Four years later he was dismissed with a pension. Paul Robeson, chairman of the left-wing Council on African Affairs, welcomed the old man as he left the NAACP. Dr. DuBois worked for various Communist front organizations, but it is likely he believed he was using them to further his own ends. The Russians interested him, but they were not Negro.

By 1952 he simply abandoned the struggle for Negro rights to give full time to world movements for world peace, for socialism, and later, to team with Kwame Nkrumah and others in promoting a Pan-Africa movement. It has never been possible to separate the man from the myth in considering W. E. B. DuBois.

Mark Lewis and I said good-bye. There was a feeling of having emerged from a place far back in time as we came out of the cool high-ceilinged house—where the talk had been of Atlanta, of the South, and of a man's more than seventy-five years of participation in the revolutionary background of changes in American educational, political, and social life—into the sun and beauty of Accra's best residential area of old walls, gardens, verandas, and flowers. Six months later in faraway Ghana W. E. B. DuBois died. It was August 28, 1963, the eve of the march on Washington, the largest demonstration for civil rights ever held. One could not help experiencing a feeling of destiny linking both events. The man who for many years had spoken with the loudest and most articulate voice was now silent while his objectives were being realized.

Web Link

1. Ralph McGill, Interview with WEB DuBois, portion, Atlantic Monthly (1965)
   http://www.theatlantic.com/past/docs/unbound/flashbks/black/mcgillbh.htm

Purpose

The purpose of this reading and exercise is to help you understand how your own beliefs about politics and government compare with those of other Americans.

Context

The concept of political ideology is an important one. *Ideology* can be defined as a set of fundamental beliefs or principles about politics and government, especially about what the scope of civil government should be, how decisions should be made, and what values should be pursued by society. The most commonly used terms used to describe people's ideologies in the U.S. are *liberal* and *conservative*. There are significant differences between liberals and conservatives in terms of the ways they approach human governance. They envision different roles for the civil government in terms of the extent to which it ought to intervene in certain behaviors, because they have different underlying assumptions about human nature, and therefore what kinds of human governance institutions are appropriate for handling certain situations.

Conservatives tend to believe that human nature is static and unchanging; that is, people today are basically the same as people were thousands of years ago. Even though culture and technology changes, people are essentially the same. Therefore, the institutions that have always existed that govern human interactions (the family, voluntary associations, and civil government) are the same as they have always been, even though their forms may change. For example, governments still exist, but most societies no longer function as monarchies, and democratic governments tend to be predominant now.

Liberals tend to believe that human nature is on an evolutionary path of perpetual improvement, such that the people, cultures and society today are superior to the people, cultures, and societies of the past. Therefore, what they view as primitive societal institutions such as the traditional family unit and churches ought to evolve away; similarly, traditional governments, geared around the nation-state, are also evolving away. Imposing earlier human governance rules, institutions, and systems on more highly-evolved societies is seen as a form of oppression.

Obviously, these differences lead to dramatically different approaches to the role of civil government. When we conceive of how these ideologies differ in terms of the appropriate role of government, other ideologies emerge; *libertarianism, socialism,* and *democratic socialism* are three other commonly-discussed ideologies. The following table summarizes how each of these ideologies envisions the role of civil government (that is, how much government planning needs to generally occur) in different areas of human interaction. Democratic socialism is related to socialism, but its forms of government are different; Socialist governments may be elected or may be imposed by revolution; in Democratic Socialism the means of establishing governments is through representative democracy.

In the area of foreign policy (how governments ought to interact with other governments in the international arena), the table summarizes how each ideology group tends to approach these inter-actions (high and low does not describe the approaches very effectively). Liberals tend to emphasize multilateral negotiations (usually through international organizations such as the United Nations) and non-military efforts (such as extended economic sanctions). Conservatives tend to be more willing to "go it alone" in the international arena, with less reliance on international organizations; they also tend to favor a more rapid application of military force, allowing less time for economic sanctions to have their effects. Modern libertarians tend to be suspicious of interventions in other countries, while socialists emphasize multilateral institutions and negotiations as venues in which state sovereignty and independent actions are de-emphasized.

Some political observers note that these broad categories don't describe many individuals beliefs about government very well. The Pew Research Center developed a new set of categories for peoples' ideology that many people have found to be helpful, because it provides different labels and takes into account current political parties and issues, instead of the more abstract ideas that lead to labels such as "liberal" and "conservative."

Governance Dimension	Civil Government's Appropriate Level of Intervention or Planning			
	Liberal	*Conservative*	*Libertarian*	*Socialist*
Economy	High	Low	Very Low	Very High; Significant Government Ownership
Social Safety Net	High	Low	Very Low	Very High
Personal Morality	Low	High	Very Low	Very Low
Foreign Policy	Multilateral and Internationalist, "Dovish"	Unilateral and Internationalist, "Hawkish"	Non-Interventionalist	Multilateral Internationalist

Thought Exercises

1. Go to http://people-press.org/typology/quiz/?src=typology-report and take the Pew "Beyond Red & Blue" ideology poll. Note the category in which the poll classifies you. Read the chapter selection and see what each group in the poll's categories believes.
2. Did your own poll results surprise you? Do you believe your overall opinions and characteristics match those in the Pew poll and report? If not, which group do you think better summarizes your thoughts about politics and government?
3. Think about the table on the previous page and the discussion that preceded it. What is your idea about human nature? Are people now basically the same as they've ever been, or have we evolved to a higher plane? What evidence do you have to support your contention?
4. If you previously considered yourself to be liberal, conservative, libertarian, or socialist, did the description and table help you to organize your thinking about people who hold different ideologies?

Web Link

1. Pew Center for People & the Press, Beyond Red vs. Blue
   http://people-press.org/report/242/beyond-red-vs-blue

15. Beyond Red vs. Blue

Republicans Divided About Role of Government—Democrats by Social and Personal Values

By Pew Research Center for The People & The Press

Coming out of the 2004 election, the American political landscape decidedly favored the Republican Party. The GOP had extensive appeal among a disparate group of voters in the middle of the electorate, drew extraordinary loyalty from its own varied constituencies, and made some inroads among conservative Democrats. These advantages outweighed continued nationwide parity in party affiliation. Looking forward, however, there is no assurance that Republicans will be able to consolidate and build upon these advantages.

Republicans have neither gained nor lost in party identification in 2005. Moreover, divisions within the Republican coalition over economic and domestic issues may loom larger in the future, given the increasing salience of these matters. The Democratic party faces its own formidable challenges, despite the fact that the public sides with them on many key values and policy questions. Their constituencies are more diverse and, while united in opposition to President Bush, the Democrats are fractured by differences over social and personal values.

These are among the conclusions of Pew's political typology study, which sorts voters into homogeneous groups based on values, political beliefs, and party affiliation. The current study is based on two public opinion surveys—a nationwide poll of 2,000 interviews conducted Dec. 1-16, 2004, and

a subsequent re-interview of 1,090 respondents conducted March 17-27 of this year. This is the fourth such typology created by the Pew Research Center for the People & the Press since 1987. Many of the groups identified in the current surveys are similar to those in past typologies, reflecting the

---

How Values Divide the Nation

Divisions *Between* Parties: Large gaps between Republicans and Democrats:

- National security
- Assertive foreign policy

Divisions *Within* Parties: Minor partisan gap, but major fissures within one or both parties:

- Environmentalism
- Government regulation
- Isolationism vs. global activism
- Immigration

Divisions Between *and* Within Parties: Partisan divides, but also intra-party gaps:

- Religious & moral values
- Welfare
- Cooperation with allies
- Business & the free market
- Cynicism about politics
- Individualism vs. fatalism

---

continuing importance of a number of key beliefs and values. These themes endure despite the consequential events of the past four years—especially the Sept. 11 terrorist attacks and the war in Iraq.

But clearly, those events—and the overall importance of national security issues—have a major impact on the typology. Foreign affairs assertiveness now almost completely distinguishes Republican-oriented voters from Democratic-oriented voters; this was a relatively minor factor in past typologies. In contrast, attitudes relating to religion and social issues are not nearly as important in determining party affiliation. Still, these issues do underscore differences within parties, especially among the Democrats. While Republican-inclined voters range from the religious to the very religious, the Democratic Party is much more divided in terms of religious and cultural values. Its core constituents include both seculars and the highly religious.

The value gaps for the GOP are, perhaps surprisingly, greatest with respect to the role of government. The Republicans' bigger tent now includes more lower-income voters than it once did, and many of these voters favor an activist government to help working class people. Government regulation to protect the environment is an issue with particular potential to divide Republicans. On this issue, wide divisions exist both within the GOP and among right-of-center voters more generally.

Yet Republicans also have much in common beyond their overwhelming support for a muscular foreign policy and broad agreement on social issues. Voters inclined toward the Republican Party are distinguished from Democrats by their personal optimism and belief in the power of the individual. While some voting blocs on the right are as financially stressed as poorer Democrats, Republicans in this situation tend to be more hopeful and positive in their outlook than their more fatalistic counterparts in the Democratic Party.

National security attitudes also generally unite the Democrats. Beyond their staunch opposition to the war in Iraq, Democrats overwhelmingly believe that effective diplomacy, rather than military strength, should serve as the basis for U.S. security policy. At home, Democrats remain committed to a strong social safety net and are joined in opposition to most domestic policy proposals from the Bush administration, from tougher bankruptcy laws to private accounts in Social Security.

The typology study's finding of significant cleavages within parties not only runs counter to the widespread impression of a nation increasingly divided into two unified camps, but also raises questions about political alignments in the future. In particular, the study suggests that if the political agenda turns away from issues of defense and security, prospects for party unity could weaken significantly. As the following chapters detail, numerous opportunities exist for building coalitions across party lines on many issues currently facing the nation—coalitions that, in many cases, include some strange political bedfellows. Overall, there are many more shades to the American political landscape than just the red and blue dividing the Electoral College maps last Nov. 2.

The Political Middle

In some ways, the biggest difference between the latest Pew Research Center typology and those in the Clinton era concerns the groups in the middle of the political spectrum. During the 1990s, the typology groups in the center were not particularly partisan, but today they lean decidedly to the GOP.

The middle groups include **Upbeats**, relatively moderate voters who have positive views of their financial situation, government performance,

The 2005 Political Typology: The Middle Groups		
	General Public	Regist. Voters
	%	%
Upbeats	11	13
Positive outlook & moderate		
Disaffecteds	9	10
Working class & discouraged		
Bystanders	10	0
Democracy's dropouts		

business, and the state of the nation in general. They are generally well-educated and fairly engaged in political news. While most Upbeats do not formally identify with either political party, they voted for Bush by more than four-to-one last November.

A second, very different group of centrist voters, the **Disaffecteds**, is much less affluent and educated than the Upbeats. Consequently, they have a distinctly different outlook on life and political matters. They are deeply cynical about government and unsatisfied with their financial situation. Even so, Disaffecteds lean toward the Republican Party and, though many did not vote in the presidential election, most of those who did supported Bush's reelection.

In effect, Republicans have succeeded in attracting two types of swing voters who could not be more different. The common threads are a highly favorable opinion of President Bush personally and support for an aggressive military stance against potential enemies of the U.S.

A third group in the center, **Bystanders**, largely consign themselves to the political sidelines. This category of mostly young people, few of whom voted in 2004, has been included in all four of the Center's political typologies.

The Right

The Republican Party's current advantage with the center makes up for the fact that the GOP-oriented groups, when taken together, account for only 29% of the public. By contrast, the three Democratic groups constitute 41% of the public. But the imbalance shifts to the GOP's favor when the inclinations of the two major groups in the center are taken into account—many of whom lean Republican and most of whom voted for George W. Bush.

The three GOP groups are highly diverse, and this is reflected in their values. The staunchly conservative **Enterprisers** have perhaps the most consistent ideological profile of any group in the typology. They are highly patriotic and strongly pro-business, oppose social welfare and overwhelmingly support an assertive foreign policy.

The 2005 Political Typology: The Republican Groups		
	General Public %	Regist. Voters %
Enterprisers	9	11
Staunch conservatives		
Social Conservatives	11	13
Religious, critical of business		
Pro-Government Conservatives	9	10
Struggling social conservatives		

This group is largely white, well-educated, affluent and male—more than three-quarters are men.

While Enterprisers are a bit less religious than the other GOP groups, they are socially conservative in most respects. Two other groups on the right are both highly religious and very conservative on moral issues. **Social Conservatives** agree with Enterprisers on most issues, but they tend to be critical of business and supportive of government regulation to protect the public good and the environment. They also express deep concerns about the growing number of immigrants in America. This largely female group includes many white evangelical Christians, and nearly half of Social Conservatives live in the South.

Pro-Government Conservatives also are broadly religious and socially conservative, but they deviate from the party line in their backing for government involvement in a wide range of policy areas, such as government regulation and more generous assistance to the poor. This relatively young, predominantly female group is under substantial financial pressure, but most feel it is within their power to get ahead. This group also is highly concentrated in the South, and, of the three core Republican groups, had the lowest turnout in the 2004 election.

Clearly, there is more than one kind of conservative. The Republican groups find common ground on cultural values, but opinions on the role of government, a defining feature of conservative philosophy for decades, are now among the most divisive for the GOP.

The 2005 Political Typology: The Democratic Groups		
	General Public %	Regist. Voters %
Liberals	17	19
Secular and anti-war		
Disadvantaged Democrats	10	10
Social welfare loyalists		
Conservative Democrats	14	15
Latter-day New Dealers		

The Left

At the other end of the political spectrum, **Liberals** have swelled to become the largest voting bloc in the typology. Liberals are opponents of an assertive foreign policy, strong supporters of environmental protection, and solid backers of government assistance to the poor.

This affluent, well-educated, highly secular group is consistently liberal on social issues, ranging from freedom of expression to abortion. In contrast, **Conservative Democrats** are quite religious, socially conservative and take more moderate positions on several key foreign policy questions. The group is older, and includes many blacks and Hispanics; of all the core Democratic groups, it has strongest sense of personal empowerment.

Disadvantaged Democrats also include many minority voters, and they are the least financially secure voting bloc. Members of this heavily female, poorly educated group are highly pessimistic about their opportunities in life, and also very mistrustful of both business and government. Nonetheless, they support government programs to help the needy.

While the Republican Party is divided over government's role, the Democrats are divided by social and personal values. Most Liberals live in a world apart from Disadvantaged Democrats and Conservative Democrats.

Other Major Findings

- For the most part, opinions about the use of force are what divides Democratic-oriented groups from the Republican groups. On other foreign policy issues, even contentious questions about working with allies, the partisan pattern is not as clear.

- Environmental protection now stands out as a major divide within the GOP's coalition. While a narrow majority of Enterprisers believe the country has gone too far in its efforts to protect the environment, most others on the GOP side disagree.

- Poorer Republicans and Democrats have strikingly different outlooks on their lives and possibilities. Pro-Government Conservatives are optimistic and positive; Disadvantaged Democrats are pessimistic and cynical.

- Immigration divides both parties. Liberals overwhelmingly believe immigrants strengthen American society, and most Enterprisers agree. Majorities of other groups in both parties say immigrants threaten traditional American customs and values.

- The Republican Party is doing a better job of standing up for its core issues than is the Democratic Party, according to their respective constituents. Liberals are particularly negative about the performance of the Democratic Party.

- A plurality of the public wants Bush to select a nominee who will keep the Supreme Court about the same as it is now. Only among Enterprisers and Social Conservatives is there substantial support for a more conservative course.

- Stem cell research deeply divides the GOP. Majorities in all three Democratic groups, and the three independent groups, favor such research. Republican groups, to varying degrees, are divided.

- Enterprisers take conservative positions on most religious and cultural issues but are less intense in their beliefs than are other GOP groups. They are more libertarian than other Republican-oriented groups.

- George W. Bush has the broadest personal appeal of any national political figure among the main independent groups, the Upbeats and Disaffecteds.

- Rudy Giuliani is widely popular with Republican groups but also has a favorable rating among majorities in both independent groups, and is viewed positively by roughly half of Conservative Democrats and Liberals.

- Bill and Hillary Clinton's favorable ratings have risen among the public, and both earn relatively high ratings from the GOP's Pro-Government Conservatives.

- Liberals stand far apart from the rest of the electorate in their strong support for gay marriage, and in opposing the public display of the Ten Commandments in government buildings.

- Enterprisers stand alone on key economic issues. Majorities in every other group—except Enterprisers—support a government guarantee of universal health insurance. Enterprisers also are the only group in which less than a majority supports increasing the minimum wage.

- Private investment accounts in Social Security draw mixed reviews. Support for Bush's plan has faded not just among Democrats, but also independents. Disaffecteds are now evenly split over the proposal; in December, they favored it by almost a two-to-one margin.

- Enterprisers are the only voters to overwhelmingly believe that the Patriot Act is a necessary tool in the war on terrorism. Liberals are the strongest opponents of the legislation.

16. Profiles of the Typology Groups

By Pew Research Center for The People & The Press

Enterprisers

Past Typology Counterpart: Staunch Conservatives, Enterprisers
9% OF ADULT POPULATION
10% OF REGISTERED VOTERS

PARTY ID: 81% Republican, 18% Independent/ No Preference, 1% Democrat (98% Rep/Lean Rep)

BASIC DESCRIPTION: As in 1994 and 1999, this extremely partisan Republican group's politics are driven by a belief in the free enterprise system and social values that reflect a conservative agenda. Enterprisers are also the strongest backers of an assertive foreign policy, which includes nearly unanimous support for the war in Iraq and strong support for such anti-terrorism efforts as the Patriot Act.

DEFINING VALUES: Assertive on foreign policy and patriotic; anti-regulation and pro-business; very little support for government help to the poor; strong belief that individuals are responsible for their own well being. Conservative on social issues such as gay marriage, but not much more religious than the nation as a whole. Very satisfied with personal financial situation.

WHO THEY ARE: Predominantly white (91%), male (76%) and financially well-off (62% have household incomes of at least $50,000, compared with 40% nationwide). Nearly half (46%) have a college degree, and 77% are married. Nearly a quarter (23%) are themselves military veterans. Only 10% are under age 30.

LIFESTYLE NOTES: 59% have a gun in the home; 53% trade stocks and bonds, and 30% are small business owners—all of which are the highest percentages among typology groups. 48% attend church weekly; 36% attend bible study or prayer group meetings.

2004 ELECTION: Bush 92%, Kerry 1%. Bush's most reliable supporters (just 4% of Enterprisers did not vote)

MEDIA USE: Enterprisers follow news about government and politics more closely than any other group, and exhibit the most knowledge about world affairs. The Fox News Channel is their primary source of news (46% cite it as a main source) followed by newspapers (42%) radio (31%) and the internet (26%).

Social Conservatives

Past Typology Counterpart: Moralists, Moderate Republicans
11% OF ADULT POPULATION
13% OF REGISTERED VOTERS

PARTY ID: 82% Republican, 18% Independent/No Preference, 0% Democrat (97% Rep/Lean Rep)

BASIC DESCRIPTION: While supportive of an assertive foreign policy, this group is somewhat more religious than are Enterprisers. In policy terms, they break from the Enterprisers in their cynical views of business, modest support for environmental and other regulation, and strong anti-immigrant sentiment.

DEFINING VALUES: Conservative on social issues ranging from gay marriage to abortion. Support an assertive foreign policy and oppose government aid for the needy, believing people need to make it on their own. Strongly worried about impact of immigrants on American society. More middle-of-the-road on economic and domestic policies, expressing some skepticism about business power and profits, and some support for government regulation to protect the environment. While not significantly better-off than the rest of the nation, most express strong feelings of financial satisfaction and security.

WHO THEY ARE: Predominantly white (91%), female (58%) and the oldest of all groups (average age is 52; 47% are 50 or older); nearly half live in the South. Most (53%) attend church weekly; 43% are white evangelical Protestants (double the national average of 21%).

LIFESTYLE NOTES: 56% have a gun in their home, and 51% attend Bible study groups.

2004 ELECTION: Bush 86%, Kerry 4%.

MEDIA USE: Half of Social Conservatives cite newspapers as a main source of news; the Fox News Channel (34%) and network evening news (30%) are their major TV news sources.

Pro-Government Conservatives

Past Typology Counterpart: Populist Republicans
9% OF ADULT POPULATION
10% OF REGISTERED VOTERS

PARTY ID: 58% Republican, 40% Independent/No Preference, 2% Democrat (86% Rep/Lean Rep)

BASIC DESCRIPTION: Pro-Government Conservatives stand out for their strong religious faith and conservative views on many moral issues. They also express broad support for a social safety net, which sets them apart from other GOP groups. Pro-Government Conservatives are skeptical about the effectiveness of the marketplace, favoring government regulation to protect the public interest and government assistance for the needy. They supported George W. Bush by roughly five-to-one.

DEFINING VALUES: Religious, financially insecure, and favorable toward government programs. Support the Iraq war and an assertive foreign policy, but less uniformly so than Enterprisers or Social Conservatives. Back government involvement in a wide range of policy areas, from poverty assistance to protecting morality and regulating industry.

WHO THEY ARE: Predominately female (62%) and relatively young; highest percentage of minority members of any Republican-leaning group (10% black, 12% Hispanic). Most (59%) have no more than a high school diploma. Poorer than other Republican groups; nearly half (49%) have household incomes of less than $30,000 (about on par with Disadvantaged Democrats). Nearly half (47%) are parents of children living at home; 42% live in the South.

LIFESTYLE NOTES: Most (52%) attend religious services at least weekly; nearly all describe religion as "very important" in their lives. Gun ownership is lower (36%) than in other GOP groups. Just 14% trade stocks and bonds in the market; 39% say someone in their home has faced unemployment in the past year.

2004 ELECTION: Bush 61%, Kerry 12%. Fully 21% said they didn't vote in November.

MEDIA USE: Most Pro-Government Conservatives consult traditional news sources, including newspapers (48%) and network TV (31%). No more or less engaged in politics than the national average.

Upbeats

Past Typology Counterpart: New Prosperity Independents, Upbeats
11% OF ADULT POPULATION
13% OF REGISTERED VOTERS

PARTY ID: 56% Independent/No Preference, 39% Republican, 5% Democrat (73% Rep/Lean Rep)

BASIC DESCRIPTION: Upbeats express positive views about the economy, government and society. Satisfied with their own financial situation and the direction the nation is heading, these voters support George W. Bush's leadership in economic matters more than on moral or foreign policy issues. Combining highly favorable views of government with equally positive views of business and the marketplace, Upbeats believe that success is in people's own hands, and that businesses make a positive contribution to society. This group also has a very favorable view of immigrants.

DEFINING VALUES: Very favorable views of government performance and responsiveness defines the group, along with similarly positive outlook on the role of business in society. While most support the war in Iraq, Upbeats have mixed views on foreign policy—but most favor preemptive military action against countries that threaten the U.S. Religious, but decidedly moderate in views about morality.

WHO THEY ARE: Relatively young (26% are under 30) and well-educated, Upbeats are among the wealthiest typology groups (39% have household incomes of $75,000 or more). The highest proportion of Catholics (30%) and white mainline Protestants (28%) of all groups, although fewer than half (46%) attend church weekly. Mostly white (87%), suburban, and married, they are evenly split between men and women.

LIFESTYLE NOTES: High rate of stock ownership (42%, 2nd after Enterprisers).

2004 ELECTION: Bush 63%, Kerry 14%.

MEDIA USE: Upbeats are second only to Liberals in citing the internet as their main news source (34% compared with 23% nationwide); 46% also cite newspapers. No more or less engaged in politics than the national average.

Disaffecteds

Past Typology Counterpart: Embittered, Disaffecteds
9% OF ADULT POPULATION
10% OF REGISTERED VOTERS

PARTY ID: 68% Independent/No Preference, 30% Republican, 2% Democrat (60% Rep/Lean Rep)

BASIC DESCRIPTION: Disaffecteds are deeply cynical about government and unsatisfied with both their own economic situation and the overall state of the nation. Under heavy financial pressure personally, this group is deeply concerned about immigration and environmental policies, particularly to the extent that they affect jobs. Alienated from politics, Disaffecteds have little interest in keeping up with news about politics and government, and few participated in the last election.

DEFINING VALUES: Despite personal financial strain—and belief that success is mostly beyond a person's control—Disaffecteds are only moderate supporters of government welfare and assistance to the poor. Strongly oppose immigration as well as regulatory and environmental policies on the grounds that government is ineffective and such measures cost jobs.

WHO THEY ARE: Less educated (70% have attended no college, compared with 49% nationwide) and predominantly male (57%). While a majority (60%) leans Republican, three-in-ten are strict independents, triple the national rate. Disaffecteds live in all parts of the country, though somewhat more are from rural and suburban areas than urban.

LIFESTYLE NOTES: Somewhat higher percentages than the national average have a gun in the home, and report that someone in their house has been unemployed in the past year.

2004 ELECTION: Bush 42%, Kerry 21%. Nearly a quarter (23%) said they didn't vote in the last election.

MEDIA USE: Disaffecteds have little interest in current events and pay little attention to the news. No single medium or network stands out as a main source.

Liberals

Past Typology Counterpart: Liberal Democrats/Seculars/60's Democrats
17% OF GENERAL POPULATION
19% OF REGISTERED VOTERS

PARTY ID: 59% Democrat; 40% Independent/No Preference, 1% Republican (92% Dem/Lean Dem)

BASIC DESCRIPTION: This group has nearly doubled in proportion since 1999. Liberal Democrats now comprise the largest share of Democrats. They are the most opposed to an assertive foreign policy, the most secular, and take the most liberal views on social issues such as homosexuality, abortion, and censorship. They differ from other Democratic groups in that they are strongly pro-environment and pro-immigration.

DEFINING VALUES: Strongest preference for diplomacy over use of military force. Pro-choice, supportive of gay marriage and strongly favor environmental protection. Low participation in religious activities. Most sympathetic of any group to immigrants as well as labor unions, and most opposed to the anti-terrorism Patriot Act.

WHO THEY ARE: Most (62%) identify themselves as liberal. Predominantly white (83%), most highly educated group (49% have a college degree or more), and youngest group after Bystanders. Least religious group in typology: 43% report they seldom or never attend religious services; nearly a quarter (22%) are seculars. More than one-third never married (36%). Largest group residing in urban areas (42%) and in the western half the country (34%). Wealthiest Democratic group (41% earn at least $75,000).

LIFESTYLE NOTES: Largest group to have been born (or whose parents were born) outside of the U.S. or Canada (20%). Least likely to have a gun in the home (23%) or attend bible study or prayer group meetings (13%).

2004 ELECTION: Bush 2%, Kerry 81%

MEDIA USE: Liberals are second only to Enterprisers in following news about government and public affairs most of the time (60%). Liberals' use of the internet to get news is the highest among all groups (37%).

Conservative Democrats

Past Typology Counterpart: Socially Conservative Democrats / New Dealers
14% OF ADULT POPULATION
15% OF REGISTERED VOTERS

PARTY ID: 89% Democrat, 11% Independent/No Preference, 0% Republican,(98% Dem/Lean Dem)

BASIC DESCRIPTION: Religious orientation and conservative views set this group apart from other Democratic-leaning groups on many social and political issues. Conservative Democrats' views are moderate with respect to key policy issues such as foreign policy, regulation of the environment and the role of government in providing a social safety net. Their neutrality on assistance to the poor is linked, at least in part, to their belief in personal responsibility.

DEFINING VALUES: Less extreme on moral beliefs than core Republican groups, but most oppose gay marriage and the acceptance of homosexuality, and support a more active role for government in protecting morality. No more conservative than the national average on other social issues such as abortion and stem-cell research. Most oppose the war in Iraq, but views of America's overall foreign policy are mixed and they are less opposed to Bush's assertive stance than are other Democratic groups.

WHO THEY ARE: Older women and blacks make up a sizeable proportion of this group (27% and 30%, respectively). Somewhat less educated and poorer than the nation overall. Allegiance to the Democratic party is quite strong (51% describe themselves as "strong" Democrats) but fully 85% describe themselves as either conservative or moderate ideologically.

LIFESTYLE NOTES: 46% attend church at least once a week, 44% attend Bible study or prayer group meetings, a third (34%) have a gun in their house.

2004 ELECTION: Bush 14%, Kerry 65%.

MEDIA USE: Emphasis on traditional providers as main news sources: newspapers (50%) and network TV news (42%).

Disadvantaged Democrats

Past Typology Counterpart: Partisan Poor
10% OF GENERAL POPULATION
10% OF REGISTERED VOTERS

PARTY ID: 84% Democrat; 16% Independent/No Preference, 0% Republican (99% Dem/Lean Dem)

BASIC DESCRIPTION: Least financially secure of all the groups, these voters are very anti-business, and strong supporters of government efforts to help the needy. Minorities account for a significant proportion of this group; nearly a third (32%) are black, roughly the same proportion as among Conservative Democrats. Levels of disapproval of George W. Bush job performance (91%) and candidate choice in 2004 (82% for Kerry) are comparable to those among Liberals.

DEFINING VALUES: Most likely to be skeptical of an individual's ability to succeed without impediments and most anti-business. Strong belief that government should do more to help the poor, yet most are disenchanted with government. Strongly supportive of organized labor (71% have a favorable view of labor unions).

WHO THEY ARE: Low average incomes (32% below $20,000 in household income); most (77%) often can't make ends meet. Six-in-ten are female. Three-in-ten (32%) are black and 14% are Hispanic. Not very well educated, 67% have at most a high-school degree. Nearly half (47%) are parents of children living at home.

LIFESTYLE NOTES: Nearly a quarter (23%) report someone in their household is a member of a labor union, and 58% report that they or someone in the home has been unemployed in the past year—both far larger proportions than in any other group. Only 27% have a gun in the home.

2004 ELECTION: 2% Bush, 82% Kerry

MEDIA USE: Largest viewership of CNN as main news source among all groups (31%). Only group in which a majority (53%) reads newspapers.

Bystanders

Past Typology Counterpart: Bystanders
10% OF ADULT POPULATION
0% OF REGISTERED VOTERS

PARTY ID: 56% Independent/No Preference, 22% Republican, 22% Democrat

BASIC DESCRIPTION: These Americans choose not to participate in or pay attention to politics, or are not eligible to do so (non-citizens).

DEFINING VALUES: Cynical about government and the political system. Uninterested in political news.

WHO THEY ARE: Young (39% are under age 30, average age is 37). Lowest education (24% have not finished high school). Less religious than any group other than Liberals (26% attend church weekly). Largely concentrated in the South and West, relatively few in the East and Midwest. One-in-five are Hispanic.

LIFESTYLE NOTES: About half (49%) say they often can't make ends meet, fewer than among Pro-Government Conservatives, Disadvantaged Democrats or Disaffecteds; 30% attend bible groups or prayer meetings; 30% own a gun.

2004 ELECTION: 96% did not vote in presidential election.

MEDIA USE: Television is the main news source for Bystanders (79%) as for all other typology groups, with network news (24%) the most frequently cited TV source; 34% read newspapers and 23% get their news from the radio.

Key Beliefs:	General Population	Enterprisers
Most corporations make a fair and reasonable amount of profit	39%	88%
Stricter environmental laws and regulations cost too many jobs and hurt the economy	31%	74%
Using overwhelming military force is the best way to defeat terrorism around the world	39%	84%
Poor people today have it easy because they can get government benefits without doing anything in return	34%	73%

Key Beliefs:	General Population	Social Conservatives
Homosexuality is a way of life that should be discouraged by society	44%	65%
The growing number of newcomers from other countries threatens traditional American customs and values	40%	68%
Poor people today have it easy because they can get government benefits without doing anything in return	34%	68%
Business corporations make too much profit	54%	66%

Key Beliefs:	General Population	Pro-gov't Conservatives
Books that contain dangerous ideas should be banned from public school libraries	44%	62%
Religion is a very important part of my life	74%	91%
The government should do more to help needy Americans, even if it means going deeper into debt	57%	80%
Government regulation of business is necessary to protect the public interest	49%	66%
We should all be willing to fight for our country, whether it is right or wrong	46%	67%

Key Beliefs:	General Population	Upbeats
Government often does a better job than people give it credit for	45%	68%
Most elected officials care what people like me think	32%	64%
Most corporations make a fair and reasonable profit	39%	78%
Immigrants strengthen our country	45%	72%
As Americans, we can always find ways to solve our problems and get what we want	59%	74%

Key Beliefs:	General Population	Disaffecteds
Immigrants today are a burden on our country because they take our jobs, housing and health care	44%	80%
Government is always wasteful and inefficient	47%	70%
Most elected officials don't care what people like me think	63%	84%
Hard work and determination are no guarantee of success for most people	28%	48%

Key Beliefs:	General Population	Liberals
Relying too much on military force to defeat terrorism creates hatred that leads to more terrorism	51%	90%
I worry the government is getting too involved in the issue of morality	51%	88%
Stricter environmental laws and regulations are worth the cost	60%	89%
Poor people have hard lives because government benefits don't go far enough to help them live decently	52%	80%

Key Beliefs:	General Population	Conservative Democrats
It is necessary to believe in God in order to be moral and have good values	50%	72%
Most people who want to get ahead can make it if they're willing to work hard	68%	82%
We should all be willing to fight for our country, whether it is right or wrong	46%	49%**
The government should do more to help needy Americans, even if it means going deeper into debt	57%	59%**

** Figures are notable for being so different from other Democratic groups.

Key Beliefs:	General Population	Disadvantaged Democrats
Hard work and determination are no guarantee of success for most people	28%	79%
Poor people have hard lives because government benefits don't go far enough to help them live decently	52%	80%
Most elected officials don't care what people like me think	63%	87%
Business corporations make too much profit	54%	76%
We should pay less attention to problems overseas and concentrate on problems here at home	49%	72%

Key Beliefs:	General Population	Bystanders
Follow what's going on in government and public affairs most/some of the time	80%	45%
Voted in 2004 Presidential election	74%	3%

Purpose

The purpose of this reading is to help you understand Dr. King's religious, social, and political thoughts on what justifies civil disobedience and political activism.

Context

This letter is considered to be one of the great documents in the American Civil Rights movement. During the 1950s, Dr. King repeatedly called upon Christian churches to endorse and come alongside his campaign of nonviolence against Jim Crow and segregation. To his chagrin, southern white pastors repeatedly criticized him instead. After being arrested in Birmingham, Alabama, he wrote this open letter, in which he justifies the timeliness and methods of the protest movement.

What political strategies should people use to bring about social change? What kinds of justifications may be used to support a strategy of civil disobedience—the intentional defiance of unjust laws? Dr. King provides us a window into his religious, social, and political rationales for political activism.

Thought Exercises

1. Read the paragraphs on pages 87-88 (from "One of the basic points" and ending with "unavoidable patience." Here, King confronts the argument that "now is not the time" for him to push for social change. What is the essence of his response to that position? Do you think his readers would find his rationale compelling? Do you?

2. Read the paragraphs on pages 88-89 (from "You express" through "that country's antireligious laws."). Here King takes on the idea of civil disobedience. What, according to Dr. King, is the difference between a just and an unjust law? In what ways does he consider segregation laws to be unjust?

3. King is addressing Christian pastors. What aspects of his argument do you think would resonate most with this group? What biblical examples does he use to support his position on civil disobedience?

4. What portions of King's line of argument do you find most important? Most compelling? Least compelling or effective? Support your answers.

Web Link

1. Martin Luther King, "Letter from a Birmingham Jail"
   http://mlk-kpp01.stanford.edu/index.php/resources/article/annotated_letter_from_birmingham/

17. Letter From the Birmingham City Jail

By Martin Luther King, Jr.

April 16, 1963

MY DEAR FELLOW CLERGYMEN:
While confined here in the Birmingham City Jail, I came across your recent statement calling our present activities "unwise and untimely." Seldom, if ever, do I pause to answer criticism of my work and ideas. If I sought to answer all the criticisms that cross my desk, my secretaries would be engaged in little else in the course of the day and I would have no time for constructive work. But since I feel that you are men of genuine goodwill and your criticisms are sincerely set forth, I would like to answer your statement in what I hope will be patient and reasonable terms.

I think I should give the reason for my being in Birmingham, since you have been influenced by the argument of "outsiders coming in." I have the honor of serving as president of the Southern Christian Leadership Conference, an organization operating in every Southern state with headquarters in Atlanta, Georgia. We have some eighty-five affiliate organizations all across the South—one being the Alabama Christian Movement for Human Rights. Whenever necessary and possible we share staff, educational, and financial resources with our affiliates. Several months ago our local affiliate here in Birmingham invited us to be on call to engage in a nonviolent direct action program if such were deemed necessary. We readily consented and when the hour came we lived up to our promises. So I am here, along with several members of my staff, because we were invited here. I am here because I have basic organizational ties here. Beyond this, I am in Birmingham because injustice is here. Just as the eighth century prophets left their little villages and carried their "thus saith the Lord" far beyond the boundaries of their home town, and just as the Apostle Paul left his little village of Tarsus and carried the gospel of Jesus Christ to practically every hamlet and city of the Graeco-Roman world, I too am compelled to carry the gospel of freedom beyond my particular home town. Like Paul, I must constantly respond to the Macedonian call for aid.

Moreover, I am cognizant of the interrelatedness of all communities and states. I cannot sit idly by in Atlanta and not be concerned about what happens in Birmingham. Injustice anywhere is a threat to justice everywhere. We are caught in an inescapable network of mutuality tied in a single garment of destiny. Whatever affects one directly affects all indirectly. Never again can we afford to live with the narrow, provincial "outside agitator" idea. Anyone who lives inside the United States can never be considered an outsider anywhere in this country.

You deplore the demonstrations that are presently taking place in Birmingham. But I am sorry that your statement did not express a similar concern for the conditions that brought the demonstrations into being. I am sure that each of you would want to go beyond the superficial social analyst who looks merely at effects, and does not grapple with underlying causes. I would not hesitate to say that it is unfortunate that so-called demonstrations are taking place in Birmingham at this time, but I would say in more emphatic terms that it is even more unfortunate that the white power structure of this city left the Negro community with no other alternative.

In any nonviolent campaign there are four basic steps: (1) Collection of the facts to determine whether injustices are alive; (2) Negotiation; (3) Self-purification; and (4) Direct action. We have gone through all of these steps in Birmingham. There can be no gainsaying of the fact that racial injustice engulfs this community. Birmingham is probably the most thoroughly segregated city in the United States. Its ugly record of police brutality is known in every section of this country. Its unjust treatment of Negroes in the courts is a notorious reality. There have been more unsolved bombings of Negro homes and churches in Birmingham than any city in this nation. These are the hard, brutal, and unbelievable facts. On the basis of these conditions Negro leaders sought to negotiate with the city fathers. But the political leaders consistently refused to engage in good faith negotiation.

Then came the opportunity last September to talk with some of the leaders of the economic community. In these negotiating sessions certain promises were made by the merchants -- such as the promise to remove the humiliating racial signs from the stores. On the basis of these promises Rev. Shuttlesworth and the leaders of the Alabama Christian Movement for Human Rights agreed to call a moratorium on any type of demonstrations. As the weeks and months unfolded we realized that we were the victims of a broken promise. The signs remained. As in so many experiences of the past we were confronted with blasted hopes, and the dark shadow of a deep disappointment

settled upon us. So we had no alternative except that of preparing for direct action, whereby we would present our very bodies as a means of laying our case before the conscience of the local and national community. We were not unmindful of the difficulties involved. So we decided to go through a process of self-purification. We started having workshops on nonviolence and repeatedly asked ourselves the questions, "Are you able to accept blows without retaliating?" "Are you able to endure the ordeals of jail?"

We decided to set our direct-action program around the Easter season, realizing that with the exception of Christmas, this was the largest shopping period of the year. Knowing that a strong economic withdrawal program would be the by-product of direct action, we felt that this was the best time to bring pressure on the merchants for the needed changes. Then it occurred to us that the March election was ahead, and so we speedily decided to postpone action until after election day. When we discovered that Mr. Connor was in the run-off, we decided again to postpone action so that the demonstrations could not be used to cloud the issues. At this time we agreed to begin our nonviolent witness the day after the run-off.

This reveals that we did not move irresponsibly into direct action. We too wanted to see Mr. Connor defeated; so we went through postponement after postponement to aid in this community need. After this we felt that direct action could be delayed no longer.

You may well ask, Why direct action? Why sit-ins, marches, etc.? Isn't negotiation a better path?" You are exactly right in your call for negotiation. Indeed, this is the purpose of direct action. Nonviolent direct action seeks to create such a crisis and establish such creative tension that a community that has constantly refused to negotiate is forced to confront the issue. It seeks so to dramatize the issue that it can no longer be ignored. I just referred to the creation of tension as a part of the work of the nonviolent resister. This may sound rather shocking. But I must confess that I am not afraid of the word tension. I have earnestly worked and preached against violent tension, but there is a type of constructive nonviolent tension that is necessary for growth. Just as Socrates felt that it was necessary to create a tension in the mind so that individuals could rise from the bondage of myths and half-truths to the unfettered realm of creative analysis and objective appraisal, we must see the need of having nonviolent gadflies to create the kind of tension in society that will help men rise from the dark depths of prejudice and racism to the majestic heights of understanding and brotherhood. So the purpose of the direct action is to create a situation so crisis-packed that it will inevitably open the door to negotiation. We, therefore, concur with you in your call for negotiation. Too long has our beloved Southland been bogged down in the tragic attempt to live in monologue rather than dialogue.

One of the basic points in your statement is that our acts are untimely. Some have asked, "Why didn't you give the new administration time to act?" The only answer that I can give to this inquiry is that the new administration must be prodded about as much as the outgoing one before it acts. We will be sadly mistaken if we feel that the election of Mr. Boutwell will bring the millennium to Birmingham. While Mr. Boutwell is much more articulate and gentle than Mr. Connor, they are both segregationists dedicated to the task of maintaining the status quo. The hope I see in Mr. Boutwell is that he will be reasonable enough to see the futility of massive resistance to desegregation. But he will not see this without pressure from the devotees of civil rights. My friends, I must say to you that we have not made a single gain in civil rights without determined legal and nonviolent pressure. History is the long and tragic story of the fact that privileged groups seldom give up their privileges voluntarily. Individuals may see the moral light and voluntarily give up their unjust posture; but as Reinhold Niebuhr has reminded us, groups are more immoral than individuals.

We know through painful experience that freedom is never voluntarily given by the oppressor; it must be demanded by the oppressed. Frankly I have never yet engaged in a direct action movement that was "well timed," according to the timetable of those who have not suffered unduly from the disease of segregation. For years now I have heard the word "Wait!" It rings in the ear of every Negro with a piercing familiarity. This "wait" has almost always meant "never." It has been a tranquilizing thalidomide, relieving the emotional stress for a moment, only to give birth to an ill-formed infant of frustration. We must come to see with the distinguished jurist of yesterday that "justice too long delayed is justice denied." We have waited for more than three hundred and forty years for our constitutional and God-given rights. The nations of Asia and Africa are moving with jet-like speed toward the goal of political independence, and we still creep at horse and buggy pace toward the gaining of a cup of coffee at a lunch counter.

I guess it is easy for those who have never felt the stinging darts of segregation to say wait. But when you have seen vicious mobs lynch your mothers and fathers at will and drown your sisters and brothers at whim; when you have seen hate filled policemen curse, kick, brutalize, and even kill your black brothers and sisters with impunity; when you see the vast majority of your twenty million Negro brothers smothering in an air-tight cage of poverty in the midst of an affluent society; when you suddenly find your tongue twisted and your speech stammering as you seek to explain to your six-year-old daughter why she can't go to the public amusement park that has just been advertised on television, and see tears welling up in her little eyes when she is told that Funtown is closed to colored children, and see the depressing clouds of inferiority begin to form in her little mental sky, and see her begin to distort her little personality by unconsciously developing a bitterness toward white people; when you have to concoct an answer for a five-year-old son asking in agonizing pathos: "Daddy, why do white people treat colored people so mean?"; when you take a cross-country drive and find it necessary to sleep night after night in the uncomfortable corners of your automobile because no motel will accept you; when you are humiliated day in and day out by nagging signs reading "white" men and "colored"; when your first name becomes "nigger" and your middle name becomes "boy" (however old you are) and your last name becomes "John," and when your wife and mother are never given the respected title "Mrs."; when you are harried by day and haunted by night by the fact that you are a Negro, living constantly at tip-toe stance never quite knowing what to expect next, and plagued with inner fears and outer resentments; when you are forever fighting a degenerating sense of "nobodiness"—then you will understand why we find it difficult to wait. There comes a time when the cup of endurance runs over, and men are no longer willing to be plunged into an abyss of injustice where they experience the bleakness of corroding despair. I hope, sirs, you can understand our legitimate and unavoidable impatience.

You express a great deal of anxiety over our willingness to break laws. This is certainly a legitimate concern. Since we so diligently urge people to obey the Supreme Court's decision of 1954 outlawing segregation in the public schools, it is rather strange and paradoxical to find us consciously breaking laws. One may well ask: "How can you advocate breaking some laws and obeying others?" The answer is found in the fact that there are two types of laws: There are just laws and there are unjust laws. I would be the first to advocate obeying just laws. One has not only a legal but moral responsibility to obey just laws. Conversely, one has a moral responsibility to disobey unjust laws. I would agree with Saint Augustine that "An unjust law is no law at all."

Now what is the difference between the two? How does one determine when a law is just or unjust? A just law is a man-made code that squares with the moral law or the law of God. An unjust law is a code that is out of harmony with the moral law. To put it in the terms of Saint Thomas Aquinas, an unjust law is a human law that is not rooted in eternal and natural law. Any law that uplifts human personality is just. Any law that degrades human personality is unjust. All segregation statutes are unjust because segregation distorts the soul and damages the personality. It gives the segregator a false sense of superiority and the segregated a false sense of inferiority. To use the words of Martin Buber, the great Jewish philosopher, segregation substitutes an "I-it" relationship for an "I-thou" relationship, and ends up relegating persons to the status of things. So segregation is not only politically, economically, and sociologically unsound, but it is morally wrong and sinful. Paul Tillich has said that sin is separation. Isn't segregation an existential expression of man's tragic separation, an expression of his awful estrangement, his terrible sinfulness? So I can urge men to obey the 1954 decision of the Supreme Court because it is morally right, and I can urge them to disobey segregation ordinances because they are morally wrong.

Let us turn to a more concrete example of just and unjust laws. An unjust law is a code that a majority inflicts on a minority that is not binding on itself. This is difference made legal. On the other hand a just law is a code that a majority compels a minority to follow that it is willing to follow itself. This is sameness made legal.

Let me give another explanation. An unjust law is a code inflicted upon a minority which that minority had no part in enacting or creating because they did not have the unhampered right to vote. Who can say that the legislature of Alabama which set up the segregation laws was democratically elected? Throughout the state of Alabama all types of conniving methods are used to prevent Negroes from becoming registered voters and there are some counties without a single Negro registered to vote despite the fact that the Negro constitutes a majority of the population. Can any law set up in such a state be considered democratically structured?

These are just a few examples of unjust and just laws. There are some instances when a law is just on its face but unjust in its application. For instance, I was arrested Friday on a charge of parading without a permit. Now there is nothing wrong with an ordinance which requires a permit for a parade, but when the ordinance is used to preserve segregation and to deny citizens the First Amendment privilege of peaceful assembly and peaceful protest, then it becomes unjust.

I hope you can see the distinction I am trying to point out. In no sense do I advocate evading or defying the law as the rabid segregationist would do. This would lead to anarchy. One who breaks an unjust law must do it openly, lovingly (not hatefully as the white mothers did in New Orleans when they were seen on television screaming "nigger, nigger, nigger") and with a willingness to accept the penalty. I submit that an individual who breaks a law that conscience tells him is unjust, and willingly accepts the penalty by staying in jail to arouse the conscience of the community over its injustice, is in reality expressing the very highest respect for law.

Of course there is nothing new about this kind of civil disobedience. It was seen sublimely in the refusal of Shadrach, Meshach, and Abednego to obey the laws of Nebuchadnezzar because a higher moral law was involved. It was practiced superbly by the early Christians who were willing to face hungry lions and the excruciating pain of chopping blocks, before submitting to certain unjust laws of the Roman Empire. To a degree academic freedom is a reality today because Socrates practiced civil disobedience.

We can never forget that everything Hitler did in Germany was "legal" and everything the Hungarian freedom fighters did in Hungary was "illegal." It was "illegal" to aid and comfort a Jew in Hitler's Germany. But I am sure that, if I had lived in Germany during that time, I would have aided and comforted my Jewish brothers even though it was illegal. If I lived in a communist country today where certain principles dear to the Christian faith are suppressed, I believe I would openly advocate disobeying these anti-religious laws.

I must make two honest confessions to you, my Christian and Jewish brothers. First, I must confess that over the last few years I have been gravely disappointed with the white moderate. I have almost reached the regrettable conclusion that the Negroes' great stumbling block in the stride toward freedom is not the White Citizen's "Counciler" or the Ku Klux Klanner, but the white moderate who is more devoted to "order" than to justice; who prefers a negative peace which is the absence of tension to a positive peace which is the presence of justice; who constantly says "I agree with you in the goal you seek, but I can't

agree with your methods of direct action"; who paternalistically feels that he can set the timetable for another man's freedom; who lives by the myth of time and who constantly advises the Negro to wait until a "more convenient season." Shallow understanding from people of good will is more frustrating than absolute misunderstanding from people of ill will. Lukewarm acceptance is much more bewildering than outright rejection.

I had hoped that the white moderate would understand that law and order exist for the purpose of establishing justice, and that when they fail to do this they become dangerously structured dams that block the flow of social progress. I had hoped that the white moderate would understand that the present tension in the South is merely a necessary phase of the transition from an obnoxious negative peace, where the Negro passively accepted his unjust plight, to a substance-filled positive peace, where all men will respect the dignity and worth of human personality. Actually, we who engage in nonviolent direct action are not the creators of tension. We merely bring to the surface the hidden tension that is already alive. We bring it out in the open where it can be seen and dealt with. Like a boil that can never be cured as long as it is covered up but must be opened with all its pus-flowing ugliness to the natural medicines of air and light, injustice must likewise be exposed, with all of the tension its exposing creates, to the light of human conscience and the air of national opinion before it can be cured.

In your statement you asserted that our actions, even though peaceful, must be condemned because they precipitate violence. But can this assertion be logically made? Isn't this like condemning the robbed man because his possession of money precipitated the evil act of robbery? Isn't this like condemning Socrates because his unswerving commitment to truth and his philosophical delvings precipitated the misguided popular mind to make him drink the hemlock? Isn't this like condemning Jesus because His unique God consciousness and never-ceasing devotion to His will precipitated the evil act of crucifixion? We must come to see, as federal courts have consistently affirmed, that it is immoral to urge an individual to withdraw his efforts to gain his basic constitutional rights because the quest precipitates violence. Society must protect the robbed and punish the robber.

I had also hoped that the white moderate would reject the myth of time. I received a letter this morning from a white brother in Texas which said: "All Christians know that the colored people will receive equal rights eventually, but is it possible that you are in too great of a religious hurry? It has taken Christianity almost 2,000 years to accomplish what it has. The teachings of Christ take time to come to earth." All that is said here grows out of a tragic misconception of time. It is the strangely irrational notion that there is something in the very flow of time that will inevitably cure all ills. Actually time is neutral. It can be used either destructively or constructively. I am coming to feel that the people of ill will have used time much more effectively than the people of good will. We will have to repent in this generation not merely for the vitriolic words and actions of the bad people, but for the appalling silence of the good people. We must come to see that human progress never rolls in on wheels of inevitability. It comes through the tireless efforts and persistent work of men willing to be co-workers with God, and without this hard work time itself becomes an ally of the forces of social stagnation.

We must use time creatively, and forever realize that the time is always ripe to do right. Now is the time to make real the promise of democracy, and transform our pending national elegy into a creative psalm of brotherhood. Now is the time to lift our national policy from the quicksand of racial injustice to the solid rock of human dignity.

You spoke of our activity in Birmingham as extreme. At first I was rather disappointed that fellow clergymen would see my nonviolent efforts as those of the extremist. I started thinking about the fact that I stand in the middle of two opposing forces in the Negro community. One is a force of complacency made up of Negroes who, as a result of long years of oppression, have been so completely drained of self-respect and a sense of "somebodiness" that they have adjusted to segregation, and of a few Negroes in the middle class who, because of a degree of academic and economic security, and because at points they profit by segregation, have unconsciously become insensitive to the problems of the masses. The other force is one of bitterness and hatred and comes perilously close to advocating violence. It is expressed in the various black nationalist groups that are springing up over the nation, the largest and best known being Elijah Muhammad's Muslim movement. This movement is nourished by the contemporary frustration over the continued existence of racial discrimination. It is made up of people who have lost faith in America, who have absolutely repudiated Christianity, and who have concluded that the white man is an incurable "devil." I have tried to stand between these two forces saying that we need not follow the "do-nothingism" of the complacent or the hatred and despair of the black nationalist. There is the more excellent way of love and nonviolent protest. I'm grateful to God that, through the Negro church, the dimension of nonviolence entered our struggle. If this philosophy had not emerged I am convinced that by now many streets of the South would be flowing with floods of blood. And I am further convinced that if our white brothers dismiss us as "rabble rousers" and "outside agitators"—those of us who are working through the channels of nonviolent direct action—and refuse to support our nonviolent efforts, millions of Negroes, out of frustration and despair, will seek solace and security in black-nationalist ideologies, a development that will lead inevitably to a frightening racial nightmare.

Oppressed people cannot remain oppressed forever. The urge for freedom will eventually come. This is what has happened to the American Negro. Something within has reminded him of his birthright of freedom; something without has reminded him that he can gain it. Consciously and unconsciously, he has been swept in by what the Germans call the Zeitgeist, and with his black brothers of Africa, and his brown and yellow brothers of Asia, South America, and the Caribbean, he is moving with a sense of cosmic urgency toward the promised land of racial justice. Recognizing this vital urge that has engulfed the Negro community, one should readily understand public demonstrations. The Negro has many pent-up resentments and latent frustrations. He has to get them out. So let him march sometime; let him have his prayer pilgrimages to the city hall; understand why he must have sit-ins and freedom rides. If his repressed emotions do not come out in these nonviolent ways, they will come out in ominous expressions of violence. This is not a threat; it is a fact of history. So I have not said to my people, "Get rid of your discontent." But I have tried to say that this normal and healthy discontent can be channeled through the creative outlet of nonviolent direct action. Now this approach is being dismissed as extremist. I must admit that I was initially disappointed in being so categorized.

But as I continued to think about the matter I gradually gained a bit of satisfaction from being considered an extremist. Was not Jesus an extremist in love? "Love your enemies, bless them that curse you, pray for them that despitefully use you." Was not Amos an extremist for justice—"Let justice roll down like waters and righteousness like a mighty stream." Was not Paul an extremist for the gospel of Jesus Christ—"I bear in my body the marks of the Lord Jesus." Was not Martin Luther an extremist—"Here I stand; I can do none other so help me God." Was not John Bunyan an extremist -- "I will stay in jail to the end of my days before I make a butchery of my conscience." Was not Abraham Lincoln an extremist—"This nation cannot survive half slave and half free." Was not Thomas Jefferson an extremist—"We hold these truths to be self-evident, that all men are created equal." So the question is not whether we will be extremist but what kind of extremist will we be. Will we be extremists for hate or will we be extremists for love? Will we be extremists for the preservation of injustice—or will we be extremists for the cause of justice? In that dramatic scene on Calvary's hill three men were crucified. We must never forget that all three were crucified for the same crime—the crime of extremism. Two were extremists for immorality, and thus fell below their environment. The other, Jesus Christ, was an extremist for love, truth, and goodness,

and thereby rose above His environment. So, after all, maybe the South, the nation, and the world are in dire need of creative extremists.

I had hoped that the white moderate would see this. Maybe I was too optimistic. Maybe I expected too much. I guess I should have realized that few members of a race that has oppressed another race can understand or appreciate the deep groans and passionate yearnings of those that have been oppressed, and still fewer have the vision to see that injustice must be rooted out by strong, persistent, and determined action. I am thankful, however, that some of our white brothers have grasped the meaning of this social revolution and committed themselves to it. They are still all too small in quantity, but they are big in quality. Some like Ralph McGill, Lillian Smith, Harry Golden, and James Dabbs have written about our struggle in eloquent, prophetic, and understanding terms. Others have marched with us down nameless streets of the South. They have languished in filthy, roach-infested jails, suffering the abuse and brutality of angry policemen who see them as "dirty nigger lovers." They, unlike so many of their moderate brothers and sisters, have recognized the urgency of the moment and sensed the need for powerful "action" antidotes to combat the disease of segregation.

Let me rush on to mention my other disappointment. I have been so greatly disappointed with the white Church and its leadership. Of course there are some notable exceptions. I am not unmindful of the fact that each of you has taken some significant stands on this issue. I commend you, Rev. Stallings, for your Christian stand on this past Sunday, in welcoming Negroes to your worship service on a non-segregated basis. I commend the Catholic leaders of this state for integrating Spring Hill College several years ago.

But despite these notable exceptions I must honestly reiterate that I have been disappointed with the Church. I do not say that as one of those negative critics who can always find something wrong with the Church. I say it as a minister of the gospel, who loves the Church; who was nurtured in its bosom; who has been sustained by its spiritual blessings and who will remain true to it as long as the cord of life shall lengthen.

I had the strange feeling when I was suddenly catapulted into the leadership of the bus protest in Montgomery several years ago that we would have the support of the white Church. I felt that the white ministers, priests, and rabbis of the South would be some of our strongest allies. Instead, some have been outright opponents, refusing to understand the freedom movement and misrepresenting its leaders; all too many others have been more cautious than courageous and have remained silent behind the anesthetizing security of the stained glass windows.

In spite of my shattered dreams of the past, I came to Birmingham with the hope that the white religious leadership of this community would see the justice of our cause and with deep moral concern, serve as the channel through which our just grievances could get to the power structure. I had hoped that each of you would understand. But again I have been disappointed.

I have heard numerous religious leaders of the South call upon their worshippers to comply with a desegregation decision because it is the law, but I have longed to hear white ministers say follow this decree because integration is morally right and the Negro is your brother. In the midst of blatant injustices inflicted upon the Negro, I have watched white churches stand on the sideline and merely mouth pious irrelevancies and sanctimonious trivialities. In the midst of a mighty struggle to rid our nation of racial and economic injustice, I have heard so many ministers say, "Those are social issues with which the gospel has no real concern," and I have watched so many churches commit themselves to a completely other-worldly religion which made a strange distinction between body and soul, the sacred and the secular.

So here we are moving toward the exit of the twentieth century with a religious community largely adjusted to the status quo, standing as a tail-light behind other community agencies rather than a headlight leading men to higher levels of justice.

I have travelled the length and breadth of Alabama, Mississippi and all the other southern states. On sweltering summer days and crisp autumn mornings I have looked at her beautiful churches with their spires pointing heavenward. I have beheld the impressive outlay of her massive religious education buildings. Over and over again I have found myself asking: "Who worships here? Who is their God? Where were their voices when the lips of Governor Barnett dripped with words of interposition and nullification? Where were they when Governor Wallace gave the clarion call for defiance and hatred? Where were their voices of support when tired, bruised, and weary Negro men and women decided to rise from the dark dungeons of complacency to the bright hills of creative protest?"

Yes, these questions are still in my mind. In deep disappointment, I have wept over the laxity of the church. But be assured that my tears have been tears of love. There can be no deep disappointment where there is not deep love. Yes, I love the Church; I love her sacred walls. How could I do otherwise? I am in the rather unique position of being the son, the grandson, and the great-grandson of preachers. Yes, I see the Church as the body of Christ. But, oh! How we have blemished and scarred that body through social neglect and fear of being nonconformist.

There was a time when the Church was very powerful. It was during that period when the early Christians rejoiced when they were deemed worthy to suffer for what they believed. In those days the Church was not merely a thermometer that recorded the ideas and principles of popular opinion; it was a thermostat that transformed the mores of society. Wherever the early Christians entered a town the power structure got disturbed and immediately sought to convict them for being "disturbers of the peace" and "outside agitators." But they went on with the conviction that they were "a colony of heaven" and had to obey God rather than man. They were small in number but big in commitment. They were too God-intoxicated to be "astronomically intimidated." They brought an end to such ancient evils as infanticide and gladiatorial contest.

Things are different now. The contemporary Church is so often a weak, ineffectual voice with an uncertain sound. It is so often the arch-supporter of the status quo. Far from being disturbed by the presence of the Church, the power structure of the average community is consoled by the Church's silent and often vocal sanction of things as they are.

But the judgment of God is upon the Church as never before. If the Church of today does not recapture the sacrificial spirit of the early Church, it will lose its authentic ring, forfeit the loyalty of millions, and be dismissed as an irrelevant social club with no meaning for the twentieth century. I am meeting young people every day whose disappointment with the Church has risen to outright disgust.

Maybe again I have been too optimistic. Is organized religion too inextricably bound to the status quo to save our nation and the world? Maybe I must turn my faith to the inner spiritual Church, the church within the Church, as the true ecclesia and the hope of the world. But again I am thankful to God that some noble souls from the ranks of organized religion have broken loose from the paralyzing chains of conformity and joined us as active partners in the struggle for freedom. They have left their secure congregations and walked the streets of Albany, Georgia, with us. They have gone through the highways of the South on torturous rides for freedom. Yes, they have gone to jail with us. Some have been kicked out of their churches and lost the support of their bishops and fellow ministers. But they have gone with the faith that right defeated is stronger than evil triumphant. These men have been the leaven in the lump of the race. Their witness has been the spiritual salt that has preserved the true meaning of the Gospel in these troubled times. They have carved a tunnel of hope through the dark mountain of disappointment.

I hope the Church as a whole will meet the challenge of this decisive hour. But even if the Church does not come to the aid of justice, I have no despair about the future. I have no fear about the outcome of our struggle in Birmingham, even if our motives are presently misunderstood. We will reach the goal of freedom in Birmingham and all over the nation, because the goal of America is

freedom. Abused and scorned though we may be, our destiny is tied up with the destiny of America. Before the pilgrims landed at Plymouth, we were here. Before the pen of Jefferson etched across the pages of history the majestic words of the Declaration of Independence, we were here. For more than two centuries our foreparents labored in this country without wages; they made cotton "king"; and they built the homes of their masters in the midst of brutal injustice and shameful humiliation—and yet out of a bottomless vitality they continued to thrive and develop. If the inexpressible cruelties of slavery could not stop us, the opposition we now face will surely fail. We will win our freedom because the sacred heritage of our nation and the eternal will of God are embodied in our echoing demands.

I must close now. But before closing I am impelled to mention one other point in your statement that troubled me profoundly. You warmly commend the Birmingham police force for keeping "order" and "preventing violence." I don't believe you would have so warmly commended the police force if you had seen its angry violent dogs literally biting six unarmed, nonviolent Negroes. I don't believe you would so quickly commend the policemen if you would observe their ugly and inhuman treatment of Negroes here in the city jail; if you would watch them push and curse old Negro women and young Negro girls; if you would see them slap and kick old Negro men and young Negro boys; if you will observe them, as they did on two occasions, refuse to give us food because we wanted to sing our grace together. I'm sorry that I can't join you in your praise for the police department.

It is true that they have been rather disciplined in their public handling of the demonstrators. In this sense they have been rather publicly "nonviolent." But for what purpose? To preserve the evil system of segregation. Over the last few years I have consistently preached that nonviolence demands the means we use must be as pure as the ends we seek. So I have tried to make it clear that it is wrong to use immoral means to attain moral ends. But now I must affirm that it is just as wrong or even more so to use moral means to preserve immoral ends. Maybe Mr. Connor and his police-men have been rather publicly nonviolent, as Chief Pritchett was in Albany, Georgia, but they have used the moral means of nonviolence to maintain the immoral end of flagrant injustice. T. S. Eliot has said that there is no greater treason than to do the right deed for the wrong reason.

I wish you had commended the Negro sit-in-ners and demonstrators of Birmingham for their sublime courage, their willingness to suffer, and their amazing discipline in the midst of the most inhuman provocation. One day the South will recognize its real heroes. They will be the James Merediths, courageously and with a majestic sense of purpose, facing jeering and hostile mobs and the agonizing loneliness that characterizes the life of the pioneer. They will be old, oppressed, battered Negro women, symbolized in a seventy-two year old woman of Montgomery, Alabama, who rose up with a sense of dignity and with her people decided not to ride the segregated buses, and responded to one who inquired about her tiredness with ungrammatical profundity: "My feets is tired, but my soul is rested." They will be the young high school and college students, young ministers of the gospel and a host of their elders courageously and nonviolently sitting-in at lunch counters and willingly going to jail for conscience sake. One day the South will know that when these disinherited children of God sat down at lunch counters they were in reality standing up for the best in the American dream and the most sacred values in our Judaeo-Christian heritage, and thus carrying our whole nation back to great wells of democracy which were dug deep by the founding fathers in the formulation of the Constitution and the Declaration of Independence.

Never before have I written a letter this long (or should I say a book?). I'm afraid it is much too long to take your precious time. I can assure you that it would have been much shorter if I had been writing from a comfortable desk, but what else is there to do when you are alone for days in the dull monotony of a narrow jail cell other than write long letters, think strange thoughts, and pray long prayers?

If I have said anything in this letter that is an overstatement of the truth and is indicative of an unreasonable impatience, I beg you to forgive me. If I have said anything in this letter that is an understatement of the truth and is indicative of my having a patience that makes me patient with anything less than brotherhood, I beg God to forgive me.

I hope this letter finds you strong in the faith. I also hope that circumstances will soon make it possible for me to meet each of you, not as an in-tegrationist or a civil rights leader, but as a fellow clergyman and a Christian brother. Let us all hope that the dark clouds of racial prejudice will soon pass away and the deep fog of misunderstanding will be lifted from our fear-drenched communi-ties and in some not too distant tomorrow the radiant stars of love and brotherhood will shine over our great nation with all their scintillating beauty.

Yours for the cause of
Peace and Brotherhood,
Martin Luther King, Jr.

Purpose

To help you understand some of the social characteristics associated with voter registration and turnout, and the reasons different people say they don't vote.

Context

Each election year, the US Government's Census Bureau surveys a large number of randomly-selected respondents about whether they registered to vote, whether they voted, and, if respondents did not vote, why not. While the government can ask information about social and demographic characteristics, such as race, ethnicity, sex, income and education, they do not ask about other factors that social scientists know are politically relevant, such as political ideology and party identification. Still, this survey provides useful information about Americans' voting – and non-voting – behavior.

Thought Exercises

1. In Table 1, look at the Citizens/Registered/Percent column. This shows the estimated percentage of US citizens who are registered to vote. Now look at the Citizens/Voted/Percent column. This shows the estimated percentage of US citizens who voted in each year. Finally, look at the Registered/Percent reported voted column. This shows the estimated percentage of US citizens who are registered to vote that said they voted. What changes do you see in each value, comparing the 1996-2008 presidential elections?

2. Table 2 looks at registration and voting rates for a wide range of demographic characteristics. For now, let's focus on the Citizens/Voted/Percent column. This compares various social groups and their voter turnout in 2008. For each grouping of social characteristics (Sex, Race and Hispanic Origin, Nativity Status, Age, Marital Status, Educational Attainment, and Annual Family Income) compare the groups' voting rates. Circle the groups with the highest percentages, and put square around those with the lowest percentages in each set of social characteristics. Which groups have the highest and lowest turnout rates? What do you think helps us explain these differences?

3. Table 6 reports the reasons people give for not registering to vote, and for not voting in 2008. Look at the Total column. Which reason is most frequently given for not voting? Now look at the columns for the four age groups under Percent Distribution. Compare the most frequent reason given by members of each of the age groups. What differences do you see? Why do you think these differences exist? Can you think of possible solutions for these reasons?

4. Now look at the part of Table 6 that lists Reasons for Not Registering. What is the most frequent reason given? What do you think about that reason? Can you think of possible solutions to that reason?

Web Link

1. Voting and Registration in 2008
   http://www.census.gov/prod/2010pubs/p20-562.pdf

18. Voting and Registration in the Election of November 2008

Current Population Reports

By Thom File and Sarah Crissey

About This Report

Voting and registration rates are historically higher in years with presidential elections than in congressional election years. For this report, we compare 2008 election data only with data from previous presidential election years (2004, 2000, 1996, etc.).

Population Characteristics

Issued May 2010

This report examines levels of voting and registration in the November 2008 presidential election, the characteristics of citizens who reported either registering or voting in the election, and the reasons why some registered individuals did not vote.

The data in this report are based on responses to the November 2008 Current Population Survey (CPS) Voting and Registration Supplement, which surveys the civilian noninstitutionalized population in the United States.[1] The estimates

[1]People in the military, U.S. citizens living abroad, and people in institutional housing, such as correctional

presented in this report may differ from those based on administrative data or exit polls. For more information, see the sections on *Measuring Voting and Registration in the Current Population Survey* and *Accuracy of the Estimates.*

Voting and Registration of the Voting-Age Citizen Population

Turnout for the November 2008 Election

In the 2008 presidential election, 64 percent of voting-age citizens voted, an estimate not statistically different from the percent that turned out in 2004, but higher than the presidential elections of 2000 and 1996 (Table 1).[2]

institutions and nursing homes, were not included in the survey. For a discussion of the differences between the official counts of votes cast and the CPS data, see the section on *Measuring Voting and Registration in the Current Population Survey.*

[2]The estimates in this report (which may be shown in text, figures, and tables) are based on responses from a sample of the population and may differ from actual values because of sampling variability or other factors. As a result, apparent differences between the estimates for two or more groups may not be statistically significant.

Overall, 131 million people voted in 2008, a turnout increase of about 5 million people since 2004. During this same 4-year period, the voting-age citizen population in the United States increased by roughly 9 million people.[3]

In 2008, 71 percent of voting-age citizens were registered to vote, a decrease compared to the 72 percent who were registered in 2004. The 2008 election had a higher registration rate than the presidential election of 2000, but was not statistically different from the 1996 rate. Overall, 146 million people were registered to vote in 2008, an increase of approximately 4 million people since 2004.

Historically, the likelihood that an individual will actually vote once registered has been high, and 2008 was no exception. Of all registered individuals, 90 percent reported voting, up slightly from 89 percent in the 2004 presidential election.

Who Votes?

This section of the report highlights voting and registration rates by selected characteristics for the voting-age citizen population.

Race and Hispanic Origin

The likelihood of voting differed among race groups and Hispanics (Table 2). Non-Hispanic Whites (66 percent) and Blacks (65 percent) had the highest levels of voter turnout in the 2008 election.[4] Voting rates for Asians and Hispanics were not statistically different from one another at about 49 percent.

Relative to the presidential election of 2004, the voting rates for Blacks, Asians, and Hispanics each increased by about 4 percentage points, while the voting rate for non-Hispanic Whites decreased by a single percentage point in 2008.[5]

Of the 5 million additional voters in 2008, about 2 million were Black, 2 million were Hispanic, and 600,000 were Asian. Meanwhile, the number of non-Hispanic White voters did not change statistically from 2004.

Historically speaking, Black citizens voted at higher levels than in any presidential election since the U.S. Census Bureau began consistently measuring citizenship status in 1996 (Figure 2). The same was true for Hispanics, while in 2008 Asians voted at a higher rate than in 2004 or 2000.[6] Although the gap separating non-Hispanic Whites from other race and ethnic groups narrowed in

those who reported Asian regardless of whether they also reported another race (the race-alone-or-in-combination concept). The body of this report (text, figures, and tables) shows data for people who reported they were the single race White and non-Hispanic, people who reported the single race Black, and people who reported the single race Asian. Use of the single-race populations does not imply that it is the preferred method of presenting or analyzing data. Because Hispanics may be any race, data in this report for Hispanics overlap slightly with data for the Black population and the Asian population. Based on the November 2008 CPS, 3 percent of the Black voting-age population and 2 percent of the Asian voting-age population were Hispanic. Of the voting-age citizen population, 2 percent of Blacks and 2 percent of Asians were Hispanic. Data for the American Indian and Alaska Native and the Native Hawaiian and Other Pacific Islander populations are not shown in this report because of their small sample size in the November 2008 CPS.

[5]For a full analysis of the 2004 election, see Kelly Holder, Voting and Registration in the Election of November 2004, *Current Population Reports* P20-556: U.S. Census Bureau, Washington, DC, 2006, <www.census.gov/prod/2006pubs/p20-556 .pdf>.

[6]The voting rate for Asians in 2008 was not statistically different from 1996.

All comparative statements have undergone statistical testing and are significant at the 90 percent confidence level unless otherwise noted.

[3]Additional historical voting and registration data, as well as detailed tables addressing each of the topics discussed in this report, are available at <www.census.gov/population/www/socdemo/voting .html>.

[4]Federal surveys now give respondents the option of reporting more than one race. Therefore, two basic ways of defining a race group are possible. A group such as Asian may be defined as those who reported Asian and no other race (the race alone or single-race concept) or as

Table 1. Reported Rates of Voting and Registration: 1996 to 2008

(Numbers in thousands)

Presidential election year	Total	Citizens						Registered	
		Total	Registered			Voted			Percent reported voted	90 percent confidence interval
			Number	Percent	90 percent confidence interval	Number	Percent	90 percent confidence interval		
2008	225,499	206,072	146,311	71.0	69.7-71.4	131,144	63.6	63.3-63.9	89.6	89.4-89.8
2004	215,694	197,005	142,070	72.1	71.8-72.4	125,736	63.8	63.5-64.1	88.5	88.3-88.7
2000	202,609	186,366	129,549	69.5	69.2-69.8	110,826	59.5	59.2-59.8	85.5	85.2-85.8
1996	193,651	179,935	127,661	70.9	70.6-71.2	105,017	58.4	58.1-58.7	82.3	82.0-82.6

Source: U.S. Census Bureau, Current Population Survey, November 1996, 2000, 2004, and 2008.

2008 compared to 2004, non-Hispanic Whites still voted at the highest level. In 2008, the voting rate for non-Hispanic Whites was lower than in 2004 but higher than 2000 or 1996.

The likelihood of registering also differed among race groups and Hispanics (Table 2). Non-Hispanic Whites (74 percent) and Blacks (70 percent) had the highest registration rates in the 2008 election, while registration rates for Hispanics (59 percent) and Asians (55 percent) were significantly lower.

Voting-Age Population

One of the primary criteria for being eligible to vote is age. Since 1972, every state has required that eligible voters be at least 18 years of age. Thus, the voting-age population, or the 18-and-older population, is a population base often used in presenting voting statistics. The Census Bureau has historically estimated voting and registration rates using this population but no longer focuses primarily on this method.

Voting-Age Citizen Population

A second criterion for voting eligibility is citizenship. In the United States, only citizens can legally vote in elections. While the Census Bureau has collected voting and registration data since 1964, the CPS has gathered citizenship data for presidential elections in a consistent way only since 1994. Removing noncitizens decreases the voting-age population base, resulting in higher turnout rates for any given election. For example, in the November 2008 election, 58 percent of the voting-age population voted, while 64 percent of the voting-age citizen population went to the polls. This report focuses on the rates of the voting-age citizen population, as this is the preferred method for analyzing elections.

Registered Population

A third criterion for voting eligibility is registration. With the exception of North Dakota, every state requires eligible voters to formally register before casting a ballot. In terms of methods and

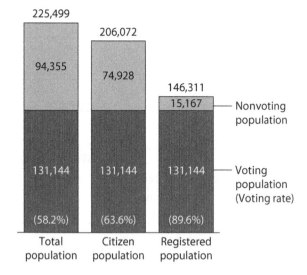

225,499

206,072

94,355

74,928

146,311

15,167 —— Nonvoting population

131,144   131,144   131,144 —— Voting population (Voting rate)

(58.2%)   (63.6%)   (89.6%)

Total population   Citizen population   Registered population

Source: U.S. Census Bureau, Current Population Survey, November 2008.
(Population 18 and older, in thousands)

Figure 1. Voters Among the Total, Citizen, and Registered Voting-Age Populations: 2008

deadlines, registration procedures vary greatly from state to state.[7]

Figure 1 illustrates the three measures of voting rates. In November 2008, of the 225 million people who were 18 and older, 206 million were citizens, and 146 million were registered. In the November election, 131 million people voted. Thus, the voting rate was 58 percent for the total population 18 and older, 64 percent for the voting-age citizen population, and 90 percent for the registered population.[8]

---

[7]Idaho, Iowa, Maine, Minnesota, Montana, New Hampshire, Wisconsin, and Wyoming all have Election-Day registration. North Dakota has no statewide voter registration requirement.

[8]A fourth criterion for voting eligibility is felony disenfranchisement, or the practice of prohibiting persons from voting based on the fact that they have been convicted of a felony. Although the Census Bureau does not currently provide a measurement of felony disenfranchisement in the CPS, some of the people who reported not being eligible to vote in Table 6 of this report were ineligible due to a felony conviction.

Age

Citizens between the ages of 18 to 24 were the only age group to show a statistically significant increase in turnout in the most recent election, reaching 49 percent in 2008, compared with 47 percent in 2004. Citizens between the ages of 45 to 64 saw their voting rates decrease to 69 percent in 2008, down slightly from 70 percent in 2004. Voting rates for citizens aged 25 to 44 and 65 years or older were statistically unchanged between 2004 and 2008.

This represents the second straight presidential election where young citizens significantly increased their voting rates. Over the last two presidential elections, young citizens have increased their voting rate by a total of 12 percent, compared to 4 percent for 25- to 44-year-olds and 1 percent for 45- to 64-year-olds.[9]

Despite this increase among young voters, voting rates did tend to increase with age. In 2008, younger citizens (18-24) had the lowest voting rate (49 percent), while citizens who fell into older age groups (25-44, 45-64, and 65 and older) had progressively higher voting rates (60 percent, 69 percent, and 70 percent, respectively).

As discussed in the previous section, about 5 million additional voters went to the polls in 2008. Young people between the ages of 18 and 24 made up about 1 million of these additional voters. Meanwhile, approximately 3 million of these voters were between the ages of 45 and 64, while approximately 1.5 million were 65 years or older.[10] The number of citizens between the ages of 25 and 44 who turned out in 2008 was not statistically different from 2004.

In 2008, registration also increased with age. Younger citizens (18-24) had the lowest registration rate (59 percent), while citizens who fell into older age groups (25-44, 45-64, and 65 and older) had progressively higher registration rates (68 percent, 75 percent, and 77 percent, respectively).

---

[9]The 2008 voting rate for individuals 65 and older was not statistically different from 2000.

[10]The number of additional voters aged 18 to 24 was not significantly different from the number of additional voters aged 65 or older.

Table 2. Reported Rates of Voting and Registration by Selected Characteristics: 2008
(Numbers in thousands)

Characteristic	Total	Citizens							Registered	
		Total	Registered			Voted			Percent reported voted	90 percent confidence interval
		Number	Number	Percent	90 percent confidence interval	Number	Percent	90 percent confidence interval		
Total, 18 years and older	225,499	206,072	146,311	71.0	69.7-71.4	131,144	63.6	63.3-63.9	89.6	89.4-89.8
Sex										
Male	108,974	98,818	68,242	69.1	68.7-69.5	60,729	61.5	61.1-61.9	89.0	88.7-89.3
Female	116,525	107,255	78,069	72.8	72.4-73.2	70,415	65.7	65.3-66.1	90.2	89.9-90.5
Race and Hispanic Origin										
White alone	183,169	169,438	122,020	72.0	71.7-72.3	109,100	64.4	64.1-64.7	89.4	89.2-89.7
White alone, non-Hispanic	154,472	151,321	111,215	73.5	73.2-73.8	100,042	66.1	65.8-66.4	90.0	89.7-90.2
Black alone	26,528	24,930	17,375	69.7	68.7-70.7	16,133	64.7	63.7-65.7	92.9	92.3-93.4
Asian alone	10,455	7,059	3,901	55.3	53.2-57.4	3,357	47.6	45.5-49.7	86.1	84.5-87.6
Hispanic (any race)	30,852	19,537	11,608	59.4	57.8-61.0	9,745	49.9	48.3-51.5	84.0	83.0-84.9
Nativity Status										
Total citizens	206,072	206,072	146,311	71.0	70.7-71.3	131,144	63.6	63.3-63.9	89.6	89.4-89.9
Native	190,683	190,683	137,001	71.8	71.5-72.1	122,839	64.4	64.1-64.7	89.7	89.4-89.9
Naturalized	15,390	15,390	9,310	60.5	59.4-61.6	8,305	54.0	52.9-55.1	89.2	88.3-90.1
Age										
18 to 24 years	28,263	25,791	15,082	58.5	57.6-59.4	12,515	48.5	47.6-49.4	83.0	82.1-83.8
25 to 34 years	40,240	34,218	22,736	66.4	65.7-67.1	19,501	57.0	56.2-57.8	85.8	85.1-86.4
35 to 44 years	41,460	36,397	25,449	69.9	69.2-70.6	22,865	62.8	62.1-63.5	89.8	89.3-90.4
45 to 54 years	44,181	41,085	30,210	73.5	72.9-74.1	27,673	67.4	66.7-68.1	91.6	91.0-92.2
55 to 64 years	33,896	32,288	24,734	76.6	75.9-77.3	23,071	71.5	70.8-72.2	93.3	92.7-93.8
65 to 74 years	20,227	19,571	15,290	78.1	77.3-78.9	14,176	72.4	71.5-73.3	92.7	92.0-93.5
75 and older	17,231	16,724	12,810	76.6	75.7-77.5	11,344	67.8	66.8-68.8	88.6	87.6-89.6

Table 2. Reported Rates of Voting and Registration by Selected Characteristics: 2008
(Numbers in thousands)

Characteristic	Total	Citizens							Registered	
		Total	Registered			Voted			Percent reported voted	90 percent confidence interval
			Number	Percent	90 percent confidence interval	Number	Percent	90 percent confidence interval		
Marital Status										
Married	125,645	113,527	86,234	76.0	75.6-76.4	79,329	69.9	69.4-70.4	92.0	91.7-92.3
Widowed	14,189	13,621	9,768	71.7	70.3-73.1	8,386	61.6	60.1-63.1	85.9	84.8-86.9
Divorced	22,935	22,012	14,905	67.7	66.6-68.8	12,977	59.0	57.8-60.2	87.1	86.3-87.9
Separated	4,833	4,209	2,707	64.3	61.7-66.9	2,252	53.5	50.8-56.2	83.2	81.1-85.3
Never married	57,896	52,703	32,698	62.0	61.2-62.8	28,200	53.5	52.7-54.3	86.2	85.7-86.8
Educational Attainment										
Less than high school graduate	30,204	22,981	11,602	50.5	49.6-51.4	9,046	39.4	38.5-40.3	78.0	76.9-79.1
High school graduate or GED	70,427	65,378	41,880	64.1	63.6-64.6	35,866	54.9	54.4-55.4	85.6	85.1-86.1
Some college or associate's degree	63,780	60,974	45,904	75.3	74.8-75.8	41,477	68.0	67.5-68.5	90.4	90.0-90.8
Bachelor's degree	40,850	38,091	30,928	81.2	80.6-81.8	29,330	77.0	76.4-77.6	94.8	94.4-95.2
Advanced degree	20,238	18,648	15,996	85.8	85.1-86.5	15,425	82.7	81.9-83.5	96.4	96.0-96.8
Annual Family Income[1]										
Total family members	168,032	153,160	110,920	72.4	72.1-72.7	100,255	65.5	65.2-65.8	90.4	90.1-90.6
Less than $20,000	15,784	12,837	8,173	63.7	62.5-64.9	6,665	51.9	50.7-53.2	81.5	80.3-82.8
$20,000 to $29,999	13,749	11,725	7,869	67.1	65.9-68.3	6,606	56.3	55.0-57.6	83.9	82.8-85.1
$30,000 to $39,999	16,150	14,144	10,051	71.1	70.0-72.2	8,793	62.2	61.0-63.4	87.5	86.6-88.4
$40,000 to $49,999	12,547	11,295	8,202	72.6	71.4-73.8	7,307	64.7	63.4-66.0	89.1	88.1-90.1
$50,000 to $74,999	29,959	27,850	21,765	78.2	77.5-78.9	19,743	70.9	70.1-71.7	90.7	90.2-91.3
$75,000 to $99,999	19,075	18,114	14,844	81.9	81.1-82.7	13,846	76.4	75.5-77.3	93.3	92.7-93.9
$100,000 and over	49,034	45,964	36,609	79.6	79.1-80.2	33,589	73.1	72.5-73.7	91.8	91.3-92.2
Income not reported	29,272	27,094	14,482	53.4	52.5-54.3	13,286	49.0	48.1-49.9	91.7	91.1-92.4

Employment Status								
In the civilian labor force	152,707	100,544	72.3	72.0-72.6	90,715	65.2	64.8-65.6	90.2	90.0-90.5
Employed	143,186	95,103	72.8	72.5-73.2	86,073	65.9	65.6-66.3	90.5	90.2-90.8
Unemployed	9,521	5,441	64.1	62.6-65.6	4,642	54.7	53.2-56.2	85.3	84.0-86.7
Not in the labor force	72,792	45,767	68.3	67.8-68.8	40,429	60.3	59.8-60.8	88.3	87.9-88.8
Duration of Residence[2]								
Less than 1 year	24,812	16,497	69.3	68.2-70.4	13,580	57.0	55.9-58.2	82.3	82.0-82.7
1 to 2 years	25,796	18,418	74.8	73.8-75.8	16,066	65.3	64.2-66.4	87.2	86.4-88.1
3 to 4 years	25,524	19,588	80.4	79.5-81.3	17,695	72.6	71.6-73.6	90.3	89.6-91.1
5 years or longer	107,826	89,805	85.3	84.9-85.7	81,979	77.8	77.3-78.3	91.3	91.0-91.6
Not reported	41,541	2,003	7.2	6.6-7.8	1,824	6.5	6.0-7.0	91.1	88.8-93.3
Region								
Northeast	41,543	26,455	69.8	69.1-70.5	23,837	62.9	62.2-63.6	90.1	89.6-90.6
Midwest	49,396	34,897	73.9	73.3-74.5	31,306	66.3	65.7-66.9	89.7	89.2-90.2
South	82,402	53,988	71.1	70.6-71.6	47,536	62.6	62.1-63.1	88.0	87.6-88.5
West	52,158	30,971	68.8	68.2-69.4	28,465	63.3	62.7-63.9	91.9	91.5-92.4
Veteran Status[3]								
Total population	225,460	146,393	71.0	70.7-71.3	131,212	63.6	63.3-63.9	89.6	89.4-89.9
Veteran	22,420	17,185	77.1	76.3-77.9	15,805	70.9	70.0-71.8	92.0	91.4-92.6
Nonveteran	203,040	129,208	70.3	70.0-70.6	115,407	62.8	62.5-63.1	89.3	89.1-89.6
Tenure								
Owner	160,889	113,717	74.5	74.1-74.9	103,560	67.8	67.4-68.2	91.1	90.8-91.4
Renter	61,842	50,812	60.9	60.1-61.7	26,239	51.6	50.8-52.4	84.8	84.0-85.5

[1] Limited to people in families.

[2] Data on duration of residence were obtained from responses to the question, "How long has (this person) lived at this address?"

[3] These estimates were derived using the veteran weight, which uses different procedures for construction than the person weight used to produce estimates elsewhere in this table; therefore, population totals differ while proportions are not affected.

Source: U.S. Census Bureau, Current Population Survey, November 2008.

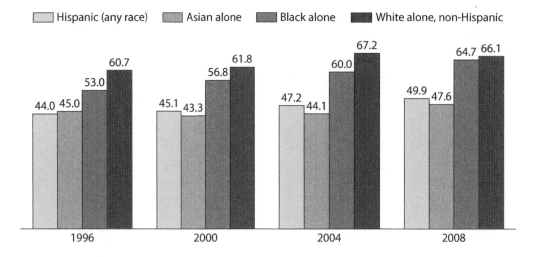

(Citizens 18 and older, in percent)

Source: U.S. Census Bureau, Current Population Survey, 1996, 2000, 2004, and 2008.

Figure 2. Voting Rates by Race and Hispanic Origin: 2008

Educational Attainment

Compared to 2004, voting rates decreased in 2008 for individuals with some college or at least a bachelor's degree (Table 2). The voting rate of citizens with at least a bachelor's degree (79 percent) was higher than that of citizens who had not received a high school diploma (39 percent), those who were high school graduates (55 percent), and individuals who had only some college or an associate's degree (68 percent).

Overall, younger adults had lower voting rates in 2008; however, for highly educated young people, the impact of being young on voter turnout was overcome by the impact of advanced education (Figure 3). Young adults with a bachelor's degree or more had a higher voting rate (70 percent) than young adults with lower levels of educational attainment (27 percent to 57 percent, respectively). Young adults with at least a bachelor's degree also had a higher voting rate than 25- to 44-year-olds with some college (64 percent), as well as most age groups with a high school diploma or less.[11]

Registration rates also increased with education in 2008. Citizens with at least a bachelor's

degree registered at a higher rate (83 percent) than those who had not received a high school diploma (51 percent), those who were high school graduates (64 percent), and individuals who had some college or an associate's degree (75 percent).

Regions

Citizens residing in the Midwest were more likely to vote than those in other regions (Table 2). In 2008, 66 percent of voting-age citizens in the Midwest voted, while the voting rates in the West, Northeast, and South were all about 63 percent.

Compared to 2004, the South was the only region to display a statistically significant increase (about 2 percentage points) in voter turnout in 2008. The Midwest and Northeast both showed significant decreases, while the voting rate in the West was not statistically different from the 2004 election.

About 4 million more voters came to the polls in the South in 2008 compared to 2004. There was also an increase of about 2 million voters in the West. The number of aggregate voters in the Northeast and Midwest did not change statistically between 2004 and 2008.

Citizens residing in the Midwest were also more likely to be registered to vote than those in other regions. In 2008, 74 percent of eligible

[11]The voting rate for young adults with at least a bachelor's degree was not statistically different from individuals 65 and older with a high school diploma.

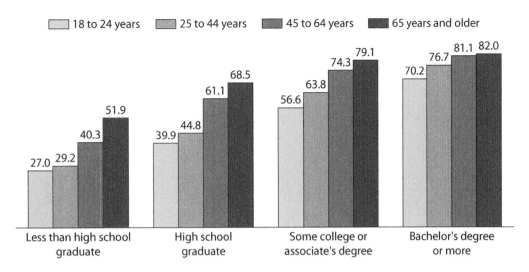

(Citizens 18 and older, in percent)

Source: U.S. Census Bureau, Current Population Survey, November 2008.

Figure 3. Voting Rates by Educational Attainment and Age Groups: 2008

individuals in the Midwest reported being registered, compared to the South (71 percent), Northeast (70 percent), and West (69 percent).

States

In 2008, 20 states showed statistically different voting rates in comparison to the election of 2004 (Table 3). As displayed in Figure 4, 8 of these states displayed an increase in voting rates, while 12 displayed a decrease. Six of the states with higher voting rates were located in the South (Mississippi, Georgia, North Carolina, Louisiana, Virginia, and the District of Columbia) while the remaining two were in the Northeast region (Connecticut and Rhode Island).

States with lower voting rates in 2008 than in 2004 were spread across the entire country and included Arizona, Arkansas, Illinois, Minnesota, Montana, North Dakota, Oklahoma,

Oregon, Pennsylvania, Utah, West Virginia, and Wisconsin.

Minnesota and the District of Columbia had some of the highest voting rates in the country (about 75 percent). Utah and Hawaii were among the states with the lowest voting rates in the country at approximately 52 percent each. Overall, 16 states had voting rates that were not statistically different from the national average of 64 percent (Figure 5).

Excluding North Dakota, which has no formal voter registration process, Maine, Minnesota, Louisiana, and the District of Columbia had among the highest levels of voter registration in the country (approximately 79 percent). Hawaii and Utah shared the lowest registration rates at about 59 percent. Overall, 19 states had registration rates that were not statistically different from the national average of 71 percent.

Table 6. Reasons for Not Registering and Voting, by Selected Characteristics: 2008
(Numbers in thousands)

Characteristic	Total	Percent distribution of reasons for not voting and registering												
		Race and Hispanic origin					Age				Educational attainment			
		White alone	White alone, non-Hispanic	Black alone, non-Hispanic	Asian alone	Hispanic (any race)	18-24 years	25-44 years	45-64 years	65 years and older	Less than high school graduate	High school graduate or GED	Some college[3]	Bachelor's degree or more
Total nonvoters	**15,167**	**12,920**	**11,172**	**1,242**	**543**	**1,862**	**2,567**	**5,819**	**4,201**	**2,581**	**2,556**	**6,015**	**4,427**	**2,169**
Reasons for not voting[1]														
Too busy, conflicting schedule	17.5	17.3	16.2	16.9	26.9	24.8	21.0	24.3	14.9	3.0	12.2	18.0	20.2	16.9
Illness or disability	14.9	15.0	15.6	20.3	6.8	10.8	3.2	6.8	14.8	45.3	25.6	14.3	10.9	12.5
Not interested	13.4	14.1	15.2	8.5	9.4	14.0	12.1	14.2	15.2	9.9	13.8	15.6	11.4	10.8
Did not like candidates or campaign issues	12.9	14.2	15.2	4.3	4.5	7.6	8.0	12.7	16.5	12.5	13.6	14.0	11.9	11.4
Other reason	11.3	11.0	10.9	12.7	11.8	11.7	11.6	11.7	12.5	8.0	10.8	10.9	11.6	12.4
Out of town	8.8	8.9	9.1	6.4	12.0	7.8	14.2	8.4	8.3	5.1	4.0	6.8	11.1	15.3
Don't know or refused	7.0	6.3	6.1	13.0	11.0	7.3	11.2	7.2	5.8	4.6	5.3	6.6	8.7	6.8
Registration problems	6.0	5.7	5.6	5.6	7.9	7.0	9.0	7.3	4.3	2.6	3.2	5.8	7.2	7.4
Inconvenient polling place	2.7	2.5	2.3	3.3	5.5	4.1	2.6	3.0	2.6	2.3	3.1	2.6	2.5	3.0
Transportation problems	2.6	2.4	2.4	4.8	1.7	2.5	2.4	1.4	3.4	4.5	4.7	2.8	1.9	1.4
Forgot to vote	2.6	2.4	2.4	3.1	2.6	2.4	4.5	2.8	1.8	1.3	3.0	2.5	2.7	1.9
Bad weather conditions	0.2	0.2	0.2	1.2	–	–	0.2	0.1	0.1	0.8	0.7	0.2	0.0	0.3
Total not registered	**30,402**	**24,848**	**20,524**	**2,961**	**1,646**	**4,663**	**6,294**	**11,882**	**8,464**	**3,763**	**7,614**	**12,799**	**7,043**	**2,947**
Reasons for not registering[2]														
Not interested in the election/not involved in politics	46.0	48.1	50.5	33.7	35.5	36.2	42.2	45.4	50.1	44.9	43.9	48.9	45.6	39.9
Did not meet registration deadlines	14.7	14.6	14.4	17.7	12.2	15.8	21.3	16.0	11.2	7.0	10.3	13.8	18.3	20.7

Not eligible to vote	8.6	7.6	5.6	14.0	12.2	17.2	7.6	10.1	8.5	5.6	11.4	8.2	6.6	7.9
Other	6.1	5.9	6.3	7.4	6.1	4.3	6.1	6.0	6.0	8.2	5.1	5.9	6.9	7.2
Permanent illness or disability	6.0	5.8	6.0	8.6	3.2	4.7	2.8	3.3	6.8	17.7	10.4	5.7	2.7	3.5
Don't know or refused	5.7	5.4	5.5	7.0	6.3	5.3	8.3	5.6	4.8	3.6	4.9	6.1	6.4	4.1
Did not know where or how to register	4.2	3.9	3.7	4.6	6.8	5.3	6.2	4.2	2.9	3.5	4.7	4.0	4.4	3.2
My vote would not make a difference	4.0	4.2	4.6	3.4	2.7	2.1	3.6	3.7	4.8	4.1	4.0	3.8	4.4	4.2
Did not meet residency requirements	3.5	3.5	2.9	2.7	5.6	5.8	3.0	4.5	3.0	2.0	2.9	2.8	3.7	7.8
Difficulty with English	1.4	0.9	0.5	0.7	9.3	3.0	0.4	1.1	1.5	3.6	2.5	0.8	1.1	1.5

- Represents zero or rounds to zero.

[1] Only individuals who reported being registered and also reported not voting were asked the question about reason for not voting.

[2] Includes only those respondents who answered "no" to the question, "Were you registered in the election of November 2008?"

[3] Includes individuals reporting an associate's degree.

Source: U.S. Census Bureau, Current Population Survey, November 2008.

Purpose

The purpose of this reading is to give you an historical perspective on how challenges the United States faced early in our history may still challenge us today.

Context

After the first eight years of the republic, President Washington gave a farewell address to the nation, in which he expressed concerns about challenges the nation would face, especially to her sense of national unity, from internal and external forces. For the first 150 years of the nation, it was common to see this speech reprinted in high school civics textbooks, because it was viewed as one of the most important speeches in America's political history. Washington has seven main concerns. As you read the speech, note how he discusses each of them. They are:

1. The ongoing sense of internal unity of the nation.
2. Geographical divisions (ie, conflicts between different regions of the country).
3. Efforts to undermine the credibility of the U.S. Constitution.
4. The "spirit of party."
5. Deterioration of religion and morality as the nation grows.
6. Excessive public debt.
7. Foreign relations, specifically, too-passionate attachments to other countries and the "insidious wiles of foreign influence."

Thought Questions

1. Which of these concerns have the most application in today's politics?
2. Which of them did not turn out to be that big of a deal?
3. Can you think of specific examples to support your answers?
4. If Washington were to advise modern political leaders, what do you think he would say?

Web Link

1. George Washington Farewell Address
   http://www.earlyamerica.com/earlyamerica/milestones/farewell/

19. Farewell Address to the People of the United States

By George Washington

Friends and Fellow-Citizens:

1. The period for a new election of a citizen, to administer the executive government of the United States, being not far distant, and the time actually arrived, when your thoughts must be employed designating the person, who is to be clothed with that important trust, it appears to me proper, especially as it may conduce to a more distinct expression of the public voice, that I should now apprize you of the resolution I have formed, to decline being considered among the number of those out of whom a choice is to be made.

2. I beg you at the same time to do me the justice to be assured that this resolution has not been taken without a strict regard to all the considerations appertaining to the relation which binds a dutiful citizen to his country; and that in withdrawing the tender of service, which silence in my situation might imply, I am influenced by no diminution of zeal for your future interest, no deficiency of grateful respect for your past kindness, but am supported by a full conviction that the step is compatible with both.

3. The acceptance of, and continuance hitherto in, the office to which your suffrages have twice called me, have been a uniform sacrifice of inclination to the opinion of duty, and to a deference for what appeared to be your desire. I constantly hoped, that it would have been much earlier in my power, consistently with motives, which I was not at liberty to disregard, to return to that retirement, from which I had been reluctantly drawn. The strength of my inclination to do this, previous to the last election, had even led to the preparation of an address to declare it to you; but mature reflection on the then perplexed and critical posture of our affairs with foreign nations, and the unanimous advice of persons entitled to my confidence impelled me to abandon the idea.

4. I rejoice, that the state of your concerns, external as well as internal, no longer renders the pursuit of inclination incompatible with the sentiment of duty, or propriety; and am persuaded, whatever partiality may be retained for my services, that, in the present circumstances of our country, you will not disapprove my determination to retire.

5. The impressions, with which I first undertook the arduous trust, were explained on the proper occasion. In the discharge of this trust, I will only say, that I have, with good intentions, contributed towards the organization and administration of the government the best exertions of which a very fallible judgment was capable. Not unconscious, in the outset, of the inferiority

of my qualifications, experience in my own eyes, perhaps still more in the eyes of others, has strengthened the motives to diffidence of myself; and every day the increasing weight of years admonishes me more and more, that the shade of retirement is as necessary to me as it will be welcome. Satisfied, that, if any circumstances have given peculiar value to my services, they were temporary, I have the consolation to believe, that, while choice and prudence invite me to quit the political scene, patriotism does not forbid it.

6. In looking forward to the moment, which is intended to terminate the career of my public life, my feelings do not permit me to suspend the deep acknowledgment of that debt of gratitude, which I owe to my beloved country for the many honors it has conferred upon me; still more for the steadfast confidence with which it has supported me; and for the opportunities I have thence enjoyed of manifesting my inviolable attachment, by services faithful and persevering, though in usefulness unequal to my zeal. If benefits have resulted to our country from these services, let it always be remembered to your praise, and as an instructive example in our annals, that under circumstances in which the passions, agitated in every direction, were liable to mislead, amidst appearances sometimes dubious, vicissitudes of fortune often discouraging, in situations in which not unfrequently want of success has countenanced the spirit of criticism, the constancy of your support was the essential prop of the efforts, and a guarantee of the plans by which they were effected. Profoundly penetrated with this idea, I shall carry it with me to my grave, as a strong incitement to unceasing vows that Heaven may continue to you the choicest tokens of its beneficence; that your union and brotherly affection may be perpetual; that the free constitution, which is the work of your hands, may be sacredly maintained; that its administration in every department may be stamped with wisdom and virtue; than, in fine, the happiness of the people of these States, under the auspices of liberty, may be made complete, by so careful a preservation and so prudent a use of this blessing, as will acquire to them the glory of

recommending it to the applause, the affection, and adoption of every nation, which is yet a stranger to it.

7. Here, perhaps I ought to stop. But a solicitude for your welfare which cannot end but with my life, and the apprehension of danger, natural to that solicitude, urge me, on an occasion like the present, to offer to your solemn contemplation, and to recommend to your frequent review, some sentiments which are the result of much reflection, of no inconsiderable observation, and which appear to me all-important to the permanency of your felicity as a people. These will be offered to you with the more freedom, as you can only see in them the disinterested warnings of a parting friend, who can possibly have no personal motive to bias his counsel. Nor can I forget, as an encouragement to it, your indulgent reception of my sentiments on a former and not dissimilar occasion.

8. Interwoven as is the love of liberty with every ligament of your hearts, no recommendation of mine is necessary to fortify or confirm the attachment.

9. The unity of Government, which constitutes you one people, is also now dear to you. It is justly so; for it is a main pillar in the edifice of your real independence, the support of your tranquillity at home, your peace abroad; of your safety; of your prosperity; of that very Liberty, which you so highly prize. But as it is easy to foresee, that, from different causes and from different quarters, much pains will be taken, many artifices employed, to weaken in your minds the conviction of this truth; as this is the point in your political fortress against which the batteries of internal and external enemies will be most constantly and actively (though often covertly and insidiously) directed, it is of infinite moment, that you should properly estimate the immense value of your national Union to your collective and individual happiness; that you should cherish a cordial, habitual, and immovable attachment to it; accustoming yourselves to think and speak of it as of the Palladium of your political safety and prosperity; watching for its preservation with jealous anxiety; discountenancing whatever may suggest even a suspicion, that it can in

any event be abandoned; and indignantly frowning upon the first dawning of every attempt to alienate any portion of our country from the rest, or to enfeeble the sacred ties which now link together the various parts.

10. For this you have every inducement of sympathy and interest. Citizens, by birth or choice, of a common country, that country has a right to concentrate your affections. The name of american, which belongs to you, in your national capacity, must always exalt the just pride of Patriotism, more than any appellation derived from local discriminations. With slight shades of difference, you have the same religion, manners, habits, and political principles. You have in a common cause fought and triumphed together; the Independence and Liberty you possess are the work of joint counsels, and joint efforts, of common dangers, sufferings, and successes.

11. But these considerations, however powerfully they address themselves to your sensibility, are greatly outweighed by those, which apply more immediately to your interest. Here every portion of our country finds the most commanding motives for carefully guarding and preserving the Union of the whole.

12. The North, in an unrestrained intercourse with the South, protected by the equal laws of a common government, finds, in the productions of the latter, great additional resources of maritime and commercial enterprise and precious materials of manufacturing industry. The South, in the same intercourse, benefiting by the agency of the North, sees its agriculture grow and its commerce expand. Turning partly into its own channels the seamen of the North, it finds its particular navigation invigorated; and, while it contributes, in different ways, to nourish and increase the general mass of the national navigation, it looks forward to the protection of a maritime strength, to which itself is unequally adapted. The East, in a like intercourse with the West, already finds, and in the progressive improvement of interior communications by land and water, will more and more find, a valuable vent for the commodities which it brings from abroad, or manufactures at home. The West derives from

the East supplies requisite to its growth and comfort, and, what is perhaps of still greater consequence, it must of necessity owe the secure enjoyment of indispensable outlets for its own productions to the weight, influence, and the future maritime strength of the Atlantic side of the Union, directed by an indissoluble community of interest as one nation. Any other tenure by which the West can hold this essential advantage, whether derived from its own separate strength, or from an apostate and unnatural connexion with any foreign power, must be intrinsically precarious.

13. While, then, every part of our country thus feels an immediate and particular interest in Union, all the parts combined cannot fail to find in the united mass of means and efforts greater strength, greater resource, proportionably greater security from external danger, a less frequent interruption of their peace by foreign nations; and, what is of inestimable value, they must derive from Union an exemption from those broils and wars between themselves, which so frequently afflict neighbouring countries not tied together by the same governments, which their own rivalships alone would be sufficient to produce, but which opposite foreign alliances, attachments, and intrigues would stimulate and embitter. Hence, likewise, they will avoid the necessity of those overgrown military establishments, which, under any form of government, are inauspicious to liberty, and which are to be regarded as particularly hostile to Republican Liberty. In this sense it is, that your Union ought to be considered as a main prop of your liberty, and that the love of the one ought to endear to you the preservation of the other.

14. These considerations speak a persuasive language to every reflecting and virtuous mind, and exhibit the continuance of the union as a primary object of Patriotic desire. Is there a doubt, whether a common government can embrace so large a sphere? Let experience solve it. To listen to mere speculation in such a case were criminal. We are authorized to hope, that a proper organization of the whole, with the auxiliary agency of governments for the respective

subdivisions, will afford a happy issue to the experiment. It is well worth a fair and full experiment. With such powerful and obvious motives to Union, affecting all parts of our country, while experience shall not have demonstrated its impracticability, there will always be reason to distrust the patriotism of those, who in any quarter may endeavour to weaken its bands.

15. In contemplating the causes, which may disturb our Union, it occurs as matter of serious concern, that any ground should have been furnished for characterizing parties by Geographical discriminations, Northern and Southern, Atlantic and Western; whence designing men may endeavour to excite a belief, that there is a real difference of local interests and views. One of the expedients of party to acquire influence, within particular districts, is to misrepresent the opinions and aims of other districts. You cannot shield yourselves too much against the jealousies and heart-burnings, which spring from these misrepresentations; they tend to render alien to each other those, who ought to be bound together by fraternal affection. The inhabitants of our western country have lately had a useful lesson on this head; they have seen, in the negotiation by the Executive, and in the unanimous ratification by the Senate, of the treaty with Spain, and in the universal satisfaction at that event, throughout the United States, a decisive proof how unfounded were the suspicions propagated among them of a policy in the General Government and in the Atlantic States unfriendly to their interests in regard to the mississippi; they have been witnesses to the formation of two treaties, that with Great Britain, and that with Spain, which secure to them every thing they could desire, in respect to our foreign relations, towards confirming their prosperity. Will it not be their wisdom to rely for the preservation of these advantages on the union by which they were procured? Will they not henceforth be deaf to those advisers, if such there are, who would sever them from their brethren, and connect them with aliens?

16. To the efficacy and permanency of your Union, a Government for the whole is indispensable. No alliances, however strict, between the parts can be an adequate substitute; they must inevitably experience the infractions and interruptions, which all alliances in all times have experienced. Sensible of this momentous truth, you have improved upon your first essay, by the adoption of a Constitution of Government better calculated than your former for an intimate Union, and for the efficacious management of your common concerns. This Government, the offspring of our own choice, uninfluenced and unawed, adopted upon full investigation and mature deliberation, completely free in its principles, in the distribution of its powers, uniting security with energy, and containing within itself a provision for its own amendment, has a just claim to your confidence and your support. Respect for its authority, compliance with its laws, acquiescence in its measures, are duties enjoined by the fundamental maxims of true Liberty. The basis of our political systems is the right of the people to make and to alter their Constitutions of Government. But the Constitution which at any time exists, till changed by an explicit and authentic act of the whole people, is sacredly obligatory upon all. The very idea of the power and the right of the people to establish Government presupposes the duty of every individual to obey the established Government.

17. All obstructions to the execution of the Laws, all combinations and associations, under whatever plausible character, with the real design to direct, control, counteract, or awe the regular deliberation and action of the constituted authorities, are destructive of this fundamental principle, and of fatal tendency. They serve to organize faction, to give it an artificial and extraordinary force; to put, in the place of the delegated will of the nation, the will of a party, often a small but artful and enterprising minority of the community; and, according to the alternate triumphs of different parties, to make the public administration the mirror of the ill-concerted and incongruous projects of faction, rather than the organ of consistent and wholesome plans digested by common counsels, and modified by mutual interests.

18. However combinations or associations of the above description may now and then answer popular ends, they are likely, in the course of time and things, to become potent engines, by which cunning, ambitious, and unprincipled men will be enabled to subvert the power of the people, and to usurp for themselves the reins of government; destroying afterwards the very engines, which have lifted them to unjust dominion.

19. Towards the preservation of your government, and the permanency of your present happy state, it is requisite, not only that you steadily discountenance irregular oppositions to its acknowledged authority, but also that you resist with care the spirit of innovation upon its principles, however specious the pretexts. One method of assault may be to effect, in the forms of the constitution, alterations, which will impair the energy of the system, and thus to undermine what cannot be directly overthrown. In all the changes to which you may be invited, remember that time and habit are at least as necessary to fix the true character of governments, as of other human institutions; that experience is the surest standard, by which to test the real tendency of the existing constitution of a country; that facility in changes, upon the credit of mere hypothesis and opinion, exposes to perpetual change, from the endless variety of hypothesis and opinion; and remember, especially, that, for the efficient management of our common interests, in a country so extensive as ours, a government of as much vigor as is consistent with the perfect security of liberty is indispensable. Liberty itself will find in such a government, with powers properly distributed and adjusted, its surest guardian. It is, indeed, little else than a name, where the government is too feeble to withstand the enterprises of faction, to confine each member of the society within the limits prescribed by the laws, and to maintain all in the secure and tranquil enjoyment of the rights of person and property.

20. I have already intimated to you the danger of parties in the state, with particular reference to the founding of them on geographical discriminations. Let me now take a more comprehensive view, and warn you in the most solemn manner against the baneful effects of the spirit of party, generally.

21. This spirit, unfortunately, is inseparable from our nature, having its root in the strongest passions of the human mind. It exists under different shapes in all governments, more or less stifled, controlled, or repressed; but, in those of the popular form, it is seen in its greatest rankness, and is truly their worst enemy.

22. The alternate domination of one faction over another, sharpened by the spirit of revenge, natural to party dissension, which in different ages and countries has perpetrated the most horrid enormities, is itself a frightful despotism. But this leads at length to a more formal and permanent despotism. The disorders and miseries, which result, gradually incline the minds of men to seek security and repose in the absolute power of an individual; and sooner or later the chief of some prevailing faction, more able or more fortunate than his competitors, turns this disposition to the purposes of his own elevation, on the ruins of Public Liberty.

23. Without looking forward to an extremity of this kind, (which nevertheless ought not to be entirely out of sight,) the common and continual mischiefs of the spirit of party are sufficient to make it the interest and duty of a wise people to discourage and restrain it.

24. It serves always to distract the Public Councils, and enfeeble the Public Administration. It agitates the Community with ill-founded jealousies and false alarms; kindles the animosity of one part against another, foments occasionally riot and insurrection. It opens the door to foreign influence and corruption, which find a facilitated access to the government itself through the channels of party passions. Thus the policy and the will of one country are subjected to the policy and will of another.

25. There is an opinion, that parties in free countries are useful checks upon the administration of the Government, and serve to keep alive the spirit of Liberty. This within certain limits is probably true; and in Governments of a Monarchical cast, Patriotism may look with indulgence, if not

with favor, upon the spirit of party. But in those of the popular character, in Governments purely elective, it is a spirit not to be encouraged. From their natural tendency, it is certain there will always be enough of that spirit for every salutary purpose. And, there being constant danger of excess, the effort ought to be, by force of public opinion, to mitigate and assuage it. A fire not to be quenched, it demands a uniform vigilance to prevent its bursting into a flame, lest, instead of warming, it should consume.

26. It is important, likewise, that the habits of thinking in a free country should inspire caution, in those intrusted with its administration, to confine themselves within their respective constitutional spheres, avoiding in the exercise of the powers of one department to encroach upon another. The spirit of encroachment tends to consolidate the powers of all the departments in one, and thus to create, whatever the form of government, a real despotism. A just estimate of that love of power, and proneness to abuse it, which predominates in the human heart, is sufficient to satisfy us of the truth of this position. The necessity of reciprocal checks in the exercise of political power, by dividing and distributing it into different depositories, and constituting each the Guardian of the Public Weal against invasions by the others, has been evinced by experiments ancient and modern; some of them in our country and under our own eyes. To preserve them must be as necessary as to institute them. If, in the opinion of the people, the distribution or modification of the constitutional powers be in any particular wrong, let it be corrected by an amendment in the way, which the constitution designates. But let there be no change by usurpation; for, though this, in one instance, may be the instrument of good, it is the customary weapon by which free governments are destroyed. The precedent must always greatly overbalance in permanent evil any partial or transient benefit, which the use can at any time yield.

27. Of all the dispositions and habits, which lead to political prosperity, Religion and Morality are indispensable supports. In vain would that man claim the tribute of Patriotism, who should labor to subvert these great pillars of human happiness, these firmest props of the duties of Men and Citizens. The mere Politician, equally with the pious man, ought to respect and to cherish them. A volume could not trace all their connexions with private and public felicity. Let it simply be asked, Where is the security for property, for reputation, for life, if the sense of religious obligation desert the oaths, which are the instruments of investigation in Courts of Justice? And let us with caution indulge the supposition, that morality can be maintained without religion. Whatever may be conceded to the influence of refined education on minds of peculiar structure, reason and experience both forbid us to expect, that national morality can prevail in exclusion of religious principle.

28. It is substantially true, that virtue or morality is a necessary spring of popular government. The rule, indeed, extends with more or less force to every species of free government. Who, that is a sincere friend to it, can look with indifference upon attempts to shake the foundation of the fabric ?

29. Promote, then, as an object of primary importance, institutions for the general diffusion of knowledge. In proportion as the structure of a government gives force to public opinion, it is essential that public opinion should be enlightened.

30. As a very important source of strength and security, cherish public credit. One method of preserving it is, to use it as sparingly as possible; avoiding occasions of expense by cultivating peace, but remembering also that timely disbursements to prepare for danger frequently prevent much greater disbursements to repel it; avoiding likewise the accumulation of debt, not only by shunning occasions of expense, but by vigorous exertions in time of peace to discharge the debts, which unavoidable wars may have occasioned, not ungenerously throwing upon posterity the burthen, which we ourselves ought to bear. The execution of these maxims belongs to your representatives, but it is necessary that public opinion should cooperate. To facilitate to them the performance of their duty, it is essential that

you should practically bear in mind, that towards the payment of debts there must be Revenue; that to have Revenue there must be taxes; that no taxes can be devised, which are not more or less inconvenient and unpleasant; that the intrinsic embarrassment, inseparable from the selection of the proper objects (which is always a choice of difficulties), ought to be a decisive motive for a candid construction of the conduct of the government in making it, and for a spirit of acquiescence in the measures for obtaining revenue, which the public exigencies may at any time dictate.

31. Observe good faith and justice towards all Nations; cultivate peace and harmony with all. Religion and Morality enjoin this conduct; and can it be, that good policy does not equally enjoin it? It will be worthy of a free, enlightened, and, at no distant period, a great Nation, to give to mankind the magnanimous and too novel example of a people always guided by an exalted justice and benevolence. Who can doubt, that, in the course of time and things, the fruits of such a plan would richly repay any temporary advantages, which might be lost by a steady adherence to it ? Can it be, that Providence has not connected the permanent felicity of a Nation with its Virtue? The experiment, at least, is recommended by every sentiment which ennobles human nature. Alas! is it rendered impossible by its vices ?

32. In the execution of such a plan, nothing is more essential, than that permanent, inveterate antipathies against particular Nations, and passionate attachments for others, should be excluded; and that, in place of them, just and amicable feelings towards all should be cultivated. The Nation, which indulges towards another an habitual hatred, or an habitual fondness, is in some degree a slave. It is a slave to its animosity or to its affection, either of which is sufficient to lead it astray from its duty and its interest. Antipathy in one nation against another disposes each more readily to offer insult and injury, to lay hold of slight causes of umbrage, and to be haughty and intractable, when accidental or trifling occasions of dispute occur. Hence frequent collisions, obstinate, envenomed, and bloody contests. The Nation, prompted by ill-will and resentment, sometimes impels to war the Government, contrary to the best calculations of policy. The Government sometimes participates in the national propensity, and adopts through passion what reason would reject; at other times, it makes the animosity of the nation subservient to projects of hostility instigated by pride, ambition, and other sinister and pernicious motives. The peace often, sometimes perhaps the liberty, of Nations has been the victim.

33. So likewise, a passionate attachment of one Nation for another produces a variety of evils. Sympathy for the favorite Nation, facilitating the illusion of an imaginary common interest, in cases where no real common interest exists, and infusing into one the enmities of the other, betrays the former into a participation in the quarrels and wars of the latter, without adequate inducement or justification. It leads also to concessions to the favorite Nation of privileges denied to others, which is apt doubly to injure the Nation making the concessions; by unnecessarily parting with what ought to have been retained; and by exciting jealousy, ill-will, and a disposition to retaliate, in the parties from whom equal privileges are withheld. And it gives to ambitious, corrupted, or deluded citizens, (who devote themselves to the favorite nation,) facility to betray or sacrifice the interests of their own country, without odium, sometimes even with popularity; gilding, with the appearances of a virtuous sense of obligation, a commendable deference for public opinion, or a laudable zeal for public good, the base or foolish compliances of ambition, corruption, or infatuation.

34. As avenues to foreign influence in innumerable ways, such attachments are particularly alarming to the truly enlightened and independent Patriot. How many opportunities do they afford to tamper with domestic factions, to practise the arts of seduction, to mislead public opinion, to influence or awe the Public Councils! Such an attachment of a small or weak, towards a great and powerful nation, dooms the former to be the satellite of the latter.

35. Against the insidious wiles of foreign influence (I conjure you to believe me, fellow-citizens,) the jealousy of a free people ought to be constantly awake; since history and experience prove, that foreign influence is one of the most baneful foes of Republican Government. But that jealousy, to be useful, must be impartial; else it becomes the instrument of the very influence to be avoided, instead of a defence against it. Excessive partiality for one foreign nation, and excessive dislike of another, cause those whom they actuate to see danger only on one side, and serve to veil and even second the arts of influence on the other. Real patriots, who may resist the intrigues of the favorite, are liable to become suspected and odious; while its tools and dupes usurp the applause and confidence of the people, to surrender their interests.

36. The great rule of conduct for us, in regard to foreign nations, is, in extending our commercial relations, to have with them as little political connexion as possible. So far as we have already formed engagements, let them be fulfilled with perfect good faith. Here let us stop.

37. Europe has a set of primary interests, which to us have none, or a very remote relation. Hence she must be engaged in frequent controversies, the causes of which are essentially foreign to our concerns. Hence, therefore, it must be unwise in us to implicate ourselves, by artificial ties, in the ordinary vicissitudes of her politics, or the ordinary combinations and collisions of her friendships or enmities.

38. Our detached and distant situation invites and enables us to pursue a different course. If we remain one people, under an efficient government, the period is not far off, when we may defy material injury from external annoyance; when we may take such an attitude as will cause the neutrality, we may at any time resolve upon, to be scrupulously respected; when belligerent nations, under the impossibility of making acquisitions upon us, will not lightly hazard the giving us provocation; when we may choose peace or war, as our interest, guided by justice, shall counsel.

39. Why forego the advantages of so peculiar a situation? Why quit our own to stand upon foreign ground? Why, by interweaving our destiny with that of any part of Europe, entangle our peace and prosperity in the toils of European ambition, rivalship, interest, humor, or caprice?

40. It is our true policy to steer clear of permanent alliances with any portion of the foreign world; so far, I mean, as we are now at liberty to do it; for let me not be understood as capable of patronizing infidelity to existing engagements. I hold the maxim no less applicable to public than to private affairs, that honesty is always the best policy. I repeat it, therefore, let those engagements be observed in their genuine sense. But, in my opinion, it is unnecessary and would be unwise to extend them.

41. Taking care always to keep ourselves, by suitable establishments, on a respectable defensive posture, we may safely trust to temporary alliances for extraordinary emergencies.

42. Harmony, liberal intercourse with all nations, are recommended by policy, humanity, and interest. But even our commercial policy should hold an equal and impartial hand; neither seeking nor granting exclusive favors or preferences; consulting the natural course of things; diffusing and diversifying by gentle means the streams of commerce, but forcing nothing; establishing, with powers so disposed, in order to give trade a stable course, to define the rights of our merchants, and to enable the government to support them, conventional rules of intercourse, the best that present circumstances and mutual opinion will permit, but temporary, and liable to be from time to time abandoned or varied, as experience and circumstances shall dictate; constantly keeping in view, that it is folly in one nation to look for disinterested favors from another; that it must pay with a portion of its independence for whatever it may accept under that character; that, by such acceptance, it may place itself in the condition of having given equivalents for nominal favors, and yet of being reproached with ingratitude for not giving more. There can be no greater error than to expect or calculate upon real favors

from nation to nation. It is an illusion, which experience must cure, which a just pride ought to discard.

43. In offering to you, my countrymen, these counsels of an old and affectionate friend, I dare not hope they will make the strong and lasting impression I could wish; that they will control the usual current of the passions, or prevent our nation from running the course, which has hitherto marked the destiny of nations. But, if I may even flatter myself, that they may be productive of some partial benefit, some occasional good; that they may now and then recur to moderate the fury of party spirit, to warn against the mischiefs of foreign intrigue, to guard against the impostures of pretended patriotism; this hope will be a full recompense for the solicitude for your welfare, by which they have been dictated.

44. How far in the discharge of my official duties, I have been guided by the principles which have been delineated, the public records and other evidences of my conduct must witness to you and to the world. To myself, the assurance of my own conscience is, that I have at least believed myself to be guided by them.

45. In relation to the still subsisting war in Europe, my Proclamation of the 22d of April 1793, is the index to my Plan. Sanctioned by your approving voice, and by that of your Representatives in both Houses of Congress, the spirit of that measure has continually governed me, uninfluenced by any attempts to deter or divert me from it.

46. After deliberate examination, with the aid of the best lights I could obtain, I was well satisfied that our country, under all the circumstances of the case, had a right to take, and was bound in duty and interest to take, a neutral position. Having taken it, I determined, as far as should depend upon me, to maintain it, with moderation, perseverance, and firmness.

47. The considerations, which respect the right to hold this conduct, it is not necessary on this occasion to detail. I will only observe, that, according to my understanding of the matter, that right, so far from being denied by any of the Belligerent Powers, has been virtually admitted by all.

48. The duty of holding a neutral conduct may be inferred, without any thing more, from the obligation which justice and humanity impose on every nation, in cases in which it is free to act, to maintain inviolate the relations of peace and amity towards other nations.

49. The inducements of interest for observing that conduct will best be referred to your own reflections and experience. With me, a predominant motive has been to endeavour to gain time to our country to settle and mature its yet recent institutions, and to progress without interruption to that degree of strength and consistency, which is necessary to give it, humanly speaking, the command of its own fortunes.

50. Though, in reviewing the incidents of my administration, I am unconscious of intentional error, I am nevertheless too sensible of my defects not to think it probable that I may have committed many errors. Whatever they may be, I fervently beseech the Almighty to avert or mitigate the evils to which they may tend. I shall also carry with me the hope, that my Country will never cease to view them with indulgence; and that, after forty-five years of my life dedicated to its service with an upright zeal, the faults of incompetent abilities will be consigned to oblivion, as myself must soon be to the mansions of rest.

51. Relying on its kindness in this as in other things, and actuated by that fervent love towards it, which is so natural to a man, who views it in the native soil of himself and his progenitors for several generations; I anticipate with pleasing expectation that retreat, in which I promise myself to realize, without alloy, the sweet enjoyment of partaking, in the midst of my fellow-citizens, the benign influence of good laws under a free government, the ever favorite object of my heart, and the happy reward, as I trust, of our mutual cares, labors, and dangers.

George Washington
United States—September 17, 1796

Source: *The Independent Chronicle*, September 26, 1796.

Purpose

The purpose of this reading is to help you compare the political behavior of young voters with that of older Americans.

Context

As we saw in the Census Bureau report from the 2008 election, peoples' ages appear to be related to their political behavior. Prior to the 1972 election, the right to vote was limited to Americans aged 21 years and older. The 26th Amendment extended the right to 18-20 year olds, but since that time, the voter turnout rates of young voters has been substantially lower than those of older voters. The Center for Information & Research on Civic Learning and Engagement (CIRCLE) researches young voters. At the end of the reading, there are listed several reports about youth voting. You can find links to them at the report's Web Link, below.

Thought Questions

1. The CIRCLE report refers to the 2010 National Election Pool, and compares young voters with older voters in several ways. What differences do they mention that you find interesting? Why do you find them interesting?
2. Graph 5 compares young voters having different educational levels. What differences does this graph show? What do those differences suggest to you about the role of education in promoting political participation like voting?
3. In the section Getting Out the Youth Vote: What Works the report suggests several campaign tactics that might increase the youth vote. What are they? How effective do you think these tactics would be? Think about these suggestions in light of the Census Bureau report from 2008 as to why young people say they didn't vote or didn't register to vote. How effective do you think the CIRCLE suggested tactics would be in addressing the reasons given for not participating in 2008?

Web Link

1. Youth Voting in the 2010 election
   http://www.civicyouth.org/quick-facts/youth-voting/

20. Youth Voting in the 2010 Election

By Circle: The Center for Information & Research on Civic Learning and Engagement

2010 Midterm Elections

An estimated 22.8 percent of all eligible young people ages 18-29 voted in the 2010 midterms. Younger voters chose Democratic House candidates over Republican House candidates by a margin of 55%–42%.

According to the 2010 National Election Pool, National Exit Poll …

- By a 62%-38% margin, younger voters approved of Barack Obama's handling of his job as president.

- Given a choice among four issues that could be the most important facing the United States, younger voters chose the economy (56%), followed by health care (26%), the war in Afghanistan (8%) and illegal immigration (6%). These choices were not much different from those of all voters or any other age group.

- Twenty-six percent of young voters supported the Tea Party, with 9% "strongly" supporting the movement. In contrast, 41% of all voters and nearly half (48%) of 60+ voters supported the Tea Party.

- Most (85%) of young adults who voted in 2010 had also voted in 2008. The 2010 young electorate was mostly a subset of the 2008 electorate.

- Younger voters were more racially and ethnically diverse than the electorate as a whole. Among younger voters, 65% were white, 16% Black, 14% Hispanic, 1% Asian, and 2% "all others." In contrast, among voters 30 and older, 80% were white, 10% Black, 7% Hispanic, 1% Asian, and 2% "all other." Seven percent of younger voters said they were gay, lesbian, or bisexual, compared to 4% of all voters.

For more information, see CIRCLE Fact Sheet "Young Voters in the 2010 Election" [www.civicyouth.org/youth-voters-in-the-2010-elections/]

Regarding turnout in presidential elections, our fact sheet can be downloaded at www.civicyouth.org/youth-voters-in-the-2010-elections/. It includes historical trends and a 50-state breakdown. Below is a graph from that report, showing turnout by age since 1972. Youth (18-29) voter turnout rose to 51 percent in 2008, an increase of two percentage points from the 2004 Presidential election.

In the 2008 election, the gap in turnout by educational attainment remained large; young people without college experience were much less likely than those with college experience to vote. Youth without college experience make up about one half of the young adult population. In the 2008 election, 36% of youth without college experience turned out to vote, compared to the 62% with college experience.

*Since 1972, young women have been more likely to vote than young men; in 2008 the voter turnout gap between genders was eight percentage points

*In 2008, 5 percent of African-American youth voted, which is the highest turnout rate of any youth racial/ethnic group since 1972.

Voting Laws & Youth Turnout

In 2008, on average, 59% of young Americans whose home state offered EDR voted; nine percentage points higher than those who did not live in EDR states.

Three of the top five states for youth voting in 2008 allowed Election Day registration (MN, IA, NH).

Other state laws that seem to increase youth voting are: early voting at convenient locations, no-excuse absentee voting, and voter registration at state motor vehicle agencies.

In states that mailed sample ballots & information about polling places and extended polling place hours, youth turnout increased by about 10 percentage points.

Our fact sheets on State Election Law Reform and Youth Voter Turnout & State Voting Laws shows which provisions (such as early voting or same-day registration) are in effect in each state and which of these rules is most likely to raise youth turnout.

Sources: "Easier Voting Methods Boost Youth Turnout"; How Postregistration Laws Affect the Turnout of Registrants; State Voting Laws, and State Election Law Reform and Youth Voter Turnout.

Getting Out the Youth Vote: What Works

- Personalized and interactive contact counts. The most effective way of getting a new voter is the in-person door knock by a peer; the least effective is an automated phone call. Canvassing costs $11 to $14 per new vote, followed closely by phone banks at $10 to $25 per new vote. Robocalls mobilize so few voters that they cost $275 per new vote. (These costs are figured per vote that would not be cast without the mobilizing effort.)
- Begin with the basics. Telling a new voter where to vote, when to vote and how to use the voting machines increases turnout.
- The medium is more important than the message. Partisan and nonpartisan, negative and positive messages seem to work about the same. The important factor is the degree to which the contact is personalized.
- In ethnic and immigrant communities, start young. Young voters in these communities are easier to reach, are more likely to speak English (cutting down translation costs), and are the most effective messengers within their communities.
- Initial mobilization produces repeat voters. If an individual has been motivated to get to the polls once, they are more likely to return. So, getting young people to vote early could be key to raising a new generation of voters.
- Leaving young voters off contact lists is a costly mistake. Some campaigns still bypass young voters, but research shows they respond cost-effectively when contacted.

Source: Young Voter Mobilization Tactics

Personally contacting young people on Election Day can significantly increase youth voter turnout, but only if they've already expressed interest in voting.

Sources: The Effects of an Election Day Voter Mobilization Campaign Targeting Young Voters by Donald P. Green

Local Political Parties and Youth

About nine-in-ten local party leaders say youth political engagement is a serious problem.

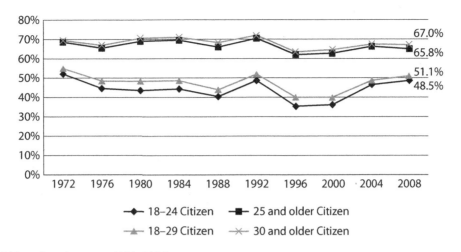

Source: CPS Nov. Supplements 1972-2008

Graph 1: Voter Turnout by Age, 1972-2008

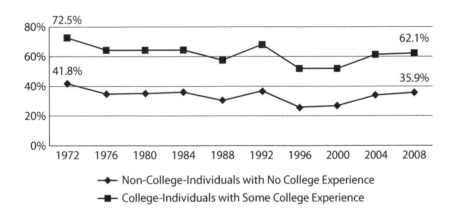

Source: CPS Nov. Supplements 1972-2008

Graph 5: l8-to-29 Year-Old Citizen Turnout by Educational Level, Presidential Years

93% of local party leaders feel local parties can make a big difference in getting young people involved in politics.

Only 8% of the party chairs identified young people as the most important demographic for the "long-term success of their party," compared to 21% who named senior citizens.

Source: Throwing a Better Party: Local Mobilizing Institutions and the Youth Vote

Resources

For more information on youth voting:

- Young Voter Mobilization Tactics

- The 2004 Youth Vote: A Comprehensive Guide
- A voter turnout time series for 1972-2004 (Excel spreadsheet)

Fact sheets:

- State Election Law Reform and Youth Voter Turnout
- The Youth Vote in 2008
- 2004 Youth (Ages 18-29) Voter Turnout Rate, Ranked by State
- Youth Voter Turnout Increases in 2006
- Young Voters in the 2006 Elections
- Voter Registration Among Young People

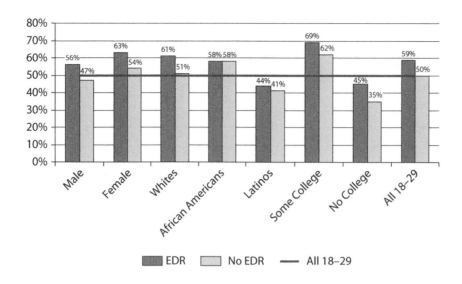

- Quick Facts About Young Voters by State: The Midterm Election Year 2006
- Quick Facts About Young Voters by Metropolitan Area: The Midterm Election Year 2006
- Young Urban Voters in the Midterm Election Year 2006
- The Youth Vote in 2004
- Electoral Engagement Among Minority Youth
- Voter Turnout Among Women and Men
- Electoral Engagement Among Non-College Attending Youth
- College students in the 2004 Election
- Youth Voter Turnout in the States during the 2004 Presidential and 2002 Midterm Elections
- Electoral Engagement Among Latino Youth

- How Young People Express Their Political Views
- Young People and Political Campaigning on the Internet
- State Voter Registration and Election Day Laws

Research Report:

- Getting Out the Vote in Local Elections

Working Papers:

- Easier Voting Methods Boost Youth Turnout
- How Postregistration Laws Affect the Turnout of Registrants
- Throwing a Better Party: Local Mobilizing Institutions and the Youth Vote

Purpose

The purpose of this reading and table is to help you understand the vote choices of a variety of demographic groups.

Context

Since 1948, the American National Election Studies have been conducted by groups working out of the University of Michigan. These surveys are some of the most important sources of information that social scientists have developed to help researchers understand the political behavior and attitudes of Americans. The tables here report the percent of a variety of demographic groups that reported voting for the Democratic or Republican candidates for president in the years 1948-2008; the "cells" marked with two asterisks (**) show either midterm election years (with no presidential election) or groups that had too few people in the survey to get accurate results. So, for example, in the first table, look at the row for Males; look at the column for '08; this shows that 52 percent of men reported voting for Barack Obama in 2008.

Thought Questions

1. Select one group in the table and trace its level of support for Democratic and Republican candidates from the earliest year possible (usually 1948 or 1952) through the present. What is the group's voting support in the early years? In later years? What changes do you see? Is there a trend, in that the group has always supported one party or has shifted in its support of one party from the earlier years to the other party in later years?

2. Select a group that might be considered "opposite" of the group you first selected (for example, males versus females, low educated versus highly educated, low income versus high income, etc.), and trace its level of support for Democratic and Republican candidates from the earliest year possible. What is the group's voting support in the early years? In later years? What changes do you see? Is there a trend, in that the group has always supported one party or has shifted in its support of one party from the earlier years to the other party in later years?

3. Compare the two groups. In what ways are they similar, and in what ways are they different? What do you think might account for the groups' support of one party over another?

4. Pick a group of which you consider yourself to be a member. Describe the patterns of political support of that group over time. Does the group's recent pattern of political support match your own political opinions? What do you think accounts for those patterns, and how you are different from or similar to the group?

Web Links

1. The ANES Guide to Public Opinion and Electoral Behavior, 2010. Table 9A.1.1, "Presidential Vote 2 Major Parties 1948-2008, PERCENT AMONG DEMOGRAPHIC GROUPS WHO RESPONDED: Democrat."
   http://www.electionstudies.org/nesguide/2ndtable/t9a_1_1.htm
2. The ANES Guide to Public Opinion and Electoral Behavior, 2010. Table 9A.1.2, "Presidential Vote 2 Major Parties 1948-2008, PERCENT AMONG DEMOGRAPHIC GROUPS WHO RESPONDED: Republican."
   http://www.electionstudies.org/nesguide/2ndtable/t9a_1_2.htm

21. The ANES Guide to Public Opinion and Electoral Behavior

(See tables on next page)

Table 1: Presidential Vote 2 Major Parties 1948-2008—Percent Among Demographic Groups Who Responded: "Democrat"

% OF GROUP:	'48	'52	'54	'56	'58	'60	'62	'64	'66	'68	'70	'72	'74	'76	'78	'80	'82	'84	'86	'88	'90	'92	'94	'96	'98	'00	'02	'04	'08
Males	56	43	**	44	**	52	**	65	**	45	**	32	**	51	**	39	**	38	**	44	**	55	**	51	**	47	**	46	52
Females	53	41	**	37	**	47	**	69	**	47	**	39	**	51	**	47	**	45	**	50	**	61	**	65	**	56	**	53	57
Whites	53	40	**	39	**	48	**	65	**	41	**	30	**	46	**	37	**	36	**	39	**	52	**	51	**	46	**	42	44
Blacks	65	80	**	64	**	71	**	100	**	97	**	87	**	95	**	93	**	89	**	92	**	94	**	99	**	92	**	90	99
Grade Sch./Some High Sch.	68	49	**	42	**	55	**	80	**	61	**	40	**	67	**	64	**	62	**	61	**	70	**	88	**	74	**	73	76
High School Diploma	54	43	**	44	**	53	**	69	**	48	**	33	**	54	**	45	**	42	**	51	**	63	**	64	**	54	**	50	59
Some College, no Degree	24	24	**	31	**	33	**	58	**	36	**	35	**	48	**	38	**	36	**	42	**	58	**	56	**	50	**	47	54
College Degree/ Post-grad	**	29	**	31	**	38	**	50	**	38	**	39	**	37	**	35	**	41	**	42	**	52	**	49	**	50	**	50	51
Income 0-16 Percentile	57	43	**	41	**	46	**	74	**	49	**	44	**	67	**	60	**	64	**	59	**	73	**	77	**	66	**	58	68
Income 17-33 Percentile	67	46	**	44	**	45	**	71	**	48	**	38	**	60	**	52	**	53	**	56	**	65	**	75	**	57	**	59	69
Income 34-67 Percentile	69	46	**	42	**	55	**	74	**	46	**	37	**	53	**	41	**	43	**	49	**	60	**	57	**	50	**	52	56
Income 68-95 Percentile	49	40	**	43	**	51	**	60	**	47	**	34	**	45	**	40	**	34	**	40	**	51	**	50	**	52	**	44	45
Income 96-100 Percentile	32	23	**	23	**	24	**	54	**	33	**	18	**	23	**	19	**	23	**	47	**	48	**	33	**	38	27
Professionals	**	31	**	33	**	42	**	54	**	40	**	34	**	41	**	39	**	39	**	45	**	57	**	53	**	51	**	56	**
White Collar	**	35	**	37	**	43	**	66	**	45	**	37	**	47	**	39	**	39	**	46	**	56	**	60	**	53	**	39	**
Blue Collar	**	56	**	49	**	63	**	79	**	54	**	39	**	66	**	51	**	49	**	50	**	66	**	67	**	53	**	55	**
Unskilled	**	66	**	63	**	33	**	90	**	80	**	53	**	66	**	42	**	72	**	57	**	59	**	62	**	76	**	76	**
Farmers	**	36	**	48	**	47	**	65	**	42	**	20	**	44	**	29	**	23	**	43	**	41	**	44	**	46	**	57	**
Housewives	**	37	**	35	**	43	**	66	**	44	**	30	**	46	**	44	**	35	**	46	**	52	**	51	**	47	**	35	**

	'48	'50	'52	'54	'56	'58	'60	'62	'64	'66	'68	'70	'72	'74	'76	'78	'80	'82	'84	'86	'88	'90	'92	'94	'96	'98	'00	'02	'04	'08
Union Households	81	56	**	53	**	64	**	83	**	56	**	43	**	64	**	55	**	57	**	59	**	68	**	75	**	61	**	64	**	60
Non-Union Households	44	36	**	44	**	62	**	43	**	33	**	47	**	40	**	37	**	44	**	57	**	54	**	50	**	46	**	**	**	54
South	**	50	**	52	**	53	**	65	**	51	**	33	**	56	**	47	**	45	**	49	**	59	**	59	**	44	**	51	**	45
Nonsouth	**	40	**	38	**	48	**	68	**	45	**	37	**	50	**	42	**	41	**	47	**	58	**	58	**	56	**	50	**	62
Born 1991 or later	**	**	**	**	**	**	**	**	**	**	**	**	**	**	**	**	**	**	**	**	**	**	**	**	**	**	**	**	**	65
Born 1975-1990	**	**	**	**	**	**	**	**	**	**	**	**	**	**	**	**	**	**	**	**	**	56	**	61	**	63	**	66	**	56
Born 1959-1974	**	**	**	**	**	**	**	**	**	**	**	**	**	**	**	52	**	42	**	48	**	58	**	58	**	46	**	45	**	54
Born 1943-1958	**	**	**	**	**	**	**	**	**	70	**	49	**	53	**	47	**	41	**	47	**	58	**	58	**	53	**	44	**	41
Born 1927-1942	70	43	**	42	**	51	**	70	**	50	**	35	**	47	**	38	**	40	**	49	**	56	**	56	**	48	**	51	**	52
Born 1911-1926	61	47	**	41	**	51	**	69	**	43	**	30	**	53	**	47	**	44	**	44	**	62	**	64	**	64	**	52	**	**
Born 1895-1910	55	39	**	39	**	49	**	66	**	32	**	46	**	32	**	47	**	50	**	42	**	47	**	58	**	57	**	0	**	**
Born before 1895	46	38	**	38	**	40	**	56	**	38	**	22	**	33	**	80	**	100	**	**	**	**	**	**	**	**	**	**	**	**
Democrats (incl leaners)	70	74	**	82	**	89	**	77	**	59	**	81	**	74	**	79	**	85	**	91	**	94	**	89	**	91	**	91	**	91
Independents	19	17	**	46	**	77	**	30	**	28	**	45	**	27	**	29	**	36	**	65	**	52	**	45	**	56	**	56	**	55
Republicans (incl leaners)	4	4	**	8	**	27	**	6	**	8	**	14	**	7	**	5	**	10	**	12	**	16	**	10	**	8	**	8	**	10
Liberals	**	**	**	**	**	**	**	**	**	**	**	**	**	69	**	78	**	72	**	82	**	92	**	94	**	84	**	92	**	90
Moderates	**	**	**	**	**	**	**	**	**	**	**	**	**	31	**	52	**	45	**	51	**	61	**	66	**	60	**	58	**	61
Conservatives	**	**	**	**	**	**	**	**	**	**	**	**	**	13	**	22	**	23	**	18	**	23	**	26	**	23	**	18	**	18

(underline) indicates 50 or fewer total respondents within group ** indicates question not asked or no cases within group 2008 NOTE: open-ended coding of occupation is not yet complete.

Source: The American National Election Studies NOTE: variable used for race grouping has changed. See Table 1A.3. (Table generated: 05AUG10)

Table 2: Presidential Vote 2 Major Parties 1948-2008—Percent Among Demographic Groups Who Responded: "Republican"

% OF GROUP:	'48	'52	'54	'56	'58	'60	'62	'64	'66	'68	'70	'72	'74	'76	'78	'80	'82	'84	'86	'88	'90	'92	'94	'96	'98	'00	'02	'04	'08
Males	44	57	**	56	**	48	**	35	**	55	**	68	**	49	**	61	**	63	**	56	**	45	**	49	**	53	**	54	48
Females	47	59	**	63	**	53	**	31	**	53	**	61	**	49	**	53	**	55	**	50	**	39	**	35	**	44	**	47	43
Whites	47	60	**	61	**	52	**	36	**	59	**	70	**	54	**	63	**	64	**	61	**	48	**	49	**	54	**	58	56
Blacks	35	20	**	36	**	29	**	0	**	3	**	13	**	5	**	7	**	11	**	8	**	6	**	1	**	8	**	10	1
Grade Sch./Some High Sch.	32	51	**	58	**	45	**	20	**	39	**	60	**	33	**	36	**	38	**	39	**	30	**	12	**	26	**	27	24
High School Diploma	46	57	**	56	**	47	**	31	**	52	**	67	**	46	**	55	**	58	**	49	**	37	**	36	**	46	**	50	41
Some College, no Degree	76	76	**	69	**	67	**	42	**	64	**	65	**	52	**	62	**	64	**	58	**	42	**	44	**	50	**	53	46
College Degree/ Post-grad	**	71	**	69	**	62	**	50	**	63	**	61	**	63	**	65	**	59	**	58	**	48	**	51	**	50	**	50	49
Income 0-16 Percentile	43	57	**	59	**	54	**	26	**	51	**	56	**	33	**	40	**	36	**	41	**	27	**	23	**	34	**	42	32
Income 17-33 Percentile	33	54	**	56	**	55	**	29	**	52	**	62	**	40	**	48	**	47	**	44	**	35	**	25	**	43	**	41	31
Income 34-67 Percentile	31	54	**	58	**	45	**	26	**	54	**	63	**	47	**	59	**	57	**	51	**	40	**	43	**	50	**	48	44
Income 68-95 Percentile	51	60	**	57	**	49	**	40	**	53	**	66	**	55	**	60	**	66	**	60	**	49	**	50	**	48	**	56	55
Income 96-100 Percentile	68	77	**	77	**	76	**	46	**	67	**	82	**	77	**	82	**	81	**	77	**	53	**	52	**	67	**	62	73
Professionals	**	69	**	67	**	58	**	46	**	60	**	66	**	59	**	61	**	61	**	55	**	43	**	47	**	49	**	44	**
White Collar	**	65	**	63	**	57	**	34	**	55	**	63	**	53	**	61	**	61	**	54	**	44	**	40	**	47	**	61	**
Blue Collar	**	44	**	51	**	37	**	21	**	46	**	61	**	34	**	49	**	51	**	50	**	34	**	33	**	47	**	46	**
Unskilled	**	34	**	37	**	67	**	10	**	20	**	47	**	34	**	58	**	28	**	43	**	41	**	38	**	24	**	24	**
Farmers	**	64	**	52	**	53	**	35	**	58	**	80	**	56	**	71	**	77	**	57	**	59	**	56	**	54	**	43	**
Housewives	**	63	**	65	**	57	**	34	**	56	**	70	**	54	**	56	**	65	**	54	**	48	**	49	**	53	**	65	**
Union Households	19	44	**	47	**	36	**	17	**	44	**	57	**	36	**	45	**	43	**	41	**	32	**	25	**	39	**	36	40
Non-Union Households	56	64	**	64	**	56	**	38	**	57	**	67	**	53	**	60	**	63	**	56	**	43	**	46	**	50	**	54	46

	'48	'52	'54	'56	'58	'60	'62	'64	'66	'68	'70	'72	'74	'76	'78	'80	'82	'84	'86	'88	'90	'92	'94	'96	'98	'00	'02	'04	'08
South	**	50	**	48	**	47	**	35	**	49	**	67	**	44	**	53	**	55	**	51	**	41	**	41	**	57	**	49	55
Nonsouth	**	60	**	62	**	52	**	32	**	55	**	64	**	50	**	58	**	59	**	53	**	42	**	42	**	44	**	50	38
Born 1991 or later	**	**	**	**	**	**	**	**	**	**	**	**	**	**	**	**	**	**	**	**	**	**	**	**	**	**	**	**	35
Born 1975-1990	**	**	**	**	**	**	**	**	**	**	**	**	**	**	**	**	**	**	**	**	**	**	**	39	**	37	**	34	44
Born 1959-1974	**	**	**	**	**	**	**	**	**	**	**	**	**	**	**	58	**	49	**	49	**	51	**	42	**	42	**	55	46
Born 1943-1958	**	**	**	**	**	**	**	**	**	48	**	58	**	59	**	51	**	47	**	48	**	44	**	44	**	52	**	56	59
Born 1927-1942	30	57	**	58	**	49	**	49	**	51	**	57	**	54	**	50	**	51	**	44	**	42	**	44	**	52	**	49	48
Born 1911-1926	39	53	**	49	**	31	**	57	**	70	**	47	**	53	**	56	**	56	**	38	**	36	**	36	**	48	**	**	**
Born 1895-1910	45	61	**	51	**	34	**	54	**	68	**	48	**	50	**	58	**	53	**	42	**	43	**	100	**	**	**	**	**
Born before 1895	54	62	**	62	**	60	**	44	**	62	**	78	**	67	**	20	**	0	**	**	**	**	**	**	**	**	**	**	**
	'48	'52	'54	'56	'58	'60	'62	'64	'66	'68	'70	'72	'74	'76	'78	'80	'82	'84	'86	'88	'90	'92	'94	'96	'98	'00	'02	'04	'08
Democrats (incl leaners)	**	30	**	18	**	26	**	11	**	23	**	41	**	20	**	26	**	21	**	15	**	9	**	9	**	11	**	6	9
Independents (incl leaners)	**	81	**	83	**	54	**	23	**	70	**	72	**	55	**	73	**	71	**	64	**	35	**	48	**	55	**	44	45
Republicans (incl leaners)	**	96	**	96	**	92	**	73	**	94	**	92	**	86	**	93	**	95	**	90	**	88	**	84	**	90	**	92	90
	'48	'52	'54	'56	'58	'60	'62	'64	'66	'68	'70	'72	'74	'76	'78	'80	'82	'84	'86	'88	'90	'92	'94	'96	'98	'00	'02	'04	'08
Liberals	**	**	**	**	**	**	**	**	**	**	**	31	**	22	**	26	**	28	**	18	**	8	**	6	**	16	**	8	10
Moderates	**	**	**	**	**	**	**	**	**	**	**	69	**	48	**	61	**	55	**	49	**	39	**	34	**	40	**	42	39
Conservatives	**	**	**	**	**	**	**	**	**	**	**	87	**	78	**	77	**	82	**	77	**	73	**	74	**	77	**	82	82

(underline) indicates 50 or fewer total respondents within group ** indicates question not asked or no cases within group 2008 NOTE: open-ended coding of occupation is not yet complete.

Source: The American National Election Studies NOTE: variable used for race grouping has changed. See Table 1A.3. (Table generated: 05AUG10)

Purpose

The purpose of this reading is to give you a background for thinking about how money influences politics and public policy.

Context

The role of money in politics is a perennial concern. Some people believe that campaign contributions from powerful "special interests" influence policies in ways that advantage powerful groups at the expense of less powerful groups. Others counter that the ability of all groups to contribute to politicians, and the wide diversity of contributing groups keeps policies from tilting to far in any one group's direction very much.

This selection is a table that shows the top 140 donors to federal politicians over the last twenty years (you can access the table with hyperlinks to the individual groups at the url on the bottom of the first page). This data is derived from required reports by the groups and by the receiving politicians submitted to the Federal Election Commission (FEC), which monitors the flow of money in national politics. OpenSecrets.org is a non-profit public interest group that distills those reports for the public.

Thought Questions

1. Look at the top ten groups on the list. What kinds of organizations are dominant in this group? Which party is the biggest beneficiary of their donations?
2. Look at the next ten groups. Does the giving pattern (in terms of types of groups and receiving parties) change much?
3. Look at the top 50 groups. How many of those groups give predominantly to Democrats, to Republicans, and how many split their giving about evenly? What about the top 100 groups?
4. Based on these numbers, which party do you think is most susceptible to influence, based on campaign contributions? What do you think the effects of these contributions have probably been? Do you think this has been a positive or negative thing for American politics? Support your answer.

Web Link

1. OpenSecrets.org, 2011. "Heavy Hitters: Top All-Time Donors, 1989-2010."
   http://www.opensecrets.org/orgs/list.php?order=A

22. Top All-Time Donors, 1989-2010

By OpenSecrets.org
Center for Responsive Politics

LEGEND: 🐘 Republican 🐴 Democrat 🏳 On the fence
🏳 = Between 40% and 59% to both parties
🐘 = Leans Dem/Repub (60%-69%)
🐴🐴 = Strongly Dem/Repub (70%-89%)
🐘🐘🐘 = Solidly Dem/Repub (over 90%)

Rank	Organization	Total	Dem %	Repub %	Tilt
1	ActBlue	$51,124,846	99%	0%	🐴🐴🐴
2	AT&T Inc	$46,292,670	44%	55%	🏳
3	American Fedn of State, County & Municipal Employees	$43,477,361	98%	1%	🐴🐴🐴
4	National Assn of Realtors	$38,721,441	49%	50%	🏳
5	Goldman Sachs	$33,387,252	61%	37%	🐴
6	American Assn for Justice	$33,143,279	90%	8%	🐴🐴🐴
7	Intl Brotherhood of Electrical Workers	$33,056,216	97%	2%	🐴🐴🐴
8	National Education Assn	$32,024,610	93%	6%	🐴🐴🐴
9	Laborers Union	$30,292,050	92%	7%	🐴🐴🐴
10	Teamsters Union	$29,319,982	93%	6%	🐴🐴🐴
11	Carpenters & Joiners Union	$29,265,808	89%	10%	🐴🐴
12	Service Employees International Union	$29,140,232	95%	3%	🐴🐴🐴
13	American Federation of Teachers	$28,733,991	98%	0%	🐴🐴🐴
14	Communications Workers of America	$28,376,306	98%	0%	🐴🐴🐴
15	Citigroup Inc	$28,065,874	50%	49%	🏳
16	American Medical Assn	$27,597,820	40%	59%	🏳
17	United Auto Workers	$27,134,252	98%	0%	🐴🐴🐴
18	National Auto Dealers Assn	$26,311,758	32%	67%	🐘

19	Machinists & Aerospace Workers Union	$26,229,477	98%	0%	Dem
20	United Parcel Service	$25,290,039	36%	62%	Rep
21	United Food & Commercial Workers Union	$25,226,733	98%	1%	Dem
22	Altria Group	$24,643,651	27%	72%	Rep
23	American Bankers Assn	$24,048,220	40%	59%	Rep
24	National Assn of Home Builders	$23,461,905	35%	64%	Rep
25	EMILY's List	$23,391,763	99%	0%	Dem
26	National Beer Wholesalers Assn	$22,757,795	34%	65%	Rep
27	JPMorgan Chase & Co	$22,514,838	51%	48%	Even
28	Microsoft Corp	$21,691,408	53%	46%	Even
29	National Assn of Letter Carriers	$20,943,434	88%	10%	Dem
30	Time Warner	$20,327,541	72%	27%	Dem
31	Morgan Stanley	$20,245,499	44%	54%	Even
32	Lockheed Martin	$19,839,004	43%	56%	Even
33	General Electric	$19,725,132	51%	48%	Even
34	Verizon Communications	$19,690,873	40%	58%	Even
35	Credit Union National Assn	$18,908,979	48%	51%	Even
36	AFL-CIO	$18,900,396	95%	4%	Dem
37	FedEx Corp	$18,816,940	40%	58%	Even
38	Bank of America	$18,699,265	46%	53%	Even
39	National Rifle Assn	$18,209,746	17%	82%	Rep
40	Blue Cross/Blue Shield	$18,197,594	39%	60%	Rep
41	Ernst & Young	$18,183,788	44%	55%	Even
42	Sheet Metal Workers Union	$18,111,313	97%	1%	Dem
43	International Assn of Fire Fighters	$17,731,993	81%	17%	Dem
44	Plumbers & Pipefitters Union	$17,635,976	94%	4%	Dem
45	American Hospital Assn	$17,562,729	53%	45%	Even
46	Deloitte Touche Tohmatsu	$17,445,497	35%	64%	Rep
47	American Dental Assn	$17,371,235	46%	53%	Even
48	Operating Engineers Union	$17,122,185	85%	14%	Dem
49	Pricewaterhouse Coopers	$16,699,488	37%	62%	Even
50	Air Line Pilots Assn	$16,586,697	84%	15%	Even
51	UBS AG	$16,428,222	40%	58%	Even
52	Natl Assn/Insurance & Financial Advisors	$15,984,854	42%	57%	Even
53	AFLAC Inc	$15,832,719	44%	55%	Rep
54	Boeing Co	$15,641,085	47%	52%	Rep
55	Pfizer Inc	$14,900,921	31%	68%	Dem
56	Union Pacific Corp	$14,883,203	25%	74%	Dem
57	United Steelworkers	$14,677,901	99%	0%	Rep
58	United Transportation Union	$14,475,010	88%	10%	Dem
59	Merrill Lynch	$14,295,360	37%	61%	Rep
60	Ironworkers Union	$14,142,975	92%	6%	Dem
61	Reynolds American	$13,687,778	24%	75%	Rep
62	Northrop Grumman	$13,560,724	43%	56%	Even
63	American Institute of CPAs	$13,367,435	42%	57%	Even
64	American Postal Workers Union	$13,312,673	95%	3%	Dem
65	Credit Suisse Group	$13,138,060	44%	55%	Even

66	National Rural Electric Cooperative Assn	$13,029,671	51%	48%	▦
67	BellSouth Corp	$12,993,782	45%	54%	▦
68	Anheuser-Busch	$12,862,221	48%	51%	▦
69	General Dynamics	$12,566,267	47%	52%	▦
70	Comcast Corp	$11,888,339	56%	43%	▦
71	American Financial Group	$11,760,437	18%	81%	🐘🐘
72	Walt Disney Co	$11,753,831	68%	31%	🫏
73	Exxon Mobil	$11,677,631	13%	85%	🐘🐘
74	National Air Traffic Controllers Assn	$11,630,988	80%	18%	🫏🫏
75	Chevron	$11,530,759	24%	75%	🐘🐘
76	GlaxoSmithKline	$11,522,090	29%	70%	🐘🐘
77	KPMG LLP	$11,478,786	34%	65%	🐘
78	Club for Growth	$11,357,288	1%	96%	🐘🐘🐘
79	DLA Piper	$11,357,157	67%	32%	🫏
80	Raytheon Co	$11,333,292	46%	52%	▦
81	News Corp	$11,270,692	58%	41%	▦
82	Natl Active & Retired Fed Employees Assn	$11,265,500	77%	21%	🫏🫏
83	Koch Industries	$11,002,235	10%	89%	🐘🐘
84	Honeywell International	$11,001,355	47%	52%	▦
85	Human Rights Campaign	$10,501,271	90%	9%	🫏🫏🫏
86	National Restaurant Assn	$10,354,545	16%	82%	🐘🐘
87	New York Life Insurance	$10,274,174	52%	46%	▦
88	Associated Builders & Contractors	$10,264,858	1%	98%	🐘🐘🐘
89	Wal-Mart Stores	$10,178,938	27%	71%	🐘🐘
90	Southern Co	$10,162,887	31%	67%	🐘
91	Saban Capital Group	$10,139,185	99%	0%	🫏🫏🫏
92	American Health Care Assn	$10,114,879	52%	46%	▦
93	American Academy of Ophthalmology	$10,043,708	52%	47%	▦
94	Prudential Financial	$10,033,181	50%	49%	▦
95	MBNA Corp	$10,029,256	17%	82%	🐘🐘
96	Newsweb Corp	$9,957,850	98%	0%	🫏🫏🫏
97	UST Inc	$9,950,761	21%	78%	🐘🐘
98	American Society of Anesthesiologists	$9,867,537	42%	57%	▦
99	MetLife Inc	$9,867,248	54%	45%	▦
100	AIG	$9,828,364	50%	49%	▦
101	Freddie Mac	$9,819,600	43%	56%	▦
102	American Crystal Sugar	$9,792,339	62%	37%	🫏
103	CSX Corp	$9,791,929	33%	65%	🐘
104	Associated General Contractors	$9,753,590	15%	84%	🐘🐘
105	Indep Insurance Agents & Brokers/America	$9,698,525	40%	59%	▦
106	General Motors	$9,678,878	39%	60%	🐘
107	Securities Industry & Financial Mkt Assn	$9,678,182	44%	55%	▦
108	Eli Lilly & Co	$9,630,679	31%	68%	🐘
109	National Cmte to Preserve Social Security & Medicare	$9,610,115	80%	18%	🫏🫏
110	Massachusetts Mutual Life Insurance	$9,606,748	39%	59%	▦
111	American Optometric Assn	$9,477,163	59%	40%	▦
112	Lehman Brothers	$9,357,030	54%	44%	▦

113	American Maritime Officers	$9,285,471	46%	52%	⚑
114	Transport Workers Union	$8,994,649	95%	4%	🐴🐴🐴🐴
115	Amway/Alticor Inc	$8,872,278	0%	99%	🐘🐘🐘🐘
116	Seafarers International Union	$8,727,594	85%	14%	🐴🐴🐴
117	National Cmte for an Effective Congress	$8,707,940	99%	0%	🐴🐴🐴🐴
118	National Fedn of Independent Business	$8,608,362	7%	92%	🐘🐘🐘
119	Archer Daniels Midland	$8,522,673	44%	55%	⚑
120	American Airlines	$8,467,294	47%	52%	⚑
121	Ford Motor Co	$8,453,192	38%	61%	🐘
122	Burlington Northern Santa Fe Corp	$8,383,535	31%	68%	🐘
123	Fannie Mae	$8,362,326	54%	45%	⚑
124	Painters & Allied Trades Union	$8,337,796	88%	10%	🐴🐴
125	National Assn of Broadcasters	$8,218,537	45%	54%	⚑
126	Skadden, Arps et al	$8,135,046	78%	21%	🐴🐴
127	MCI Inc	$8,092,972	46%	53%	⚑
128	Wachovia Corp	$8,059,347	31%	68%	🐘
129	American Council of Life Insurers	$7,930,665	38%	61%	🐘
130	Amalgamated Transit Union	$7,776,918	93%	6%	🐴🐴🐴🐴
131	Aircraft Owners & Pilots Assn	$7,713,366	45%	54%	⚑
132	American Trucking Assns	$7,704,240	28%	71%	🐘🐘
133	Marine Engineers Beneficial Assn	$7,598,877	74%	24%	🐴🐴
134	Bristol-Myers Squibb	$7,370,699	22%	77%	🐘🐘
135	Bear Stearns	$7,145,772	55%	43%	⚑
136	Enron Corp	$6,548,235	28%	71%	🐘🐘
137	Andersen	$6,253,977	37%	62%	🐘
138	BP	$6,231,474	28%	70%	🐘🐘
139	MGM Resorts International	$6,190,170	48%	51%	⚑
140	Vivendi	$4,704,596	66%	32%	🐴

Purpose

The purpose of this reading is to help you think about Americans' use of the media, and the role that the media plays in communicating political information.

Context

The mass media is a very important for communicating political information to the public, and thus the extent to which people believe what they media tells them is an important topic. This report from the Pew Center for The People & The Press surveyed a random sample of Americans about their media use and their views on the credibility of various major mass media sources.

Thought Questions

1. Which news outlets are the most credible to most Americans? Which are the least credible?
2. How has the credibility of news sources changed over time? Which have come to be more credible? Which are less credible now?
3. How is the perceived credibility of a mass media source connected to people's party identification? That is, do Democrats and Republicans have differing views on mass media source credibility? What are those differences?
4. Which of these news sources do you go to for information? How credible do you believe they are? Are you satisfied with their levels of credibility? Why or why not? What difference does it make in the way you evaluate the information the news media provides?

Web Link

1. Pew Research Center for the People & the Press, 2010, "Americans Spending More Time Following the News," News Media Credibility.
   http://people-press.org/2010/09/12/section-5-news-media-credibility/

23. News Media Credibility

Excerpt from Section 5 of "Americans Spending More Time Following the News"

By The Pew Research Center for The People & The Press

The public continues to take a skeptical view of reporting from the major news outlets. No more than a third says they can believe all or most of the reporting by 14 major news organizations.

There has been little change in public views of media credibility since 2008. Since the late 1990's, however, there has been significant erosion in the believability ratings of several news organizations.

For example, since 1998 ABC News, CBS News and NBC News have all seen substantial declines in the percentages saying they believe all or most of what they say (among those who say they can rate those organizations). Currently, about two-in-ten say they believe all or most information from ABC News (21%), CBS News (21%) and NBC News (20%)—down from about three-in-ten in 1998.

The longer-term declines can be seen across different media groups as well. Since 1998, CNN and the Wall Street Journal, for example, have experienced double-digit declines in the percentages saying they can believe all or most of their reporting (a rating of four on a scale of one to four). Currently, 29% say they can believe all or most of the reporting of CNN and 25% say the same about the Wall Street Journal.

The credibility ratings for Fox News (27% today) and 60 Minutes (33%) have shown less change over the past decade. And NPR is the only news organization whose credibility rating has improved since 1998—28% now give it the top rating compared with 19% a dozen years ago.

National newspapers fare relatively poorly when it comes to public perceptions of media credibility. Just two-in-ten (20%) of those who offer a rating for the New York Times say they can believe all or most of what it says and just 17% say the same about USA Today. Those numbers have fluctuated only slightly since 2004. Local daily news newspapers are seen in largely the same way (21% get the highest credibility rating).

Majorities give each of the news organizations included on the survey a credibility rating of three or four on the four-point scale. Relatively small percentages give the organizations a one—meaning they can believe "almost nothing" of what the news organization reports.

Partisan Gaps in Credibility Ratings

Republicans have long viewed the overall media more skeptically than Democrats and this continues to be reflected in credibility ratings for individual news outlets. Republicans express far less confidence than Democrats in most major outlets. The Fox News Channel stands out as the only news organization that more Republicans than Democrats view as highly credible.

Democrats are at least twice as likely as Republicans to give the highest believability ratings to CNN, NPR, MSNBC and the New York Times.

About four-in-ten (41%) Republicans say they believe all or most of what the Fox News Channel says, by far the highest believability rating offered by Republicans. By contrast, 21% of Democrats give a believability rating of four to Fox News, among the lowest rating given by Democrats to any outlet.

Local TV news, the Wall Street Journal, and USA Today receive about the same ratings from Republicans and Democrats. For example, 28% of Republicans and 33% of Democrats say they believe all or most of what the Wall Street Journal says.

Widening Gaps in Credibility Ratings of Cable News Channels

In recent years, the divides between Democrats and Republicans have grown in judging the credibility of the cable news outlets. In 2000, about equal percentages of each said they could believe all or most of what Fox News said (26% Republicans, 27% Democrats). Since that time, Fox News' credibility rating among Republicans has increased (now 41%). As a result, there is now a 20-point partisan gap in Fox News' credibility ratings.

Republican credibility ratings for MSNBC have fallen over the past decade, from 24% in 2000 to 13% today. Democrats' ratings have changed little over this period (now 34%). As a result, partisan differences over MSNBC's credibility (21 points) are as large as those over Fox News.

Similarly, there is sizable partisan divide in perceptions of CNN's credibility; 19% of Republicans say they believe all or most of what they see or hear on CNN, compared with 40% of Democrats.

Partisanship and Credibility

Believe "all or most" of what org. says …	Rep %	Dem %	Ind %	R-D gap %
CNN	19	40	26	-21
NPR	16	37	29	-21
MSNBC	13	34	17	-21
60 Minutes	25	42	31	-17
New York Times	14	31	16	-17
C-SPAN	16	31	22	-15
NBC News	17	30	12	-13
CBS News	16	29	16	-13
ABC News	16	28	15	-12
Your daily newspaper	18	27	17	-9
Local TV News	27	33	25	-6
Wall Street Journal	28	33	19	-5
USA Today	16	20	13	-4
Fox News	41	21	22	+ 20

PEW RESEARCH CENTER July 8-11, 2010. PEW 11a-l, n-o. Percentages based on those who could rate each organization.

News Organization Believability

	Believe all or most		Believe almost nothing			
	4%	3%	2%	1%	N	Can't rate%
60 Minutes	33	34	22	11=100	859	15
Local TV news	29	40	23	8=100	931	7
CNN	29	36	22	13=100	894	10
NPR	28	32	25	16=100	696	28
Fox News	27	29	22	22=100	900	8
Wall Street Journal	25	37	23	14=100	701	27
C-SPAN	23	35	25	17=100	658	32
MSNBC	22	38	21	19=100	839	15
ABC News	21	43	23	13=100	901	9
CBS News	21	41	24	15=100	889	12
Your daily newspaper	21	38	27	14=100	921	9
NBC News	20	43	23	14=100	914	7
New York Times	20	38	21	21=100	707	27
USA Today	17	39	28	15=100	744	23

PEW RESEARCH CENTER July 8-11, 2010. PEW 11a-l, n-o. Figures may not add to 100% because of rounding. Percentages based on those who could rate each organization.

Believability Trends

Believe "all or most" of what organization says …	1998 %	2000 %	2002 %	2004 %	2006 %	2008 %	2010 %
60 Minutes	35	34	34	33	27	29	33
Local TV news	34	33	27	25	23	28	29
CNN	42	39	37	32	28	30	29
NPR	19	25	23	23	22	27	28
Fox News	--	26	24	25	25	23	27
Wall Street Journal	41	41	33	24	26	25	25
C-SPAN	32	33	30	27	25	26	23
MSNBC	--	28	28	22	21	24	22
ABC News	30	30	24	24	22	24	21
CBS News	28	29	26	24	22	22	21
Your daily newspaper	29	25	21	19	19	22	21
NBC News	30	29	25	24	23	24	20
New York Times	--	--	--	21	20	18	20
USA Today	23	23	19	19	18	16	17

PEW RESEARCH CENTER July 8-11, 2010. PEW 11a-l, n-o. Percentages based on those who could rate each organization.

News Media Credibility Ratings by Party, 2000-2010

Believe all or most from	Republicans						Democrats						R-D Gap			
	00 %	02 %	04 %	06 %	08 %	10 %	00 %	02 %	04 %	06 %	08 %	10 %	04 %	06 %	08 %	10 %
CNN	33	32	26	22	22	19	48	45	45	32	35	40	-19	-10	-13	-21
NPR	20	16	15	15	18	16	36	24	33	30	37	37	-18	-15	-19	-21
MSNBC	24	22	14	18	18	13	36	30	29	25	29	34	-15	-7	-11	-21
60 Minutes	--	23	25	20	24	25	--	45	42	32	37	42	-17	-12	-13	-17
NY Times	--	--	14	16	10	14	--	--	31	23	24	31	-17	-7	-14	-17
C-SPAN	32	27	23	21	17	16	38	31	36	28	31	31	-13	-7	-14	-15
NBC News	29	19	16	19	16	17	37	31	29	26	31	30	-13	-7	-15	-13
CBS News	27	17	15	15	18	16	36	33	34	26	26	29	-19	-11	-8	-13
ABC News	25	17	17	18	19	16	37	31	35	27	28	28	-18	-9	-9	-12
Your daily newspaper	21	18	16	12	19	18	31	28	23	26	29	27	-7	-14	-10	-9
Local TV News	--	26	21	17	27	27	--	31	29	28	32	33	-8	-11	-5	-6
Wall St. Journal	46	35	23	29	29	28	40	29	29	26	24	33	-6	+3	+5	-5
USA Today	--	13	14	15	16	16	--	22	25	22	15	20	-11	-7	-1	-4
Fox News	26	28	29	32	34	41	27	27	24	22	19	21	+5	+10	+15	+20

PEW RESEARCH CENTER July 8-11, 2010. PEW 11a-l, n-o. Percentages based on those who could rate each organization.

Purpose

The purpose of this reading is to give you insight as to how members of Congress really make their decisions.

Context

There are many factors that might explain why members of Congress vote on bills the way they do. In this reading, former US Representative Hamilton attempts to explain the many factors that make congressional votes complicated and challenging. While the recent impression is that members simply vote with the leaders of their political parties, you'll see that it isn't quite that simple.

Thought Questions

1. What are the factors Rep. Hamilton mentions as possible influences on a member's vote?
2. Why does he say the vote decision is very challenging?
3. Why does he say that getting the time to think about congressional votes is also challenging?
4. What impression do you now have about members of Congress? Is it easy or hard to hold them accountable for their decisions? Why or why not?

Web Link

1. Lee Hamilton, "How Members Vote"
   http://67.192.5.107/how-members-vote

24. How Members Vote

By Former U.S. Representative Lee Hamilton

Wednesday, October 24, 2001

As I was chatting with a constituent one day, he brought me up short with a simple question: "What's the toughest part of your job?" At the time, I'd represented southern Indiana in Congress for well over two decades, but I had to pause to sort through the possible answers. The long hours? The time spent away from home? The criticism? The heavy lobbying? Suddenly, it came to me that the answer had nothing to do with the frustrations of the job, but with its essence: The toughest part of serving in Congress is voting on legislation.

This might come as a surprise. Certainly, it surprised my constituent to hear me say so. In the popular imagination, members of Congress don't have to work very hard to make voting decisions. They listen to their biggest campaign donors, or to powerful special interests, or to the polls, and then vote accordingly. Or perhaps they're captives of a particular ideology: Whatever the conservative or liberal line might be on a given bill, that's where they come down. As with many common perceptions about Congress, there's a germ of truth in all of this, but the reality is far more interesting.

In fact, before a major vote members of Congress are overwhelmed by differing opinions. They get constituent letters, e-mails, faxes, and telephone calls by the hundreds or even thousands; they have stacks of background material sent out by special-interest groups and think tanks; they can read page after page of testimony collected by congressional committees; colleagues in Congress send out letters with recommendations; the Administration—and, on significant occasions, the President himself—will often weigh in as well. So are members of Congress influenced in their votes by what others tell them? Of course they are—if they're doing their jobs.

Deciding how to vote is challenging because it involves complicated issues not as simple as the TV "sound bite" makes it out to be and complex interactions between members and everyone from the President to the party leadership to constituents to colleagues to special interest groups to contributors to the media. On some issues, members of Congress will vote their consciences or their own personal assessment of the reasons for the bill; on others, they'll vote what they think are the wishes of most of their constituents; on still others, of less importance to their own districts, they'll stick with their party leaders and other groups—often in hopes of getting support later on bills that matter more to them. Each bill that comes up involves a different calculation—but it always involves a calculation.

Imagine yourself in Congress, for instance, considering the Justice Department package of some 40 changes to make it easier for law-enforcement officials to fight terrorism. Every day, your office staff has to deal with letters and calls from constituents urging you—in the most heartfelt terms—either to go along in the name of security or to go slowly in the interest of safeguarding basic American liberties. Every day, you hear from a host of experts and interests on both sides of the issue advising you on the right course to take. An easy decision? Hardly. In the end, your vote will be black or white—Aye or Nay—but casting it will involve a thorny analysis of shades of gray.

And this is just one issue. As a member of Congress, you might cast 400 votes a year on everything from basic constitutional questions to cotton subsidies to tiny changes in a time zone. Though you might become well-versed in a few subjects, you can't possibly get to know them all. Yet on every single one you'll be expected to have an opinion and to be able to defend it. And with lobbyists demanding to see you and constituents never shy about expressing their opinion, finding the time actually to arrive at a decision can be a challenge.

When I first came to Congress in 1965, journalist James Reston gave a talk to a handful of us in which he said that every now and then, we had to shut the door, ignore the phone, put our feet up on the table and think about what was the right thing to do for the country. Even then, 35 years ago, he knew that was difficult. These days it's next to impossible. Yet almost every day that Congress is in session, 535 men and women struggle to find their way to a moment of clarity about how they'll vote. It's the toughest thing they'll do in their job, and the next day—and the next—they'll have to do it all over again.

(Lee Hamilton is Director of the Center on Congress at Indiana University. He was a member of the U.S. House of Representatives for 34 years.)

Purpose

The purpose of this reading is to help you understand the rationale for checks and balances and separation of powers as guiding principles in the Constitution's construction of our government.

Context

One of the major concerns about the second US Constitution was that it would concentrate a great deal of power in the national (federal) government, even though the nation's experience under the Articles of Confederation was of having too little power in the government. This topic was quite controversial, and this Federalist Paper explains how the structure of the government would actually protect Americans' liberty, and keep the overall government from becoming too powerful.

Thought Questions

1. What are the five ways in which Madison argues that the proposed constitution would protect against the concentration of power in the government?
2. The core of Madison's rationale for this structure is in the fourth paragraph. The lines beginning with "Ambition must be made to counter ambition." are some of the most famous in American political writing. What does this paragraph tell you about Madison's view of politicians? Why do we need "auxiliary precautions" against them, instead of simply trusting them to do the right thing? How applicable are his concerns about politicians today?

25. Federalist No. 51 Excerpt

**The Federalist No. 51 Excerpt
The Structure of the Government Must
Furnish the Proper Checks and Balances
Between the Different Departments**

Independent Journal
Wednesday, February 6, 1788
[James Madison]

To the People of the State of New York:

TO WHAT expedient, then, shall we finally resort, for maintaining in practice the necessary partition of power among the several departments [the branches of government], as laid down in the Constitution? The only answer that can be given is, that as all these exterior provisions are found to be inadequate, the defect must be supplied, by so contriving the interior structure of the government as that its several constituent parts may, by their mutual relations, be the means of keeping each other in their proper places. ...

In order to lay a due foundation for that separate and distinct exercise of the different powers of government, ... it is evident that each department should have a will of its own; and consequently should be so constituted that the members of each should have as little agency as possible in the appointment of the members of the others. Were this principle rigorously adhered to, it would require that all the appointments for the supreme executive, legislative, and judiciary magistracies should be drawn from the same fountain of authority, the people ... Some deviations. from the principle must be admitted. In the constitution of the judiciary department in particular, it might be inexpedient to insist rigorously on the principle: first, because peculiar qualifications being essential in the members, the primary consideration ought to be to select that mode of choice which best secures these qualifications; secondly, because the permanent tenure by which the appointments are held in that department, must soon destroy all sense of dependence on the authority conferring them.

It is equally evident, that the members of each department should be as little dependent as possible on those of the others, for the emoluments annexed to their offices. ...

But the great security against a gradual concentration of the several powers in the same department, consists in giving to those who administer each department the necessary constitutional means and personal motives to resist encroachments of the others. The provision for defense must in this, as in all other cases, be made commensurate to the danger of attack. Ambition must be made to counteract ambition. The interest of the man must be connected with the constitutional rights of the place. It may be a reflection on human nature, that such devices should be necessary to control the abuses of government. But what is government itself, but the greatest of all reflections on human nature? If men were angels, no government would be necessary. If angels were to govern men, neither external nor internal controls on government would be necessary. In framing a government which is to be administered by men over men, the great difficulty lies in this: you must first enable the government to control the governed; and in the next place oblige it to control itself. A dependence on the people is, no doubt, the primary control on the government; but experience has taught mankind the necessity of auxiliary precautions. …

But it is not possible to give to each department an equal power of self-defense. In republican government, the legislative authority necessarily predominates. The remedy for this inconveniency is to divide the legislature into different branches; and to render them, by different modes of election and different principles of action, as little connected with each other as the nature of their common functions and their common dependence on the society will admit. It may even be necessary to guard against dangerous encroachments by still further precautions. As the weight of the legislative authority requires that it should be thus divided, the weakness of the executive may require, on the other hand, that it should be fortified. An absolute negative on the legislature appears, at first view, to be the natural defense with which the executive magistrate should be armed. But perhaps it would be neither altogether safe nor alone sufficient. …

There are, moreover, two considerations particularly applicable to the federal system of America, which place that system in a very interesting point of view.

First. In a single republic, all the power surrendered by the people is submitted to the administration of a single government; and the usurpations are guarded against by a division of the government into distinct and separate departments. In the compound republic of America, the power surrendered by the people is first divided between two distinct governments, and then the portion allotted to each subdivided among distinct and separate departments. Hence a double security arises to the rights of the people. The different governments will control each other, at the same time that each will be controlled by itself.

Second. It is of great importance in a republic not only to guard the society against the oppression of its rulers, but to guard one part of the society against the injustice of the other part. Different interests necessarily exist in different classes of citizens. If a majority be united by a common interest, the rights of the minority will be insecure. There are but two methods of providing against this evil: the one by creating a will in the community independent of the majority—that is, of the society itself; the other, by comprehending in the society so many separate descriptions of citizens as will render an unjust combination of a majority of the whole very improbable, if not impracticable. [This process is the topic of Federalists 9 and 10.]

Justice is the end of government. It is the end of civil society. It ever has been and ever will be pursued until it be obtained, or until liberty be lost in the pursuit. In a society under the forms of which the stronger faction can readily unite and oppress the weaker, anarchy may as truly be said to reign as in a state of nature, where the weaker individual is not secured against the violence of the stronger; and as, in the latter state, even the stronger individuals are prompted, by the uncertainty of their condition, to submit to a government which may protect the weak as well as themselves; so, in the former state, will the more powerful factions or parties be gradually induced, by a like motive, to wish for a government which will protect all parties, the weaker as well as the more powerful. … In the extended republic of the United States, and among the great variety of interests, parties, and sects which it embraces, a coalition of a majority of the whole society could seldom take place on any other principles than those of justice and the general good; … the larger the society, provided it lie within a practical sphere, the more duly capable it will be of self-government. And happily for the republican cause, the practicable sphere may be carried to a very great extent, by a judicious modification and mixture of the federal principle.

PUBLIUS

Purpose

The purpose of these materials is to help you understand the reapportionment process, and to think about the political implications of the changes in representation that occur as a function of reapportionment.

Context

Apportionment is the process of dividing the seats in the House of Representatives among the 50 states based on the population figures collected during the decennial census. The number of seats in the House has grown with the country. The Constitution set the number of representatives at 65 from 1787 until the first Census of 1790, when it was increased to 105 members. Congress sets the number in law and increased the number to 435 in 1913, where it has remained ever since. As the US population changes, seats get redistributed, so states that have a smaller portion of the nation's population have fewer seats, states with larger portions have more seats. When a state's relative share of the population falls, its number of seats in the House may decrease as well; as a state's relative share of the population rises, it's number of seats in the House may increase. Following the 2010 census, the 435 seats in the U.S. House were reapportioned, and the map on page 151 shows the results.

Thought Questions

1. How does apportionment work? Go to http://2010.census.gov/mediacenter/census-data/census-apportionment-machine.php. Through animation, the U.S. Census Bureau helps explain how the apportionment formula is used to ensure equal representation for all, just like the Founding Fathers planned. Watch the video linked below, and then answer the questions.
   - Briefly describe how apportionment works.
   - How many people were originally represented by each member of the House? How many are represented now?
2. Look at the map in this Reader that show changes in the apportionment of seats in the US House. Which states gained seats in 2010, and which states lost? What does this tell you about population shifts between 2000 and 2010?
3. On the table that tracks changes from 1940 to 2010, look at the states that have gained 3 or more seats in that time; compare them with the states that have lost 3 or more seats. What do the gainers seem to have in common; what do the losers seem to have in common?
4. What do you think these changes in representation (and therefore votes in the House) mean for the people who live in the gaining and losing states?

Web Links

1. U.S. Bureau of the Census, 2011. "Change in Number of Seats in the U.S. House of Representatives, by Region: 1940 to 2010."
   http://www.census.gov/population/apportionment/data/files/1940-2010%20seat%20change%20by%20state.pdf
2. U.S. Bureau of the Census, 2011. "Apportionment of the U.S. House of Representatives Based on the 2010 Census."
   http://www.census.gov/population/apportionment/data/files/2010mapbw.pdf

26. Apportionment of the U.S. House of Representatives Based on the 2010 Census

By U.S. Census Bureau

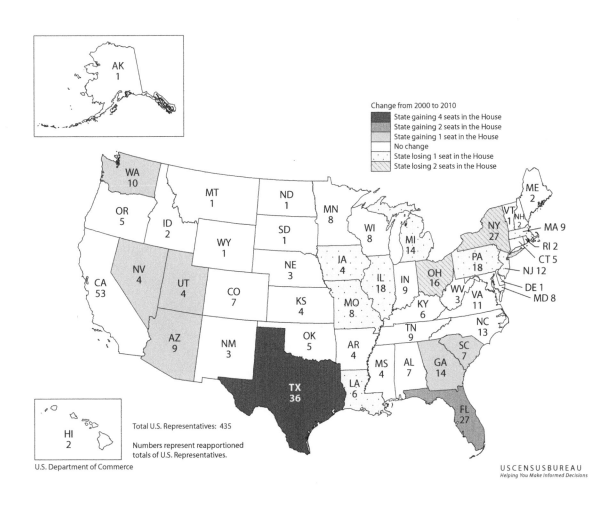

Change from 2000 to 2010
- State gaining 4 seats in the House
- State gaining 2 seats in the House
- State gaining 1 seat in the House
- No change
- State losing 1 seat in the House
- State losing 2 seats in the House

AK 1

WA 10
OR 5
ID 2
MT 1
ND 1
MN 8
ME 2
VT 1
NH 2
NY 27
MA 9
WI 8
MI 14
RI 2
CT 5
PA 18
NJ 12
DE 1
MD 8
SD 1
WY 1
NV 4
UT 4
CA 53
CO 7
NE 3
IA 4
IL 18
IN 9
OH 16
WV 3
VA 11
KS 4
MO 8
KY 6
NC 13
AZ 9
NM 3
OK 5
AR 4
TN 9
SC 7
MS 4
AL 7
GA 14
TX 36
LA 6
FL 27

HI 2

Total U.S. Representatives: 435

Numbers represent reapportioned totals of U.S. Representatives.

U.S. Department of Commerce

USCENSUSBUREAU
Helping You Make Informed Decisions

27. Change in Number of Seats in the U.S. House of Representatives by Region: 1940–2010

U.S. Department of Commerce
U.S. Census Bureau

Change in Number of Seats in the U.S. House of Representatives, by State, Ordered by Seats Gained and Lost: 1940 to 2010

State	Number of Seats in 1940	Number of Seats in 2010	Change
UNITED STATES	435	435	0
California	23	53	+30
Florida	6	27	+21
Texas	21	36	+15
Arizona	2	9	+7
Georgia	10	14	+4
Washington	6	10	+4
Colorado	4	7	+3
Nevada	1	4	+3
Hawaii	*	2	+2
Maryland	6	8	+2
Utah	2	4	+2
Virginia	9	11	+2
Alaska	*	1	+1
New Mexico	2	3	+1
North Carolina	12	13	+1
Oregon	4	5	+1
South Carolina	6	7	+1
Delaware	1	1	0
Idaho	2	2	0
New Hampshire	2	2	0

"Change in Number of Seats in the U.S. House of Representatives, by State, Ordered by Seats Gained and Lost: 1940 to 2010," U.S. Census Bureau, U.S. Department of Commerce. Copyright in the Public Domain.

Rhode Island	2	2	0
Vermont	1	1	0
Wyoming	1	1	0
Connecticut	6	5	-1
Maine	3	2	-1
Minnesota	9	8	-1
Montana	2	1	-1
Nebraska	4	3	-1
North Dakota	2	1	-1
South Dakota	2	1	-1
Tennessee	10	9	-1
Alabama	9	7	-2
Indiana	11	9	-2
Kansas	6	4	-2
Louisiana	8	6	-2
New Jersey	14	12	-2
Wisconsin	10	8	-2
Arkansas	7	4	-3
Kentucky	9	6	-3
Michigan	17	14	-3
Mississippi	7	4	-3
Oklahoma	8	5	-3
West Virginia	6	3	-3
Iowa	8	4	-4
Massachusetts	14	9	-5
Missouri	13	8	-5
Ohio	23	16	-7
Illinois	26	18	-8
Pennsylvania	33	18	-15
New York	45	27	-18

* Not a state in 1940.

Purpose

The purpose of this reading is to help you identify the major political events that influence presidential approval.

Context

Presidential popularity depends on many factors. Political scientists often refer to a president's "honeymoon" period (early popularity) but circumstances usually tend to produce nearly inevitable declines in popularity. Events that can decrease a president's popularity include economic downturns, scandals, and unpopular policies. Events that can increase a president's popularity include economic "boom" times, international crises and events, and reelection campaigns. This reading shows you the entire, week-by-week Gallup Poll approval ratings for President George W. Bush. The numbers represent the percent of Americans reporting that they approve of the job Bush was doing in each week.

Thought Questions

1. Note the big jump in Bush's approval ratings, where it leapt from 51% to 86%. This occurred during the second week of September, 2001. What event occurred that week that caused his approval to rise? What exactly did Bush do to deserve such high levels of support? Why do you think Americans changed their opinions of Bush so rapidly?

2. Look at the "spikes" in approval in April 2003 (from 58 to 71 percent) and in December of 2003 (from about 50 to 63%). What events occurred during those weeks that caused his approval to rise? How long did the effects of those events last before the approval returned to its pre-spike level?

3. Go to the Gallup Poll's Presidential Job Approval Center website (http://www.gallup.com/poll/124922/Presidential-Job-Approval-Center.aspx), and click on Barack Obama's picture to see his overall job approval values. In the figure that appears, note the trend of the President's approval ratings. (The solid light gray line in the middle of the graph shows the 50% approval level; the gray hashed line - - - represents the average presidential approval ratings for each president, Truman through Bush, at each point in their presidential administrations.) What do you observe? Note the spike that appears shortly after day 800 (this the first week of May, 2011). What change occurs? What happened at that time to increase the public's approval of the President's job performance? How long did the effects of that event last before the approval returned to its pre-spike level?

4. Now hover over President Obama's picture and select Democrats, Republicans, and Independents; individual trends for each of these groups should now appear on your chart. What do you observe about the approval ratings for each group, and how they have changed over time? If you were working for Mr. Obama, would anything about this chart worry you as you look forward to reelection in 2012? Why or why not?

Web Link

1. *http://www.pollster.com/blogs/us_bush_approval_avg_gallup200.php?nr=1*

28. U.S. Bush Approval Average (Gallup 2001–2008)

By Jeffrey M. Jones

National
George W. Bush's Job Approval Ratings Trend

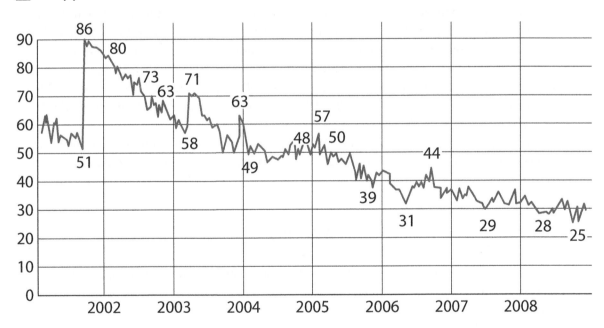

"Because of these ups and downs, Bush's 49% approval average for his presidency will rank him in the middle of the pack (7th of 11) of post-World War II presidents. His average to-date of 49.4% is similar to Richard Nixon's 49.1% but slightly better than Harry Truman's and Jimmy Carter's historical lows below 46%."

Jeffrey M. Jones, Excerpts from: "Despite Recent Lows, Bush Approval Average Is Midrange: Extreme High and Low Ratings Characterize Bush Presidency." Copyright © 2009 by Gallup, Inc. Reprinted with permission.

Purpose

The purpose of this reading is to help you understand the importance of judicial independence for the U.S. Supreme Court, but also why the court needs the cooperation of the other branches.

Context

The principles of separation of powers and checks and balances are central organizing features of the U.S. Constitution. But more than the other branches, the Supreme Court needs the cooperation of the other branches of government, especially when the court makes a decision that is likely to be very unpopular. In these readings, which can be viewed as videos at the Web Links below, former Justice Sandra Day O'Connor and Chief Justice John Roberts discuss why these are important for the way the U.S. Supreme Court works.

Thought Questions

1. Why, according to Justice O'Connor, is Separation of Powers important to the Supreme Court?
2. In spite of the separation of powers, why does the Supreme Court need the other branches when it makes a decision? What two examples are used to illustrate the answer to this question?
3. One way Separation of Powers is important to the Supreme Court is that its members aren't elected to the office, and have a lifetime appointment. This keeps the court somewhat insulated from the pressures of elections. Why does Chief Justice Roberts say that it is important that the court be insulated from elections?
4. What do you think of these arguments? What would happen if the members of the court were selected by popular election, or could be removed if Congress or the President didn't like their decisions?

Web Links

PBS.org, Chief Justice John Roberts and Former Associate Justice Sandra Day O'Connor on Separation of Powers and Judicial Independence.
1. *http://www.pbs.org/wnet/supremecourt/bonus/sandra1.html*
2. *http://www.pbs.org/wnet/supremecourt/bonus/sandra4.html*
3. *http://www.pbs.org/wnet/supremecourt/bonus/john8.html*

29. Preserving the Separation of Powers and The Court's Ability to Enforce its Decisions

By Sandra Day O'Connor, Former Supreme Court Justice

On the Role of the Court in Preserving the Separation of Powers

Transcript

The Supreme Court in the United States plays a very important role in preserving, I think, the structure of government that the framers of our Constitution had in mind. The unusual thing that the framers achieved in drafting the Constitution was to set up three separate branches of government each with some power over the other two but no one branch being supreme in the final sense. It was this balance that they achieved among the three branches that was different than what any other country had achieved that made the difference in the long run. Now, the system the framers created with the three branches is not designed for maximum efficiency in government. It makes it a lot harder to get anything accomplished. The British model, the Parliamentary system, where the party who gets the most members in the Parliament can do anything it wants. And that party is the one that then selects the Prime Minister and is in control of what happens in terms of legislation. And under the British model it's not it was not possible, until recently, for Britain's highest court to declare a law passed by the Parliament as

unconstitutional. That model was rejected by the framers of our Constitution.

On the history of the Court's ability to enforce its decisions

Transcript

One of the great blessings of the system of government created by the framers has been that by and large the public and the other branches of government in the United States have followed and respected the holdings of the Supreme Court of the United States, have applied them even if they might not personally have agreed. One of the prime examples of that is Brown versus Board of Education, the case that held that states in providing public benefits, such as a public school education, may not discriminate on the basis of the color of one's skin, may not deny for instance African American children the benefits of being in a public school with non African American students because that isn't equal protection of the law. Now, when that decision was handed down President Eisenhower did not, I think, agree with it. And yet he enforced it by sending federal troops to Little Rock, Arkansas to make sure that the children could enter the public school in that state where they were being barred at the door. And there are only a couple of examples in all of the history of our country where presidents did not enforce some relevant applicable decision of the Supreme Court. One was President Andrew Jackson who, in the case involving the Cherokee Indians that was handed down by the United States Supreme Court saying that Indians owned certain property in the state, President Jackson said the Supreme Court made its decision now let them enforce it. And he said that very cynically because he knew that the Supreme Court had no power of enforcement other than the power of persuasion, the ability to persuade the other branches that yes, that must be followed. And the result was disaster for the Cherokee Indians. He did not enforce the judgment of the Court in the case. And another example was beloved President Abraham Lincoln who, during the Civil War, without the consent of Congress at the time because Congress wasn't in session, he suspended the writ of habeas corpus. Now that's a constitutional right of someone being held in custody to bring some petition before a court and say I'm being held unlawfully. And President Lincoln suspended that for a time during the Civil War.

The Importance of Judicial Independence

By John Roberts, Supreme Court Chief Justice

On the importance of Judicial Independence

Transcript

The role of the Court under the Constitution is, as Chief Justice Marshall put it in Marbury versus Madison, to say what the law is. And if you have a Supreme Court whose decisions are not followed, then you have a Constitution that is no longer interpreted by the courts as law. It becomes simply a political document as it is in many other countries throughout history and around the world. And disputes about what the Constitution means will be resolved by political means. And a number of things follow from that. If by political means you talk, you mean elections, there's going to be a dispute of constitutional law that's going to be settled solely by elections then our Constitution's role in protecting the rights of minorities is forfeited. The Constitution will only afford such protection as the people are willing to confer, as the majority is willing to confer. Having the judiciary as the interpreter of the Constitution a judiciary that is protected from popular pressure and sentiment insures that minorities will have greater protection under our Constitution. Or if you have the Constitution solely as a political document, not as a legal document given final interpretation by the judiciary, then constitutional issues may be decided by means other than the elections as so often happens in other countries around the world where it's decided by force. So, the genius of the framers, as interpreted by Marshall in Marbury versus Madison in viewing the Constitution as law not simply as a political document, and understanding that from that flowed the fact that its meaning is going to be determined by courts, because it's the job of courts to tell you what the law is. That has very significant consequences ultimately insuring the protection of minorities under the Constitution, insuring that the rule of law is settled by judicial decision and not by elections which would eliminate the protection of minority, or not by force which would eliminate the rule of law.

Purpose

The purpose of this reading is to help you think about the implications of changing government policies, and the effects, positive and negative, that policy changes can have on people.

Context

Bill Clinton signed into law a reform that sent welfare recipients looking for jobs, with their cash benefits on a timer. In this article from 2006, the effects of those changes over time could be assessed. For some, the nudge to find work landed them a career. Others were stuck in low-wage jobs that don't pay the bills. The bill was highly controversial, but by many measures, it had the intended effect—getting many people of the public assistance rolls and into work. Some problems remain, however.

Thought Questions

1. What was the Personal Responsibility and Work Opportunity Reconciliation Act of 1996 meant to do?
2. What support does the act provide for those who have found jobs? What was the partisan reaction to Clinton's welfare reform, and why were opponents so vehemently opposed to it?
3. How well did the reform work between 1996 and 2006?

Web Link

1. "How Welfare Reform Changed America," *USA Today*
   http://www.usatoday.com/news/nation/2006-07-17-welfare-reform-cover_x.htm

30. How Welfare Reform Changed America

By Richard Wolf

KANSAS CITY, Mo.—Michelle Gordon was 30, a poor, single mother with four kids between 5 and 13, when the federal government decided in 1996 that parents on welfare should go to work.

Since then, Gordon's life has been "a little bit of a roller coaster." She has held about 10 jobs—at a call center, as a nurse's aide, as a janitorial supervisor, most recently at a grocery store. She lost that job on April 19, her 40th birthday. It took her two months to find another. For 25 hours a week, she cleans bathrooms and vacuums floors at a drug rehabilitation center.

Mary Bradford was 45 in 1996, with three children between 11 and 25, when she traded welfare for a job filling orders at Victorian Trading Co. Ten years later, her office has moved from Missouri to Kansas, and she's still with the company. She's a production supervisor, and her earnings have more than doubled from the $7 an hour she made in 1996. "Most likely, I'll retire from here," Bradford says.

"She's reliable as the sun coming up," says Randy Rolston, the company's co-founder. "I can't think of a day she's missed."

The paths that Gordon and Bradford have traveled illustrate the successes and frustrations in the decade since the nation's welfare system was overhauled to require work and limit benefits.

THEN AND NOW: How three families have come through | Your thoughts?

The law signed by President Clinton on Aug. 22, 1996, has transformed the way the nation helps its neediest citizens. Gone is the promise of a government check for parents raising children in poverty. In its place are 50 state programs to help those parents get jobs.

In the 12 years since caseloads peaked at 5.1 million families in 1994, millions have left the welfare rolls for low-paying jobs. Nearly 1 million more have been kicked off for not following states' rules or have used up all the benefits they're allowed under time limits. Today, 1.9 million families get cash benefits; in one-third of them, only the children qualify for aid. About 38% of those still on welfare are black, 33% white and 24% Hispanic.

Three in four families on welfare are headed by unmarried women. As a result, employment rates for all single women rose 25% before declining slightly since 2001. Earnings for the poorest 40% of families headed by women doubled from 1994 to 2000, before recession wiped out nearly half the gains. Poverty rates for children fell 25% before rising 10% since 2000.

"It was a profoundly important philosophic shift," says Health and Human Services (HHS) Secretary Michael Leavitt, who was governor of Utah when the law was implemented. "This was

.... one of the few things in a decade you can look at and say the world really changed."

Many welfare experts, however, cite continuing problems. Liberals such as Olivia Golden of the Urban Institute, who ran the nation's welfare program in 1996, say more government services such as child care assistance are needed to help single parents succeed in the workplace. Conservatives such as Robert Rector of the Heritage Foundation say states should be forcing more of those who remain on welfare to prepare for work. Ron Haskins of the Brookings Institution, who helped write the new law when he worked for Congress, worries that too many women on welfare have turned into the working poor.

Gordon typifies that concern. Between her many jobs, she used up her cash benefits under the five-year time limit imposed by the welfare overhaul. Without work, she lost her federal housing subsidy, which helped pay her rent. So in October, she and three of her kids moved in with her mother. Her oldest son is in jail; she cares for his 6-year-old daughter. The three fathers of her children pay no child support. She gets about $500 a month in food stamps.

These days, the family mows lawns to help make ends meet. "Things are really rough out here," Gordon says. "We do what we need to do to have money."

Worst fears didn't come true

When Clinton signed the Personal Responsibility and Work Opportunity Reconciliation Act, conservatives celebrated and liberals screamed; three administration officials quit their jobs in protest. The act ended a 60-year-old federal guarantee of cash aid for the poor.

The law, modeled on state pilot programs begun in 1994 with federal approval, was intended to prod welfare mothers and fathers into the workplace with a series of carrots and sticks.

Work, and you got help with child care, job training, transportation. Refuse, and you risked sanctions and being cut off by time limits.

A decade later, the worst fears of liberals haven't materialized. States did not enter what critics feared would be a money-saving "race to the bottom." Thousands of poor children did not wind up "sleeping on grates," as Democratic senator Daniel Patrick Moynihan predicted.

Major employers hired thousands of welfare recipients. UPS hired 52,000; CVS/pharmacy hired 45,000, 60% of whom remain. Welfare offices have shed the look and language of their first 60 years for the aura of job-services agencies.

Nearly 70% of all single women are working, compared with 66% of married women, a reversal of the past. Single women's incomes have risen, thanks in part to the expansion of the earned income tax credit, a tax break of up to $4,400 for low-income workers. Child poverty rates have dropped, particularly among blacks and Hispanics. Teen pregnancies are down. Child support collections are up.

"Everything has worked," says conservative Douglas Besharov of the American Enterprise Institute. "Every critique one might have is about what could have gone better, not something that has gone poorly."

Among the things that experts say could be going better:

- Most of the women who left welfare remain in low-paying, unskilled jobs. Those with the greatest burdens—mental illness, substance abuse, criminal records—seldom make it easily from welfare to work. "They became the working poor," says Sheri Steisel, a welfare expert at the National Conference of State Legislatures. "Many of these families are still struggling."
- More than half of those still on welfare aren't looking for work, honing their skills or going to school. That has led to a crackdown by the Bush administration, which last month issued tough new regulations designed to ensure that at least half the people on welfare are involved in activities such as job training or community service.

"There's now a reciprocal responsibility," says Wade Horn, HHS assistant secretary for children and families. "In exchange for the cash assistance, you're supposed to be doing something."

- More than half of those eligible for welfare payments don't get them—a sign, critics say, that the new system discourages people who need help from applying. "We now simply have a system that provides less help in times when people are without work," says Mark Greenberg, a liberal welfare expert at the Center for American Progress, a think tank.
- While welfare was trimmed, other parts of the nation's social safety net were expanding. The number of people receiving Medicaid and food stamps has soared by 50% since 2000.

Medicaid is now the nation's largest entitlement program, with 53 million recipients; 25 million people get food stamps. That upsets conservatives who applauded welfare reform. "The bulk of the welfare system is exactly the way it was back in 1972," Rector says, "except that it's bigger and more expensive."

A need to 'skill them up'

In Kansas City, a team of civic leaders working with the state and county governments enjoyed success in the mid-1990s moving women from welfare to work. Caseloads declined by about 60%, leaving only about 6,000 families on welfare rolls.

In recent years, however, the state stopped subsidizing employers, making the program less inviting. State aid for work supports such as case managers has declined. The welfare caseload has held steady since 1999.

"I think we're back at the drawing board," says Marge Randle, family support director for the Kansas City regional office of the state Department of Social Services.

The state faces new pressure from Washington to move those remaining on welfare to work. Even parents who make the jump often remain mired in $6.50-an-hour jobs. That's a big step up from the average national welfare grant of $445 a month for a family of three. But until they double those wages, the gains they make are roughly offset by

cuts in food stamps, health care, child care and energy assistance, which are based on income.

"We're punishing the people who won't work, and we're punishing the people who will work," says Berta Sailer, who helps run a child care and family services center for low- income Kansas City residents. The average income for a family of four in her program is $12,000, well below the federal poverty threshold of $19,307. "I think our moms really feel that they're headed nowhere," she says.

While a $6.50-an-hour job might have seemed like enough in 1996, it's insufficient today, officials agree. Clyde McQueen, president of the local Full Employment Council, a private non-profit corporation, stresses the importance of vocational education. In the 1990s, many of those on welfare who were placed easily in jobs had skills and experience, he says. Most of those who are left on the rolls have fewer skills and need education as well as job training. "Let's take the people who are non-skilled and skill them up for the jobs that are available," McQueen says.

Employers who have hired people off welfare here report mixed results.

Tom Davidson says only "one or two" of the 30 to 40 people he hired from welfare succeeded at his former archives business. "Their personal management skills are horrible," he says. Still, he calls the program "a noble experiment."

'This job saved me'

Parents who have left welfare are spread throughout Kansas City and the nation. Some are succeeding. Others are struggling.

- At the local welfare office, workers Carol Ward and Charlese Henderson are thriving. Ward, 52, got a high school equivalency diploma, job training and child care through the welfare-to-work program. Now she's a clerical aide earning about $17,000 a year. "This job saved me," she says.

Henderson, 31, who had the first of her four children at 14, is a $26,000-a-year caseworker after running through about a dozen lesser jobs over the past 15 years. She has little sympathy for clients who aren't motivated to work. "I had a co-worker tell me that I'm not very compassionate," she says.

- At home and out of work, Patricia Williams is struggling. She needs a few months of cash benefits to get through the summer, until her part-time job in the kitchen of a charter high school resumes. Welfare officials say she's used up 54 of her 60 months under the law. "You have to get out and look for a job," Williams, 43, says. "You just can't rely on the system anymore."
- At a local business and technology community college, Sandy Carson and Gary Trimble are somewhere in between. They are getting nearly a year's training for jobs in manufacturing. Trimble, 50, a self-employed carpenter who cares for his 16-year-old son, wound up on welfare after a seven-month jail term for a child-support violation. "I really felt lost," he says. "I went in telling them right out of the gate, 'I want school.'"

Carson, 42, left her postal clerk's job seven years ago to care for a son, then 3, with a disability. She wants to work with animals, but she considers herself lucky to be in the manufacturing course. "It's not my dream job, but it's something I can do," she says.

For Michelle Gordon, making ends meet these days depends on two lawn mowers, two trimmers and a broom. "I'm living with my mother. I'm 40 years old," she says.

She uses her experience as a lesson to her children. Daughter Essence, 19, has a high school diploma and a job and is attending college. Son Geno, 17, also has a summer job. Daughter Zoila, 15, says she won't have kids until she's married and established in life. The family gets food stamps, and the youngest two are on Medicaid, but they no longer get cash benefits.

The roller coaster Gordon has been riding for 10 years has made her less dependent on the government and more of a role model for her kids, she says.

"I'm not making $50,000 a year," she says, "but I'm keeping my head up, and I'm surviving."

Welfare rolls slashed across the U.S.

Welfare caseloads nationwide have declined by nearly 58% since the landmark overhaul of the nation's welfare system in 1996. How the numbers of families receiving welfare has changed, by state and territory (December 2005 figures are the most recent available):

State	Aug. 1996 families	Dec. 2005 families	Pct. change	State	Aug. 1996 families	Dec. 2005 families	Pct. change	State	Aug. 1996 families	Dec. 2005 families	Pct. change
Ala.	41,032	20,316	-50.5%	La.	67,467	13,888	-79.4%	Ore.	29,917	20,194	-32.5%
Alaska	12,159	3,590	-70.5%	Maine	20,007	9,516	-52.4%	Pa.	186,342	97,469	-47.7%
Ariz.	62,404	41,943	-32.8%	Md.	70,665	22,530	-68.1%	Puerto Rico	49,871	14,562	-70.8%
Ark.	22,069	8,283	-62.5%	Mass.	84,700	47,950	-43.4%	R.I.	20,670	10,063	-51.3%
Calif.	880,378	453,819	-48.5%	Mich.	169,997	81,882	-51.8%	S.C.	44,060	16,234	-63.2%
Colo.	34,486	15,303	-55.6%	Minn.	57,741	27,589	-52.2%	S.D.	5,829	2,876	-50.7%
Conn.	57,326	18,685	-67.4%	Miss.	46,428	14,636	-68.5%	Tenn.	97,187	69,361	-28.6%
Del.	10,585	5,744	-45.7%	Mo.	80,123	39,715	-50.4%	Texas	243,504	77,693	-68.1%
D.C.	25,350	16,209	-36.1%	Mont.	10,114	3,947	-61.0%	Utah	14,221	8,151	-42.7%
Fla.	200,922	57,361	-71.5%	Neb.	14,435	10,016	-30.6%	Vt.	8,765	4,479	-48.9%
Ga.	123,329	35,621	-71.1%	Nev.	13,712	5,691	-58.5%	Virgin Islands	1,371	421	-69.3%
Guam	2,243	3,072	37.0%	N.H.	9,100	6,150	-32.4%	Va.	61,905	9,615	-84.5%
Hawaii	21,894	7,243	-66.9%	N.J.	101,704	42,198	-58.5%	Wash.	97,492	55,910	-42.7%
Idaho	8,607	1,870	-78.3%	N.M.	33,353	17,773	-46.7%	W.Va.	37,044	11,275	-69.6%
Ill.	220,297	38,129	-82.7%	N.Y.	418,338	139,220	-66.7%	Wis.	51,924	17,970	-65.4%
Ind.	51,437	48,213	-6.3%	N.C.	110,060	31,746	-71.2%	Wyo.	4,312	294	-93.2%
Iowa	31,579	17,215	-45.5%	N.D.	4,773	2,789	-41.6%	U.S. total	4,408,508	1,870,039	-57.6%
Km.	23,790	17,-400	-26.9%	Ohio	204,240	81,425	-60.1%>				
Ky.	71,264	33,691	-52.7%	Okla.	35,986	11,104	-69.1%				

Source: Department of Health and Human Services

Purpose

The purpose of this reading is to help you understand the role the president plays in setting goals for US foreign policy and managing the United States' leadership role in world politics.

Context

President Obama won the prestigious Nobel Peace Prize in 2009. While receiving this award was controversial since he won it mere months after taking office, the speech gave him the opportunity to make very broad statements about the United States and her role in international politics, both in terms of promoting peace and in promoting US interests in the international arena.

Thought Questions

1. What does President Obama say about the need for the military actions to combat political violence and oppression? Under what circumstances is it warranted? What processes does he suggest for the application of military force?
2. In the speech, what alternatives does he pose to the use of military action? Is the combination of approaches he suggests practical, given the realities of human nature? Why or why not?
3. Some observers noted that, for a "peace prize" speech, there was a lot of talk in it of the US's willingness to apply military force. What do you think? Should he have been more "peaceful"? Or does the maintenance of peace in the international arena require some nations to have very strong military forces in order to hold megalomaniacs in check? Why or why not?

Web Link

1. Barack Obama, Nobel Peace Prize Acceptance Speech
   http://www.whitehouse.gov/the-press-office/remarks-president-acceptance-nobel-peace-prize

31. Remarks by the President at the Acceptance of the Nobel Peace Prize

Oslo, Norway

By Barack Obama

1:44 P.M. CET

THE PRESIDENT: Your Majesties, Your Royal Highnesses, distinguished members of the Norwegian Nobel Committee, citizens of America, and citizens of the world:

I receive this honor with deep gratitude and great humility. It is an award that speaks to our highest aspirations—that for all the cruelty and hardship of our world, we are not mere prisoners of fate. Our actions matter, and can bend history in the direction of justice.

And yet I would be remiss if I did not acknowledge the considerable controversy that your generous decision has generated. (Laughter.) In part, this is because I am at the beginning, and not the end, of my labors on the world stage. Compared to some of the giants of history who've received this prize—Schweitzer and King; Marshall and Mandela—my accomplishments are slight. And then there are the men and women around the world who have been jailed and beaten in the pursuit of justice; those who toil in humanitarian organizations to relieve suffering; the unrecognized millions whose quiet acts of courage and compassion inspire even the most hardened cynics. I cannot argue with those who find these men and women—some known, some obscure to all but those they help—to be far more deserving of this honor than I.

But perhaps the most profound issue surrounding my receipt of this prize is the fact that I am the Commander-in-Chief of the military of a nation in the midst of two wars. One of these wars is winding down. The other is a conflict that America did not seek; one in which we are joined by 42 other countries—including Norway—in an effort to defend ourselves and all nations from further attacks.

Still, we are at war, and I'm responsible for the deployment of thousands of young Americans to battle in a distant land. Some will kill, and some will be killed. And so I come here with an acute sense of the costs of armed conflict—filled with difficult questions about the relationship between war and peace, and our effort to replace one with the other.

Now these questions are not new. War, in one form or another, appeared with the first man. At the dawn of history, its morality was not questioned; it was simply a fact, like drought or disease—the manner in which tribes and then civilizations sought power and settled their differences.

And over time, as codes of law sought to control violence within groups, so did philosophers and clerics and statesmen seek to regulate the destructive power of war. The concept of a "just war" emerged, suggesting that war is justified only when certain conditions were met: if it is waged as a last resort or in self-defense; if the force used is proportional; and if, whenever possible, civilians are spared from violence.

Of course, we know that for most of history, this concept of "just war" was rarely observed. The capacity of human beings to think up new ways to kill one another proved inexhaustible, as did our capacity to exempt from mercy those who look different or pray to a different God. Wars between armies gave way to wars between nations—total wars in which the distinction between combatant and civilian became blurred. In the span of 30 years, such carnage would twice engulf this continent. And while it's hard to conceive of a cause more just than the defeat of the Third Reich and the Axis powers, World War II was a conflict in which the total number of civilians who died exceeded the number of soldiers who perished.

In the wake of such destruction, and with the advent of the nuclear age, it became clear to victor and vanquished alike that the world needed institutions to prevent another world war. And so, a quarter century after the United States Senate rejected the League of Nations—an idea for which Woodrow Wilson received this prize—America led the world in constructing an architecture to keep the peace: a Marshall Plan and a United Nations, mechanisms to govern the waging of war, treaties to protect human rights, prevent genocide, restrict the most dangerous weapons.

In many ways, these efforts succeeded. Yes, terrible wars have been fought, and atrocities committed. But there has been no Third World War. The Cold War ended with jubilant crowds dismantling a wall. Commerce has stitched much of the world together. Billions have been lifted from poverty. The ideals of liberty and self-determination, equality and the rule of law have haltingly advanced. We are the heirs of the fortitude and foresight of generations past, and it is a legacy for which my own country is rightfully proud.

And yet, a decade into a new century, this old architecture is buckling under the weight of new threats. The world may no longer shudder at the prospect of war between two nuclear superpowers, but proliferation may increase the risk of catastrophe. Terrorism has long been a tactic, but modern technology allows a few small men with outsized rage to murder innocents on a horrific scale.

Moreover, wars between nations have increasingly given way to wars within nations. The resurgence of ethnic or sectarian conflicts; the growth of secessionist movements, insurgencies, and failed states—all these things have increasingly trapped civilians in unending chaos. In today's wars, many more civilians are killed than soldiers; the seeds of future conflict are sown, economies are wrecked, civil societies torn asunder, refugees amassed, children scarred.

I do not bring with me today a definitive solution to the problems of war. What I do know is that meeting these challenges will require the same vision, hard work, and persistence of those men and women who acted so boldly decades ago. And it will require us to think in new ways about the notions of just war and the imperatives of a just peace.

We must begin by acknowledging the hard truth: We will not eradicate violent conflict in our lifetimes. There will be times when nations—acting individually or in concert—will find the use of force not only necessary but morally justified.

I make this statement mindful of what Martin Luther King Jr. said in this same ceremony years ago: "Violence never brings permanent peace. It solves no social problem: it merely creates new and more complicated ones." As someone who stands here as a direct consequence of Dr. King's life work, I am living testimony to the moral force of non-violence. I know there's nothing weak—nothing passive—nothing naive—in the creed and lives of Gandhi and King.

But as a head of state sworn to protect and defend my nation, I cannot be guided by their examples alone. I face the world as it is, and cannot stand idle in the face of threats to the American people. For make no mistake: Evil does exist in the world. A non-violent movement could not have halted Hitler's armies. Negotiations cannot convince al Qaeda's leaders to lay down their arms. To say that force may sometimes be necessary is not a call to cynicism—it is a recognition of history; the imperfections of man and the limits of reason.

I raise this point, I begin with this point because in many countries there is a deep ambivalence about military action today, no matter what the cause. And at times, this is joined by a reflexive suspicion of America, the world's sole military superpower.

But the world must remember that it was not simply international institutions—not just treaties and declarations—that brought stability to a post-World War II world. Whatever mistakes we have made, the plain fact is this: The United States of America has helped underwrite global security for more than six decades with the blood of our citizens and the strength of our arms. The service and sacrifice of our men and women in uniform has promoted peace and prosperity from Germany to Korea, and enabled democracy to take hold in places like the Balkans. We have borne this burden not because we seek to impose our will. We have done so out of enlightened self-interest—because we seek a better future for our children and grandchildren, and we believe that their lives will be better if others' children and grandchildren can live in freedom and prosperity.

So yes, the instruments of war do have a role to play in preserving the peace. And yet this truth must coexist with another—that no matter how justified, war promises human tragedy. The soldier's courage and sacrifice is full of glory, expressing devotion to country, to cause, to comrades in arms. But war itself is never glorious, and we must never trumpet it as such.

So part of our challenge is reconciling these two seemingly irreconcilable truths—that war is sometimes necessary, and war at some level is an expression of human folly. Concretely, we must direct our effort to the task that President Kennedy called for long ago. "Let us focus," he said, "on a more practical, more attainable peace, based not on a sudden revolution in human nature but on a gradual evolution in human institutions." A gradual evolution of human institutions.

What might this evolution look like? What might these practical steps be?

To begin with, I believe that all nations—strong and weak alike—must adhere to standards that govern the use of force. I—like any head of state—reserve the right to act unilaterally if necessary to defend my nation. Nevertheless, I am convinced that adhering to standards, international standards, strengthens those who do, and isolates and weakens those who don't.

The world rallied around America after the 9/11 attacks, and continues to support our efforts in Afghanistan, because of the horror of those senseless attacks and the recognized principle of self-defense. Likewise, the world recognized the need to confront Saddam Hussein when he invaded Kuwait—a consensus that sent a clear message to all about the cost of aggression.

Furthermore, America—in fact, no nation—can insist that others follow the rules of the road if we refuse to follow them ourselves. For when we don't, our actions appear arbitrary and undercut the legitimacy of future interventions, no matter how justified.

And this becomes particularly important when the purpose of military action extends beyond self-defense or the defense of one nation against an aggressor. More and more, we all confront difficult questions about how to prevent the slaughter of civilians by their own government, or to stop a civil war whose violence and suffering can engulf an entire region.

I believe that force can be justified on humanitarian grounds, as it was in the Balkans, or in other places that have been scarred by war. Inaction tears at our conscience and can lead to more costly intervention later. That's why all responsible nations must embrace the role that militaries with a clear mandate can play to keep the peace.

America's commitment to global security will never waver. But in a world in which threats are more diffuse, and missions more complex, America cannot act alone. America alone cannot secure the peace. This is true in Afghanistan. This is true in failed states like Somalia, where terrorism and piracy is joined by famine and human suffering. And sadly, it will continue to be true in unstable regions for years to come.

The leaders and soldiers of NATO countries, and other friends and allies, demonstrate this truth through the capacity and courage they've shown in Afghanistan. But in many countries, there is a disconnect between the efforts of those who serve and the ambivalence of the broader public. I understand why war is not popular, but I also know this: The belief that peace is desirable is rarely enough to achieve it. Peace requires responsibility. Peace entails sacrifice. That's why NATO continues to be indispensable. That's why we must strengthen U.N. and regional peacekeeping, and not leave the task to a few countries. That's why we honor those who return home from peacekeeping and training abroad to Oslo and Rome; to Ottawa and Sydney; to Dhaka and Kigali—we honor them not as makers of war, but of wagers—but as wagers of peace.

Let me make one final point about the use of force. Even as we make difficult decisions about going to war, we must also think clearly about how we fight it. The Nobel Committee recognized this truth in awarding its first prize for peace to Henry Dunant—the founder of the Red Cross, and a driving force behind the Geneva Conventions.

Where force is necessary, we have a moral and strategic interest in binding ourselves to certain rules of conduct. And even as we confront a vicious adversary that abides by no rules, I believe the United States of America must remain a standard bearer in the conduct of war. That is what makes us different from those whom we fight. That is a source of our strength. That is why I prohibited torture. That is why I ordered the prison at Guantanamo Bay closed. And that is why I have reaffirmed America's commitment to abide by the Geneva Conventions. We lose ourselves when we compromise the very ideals that we fight to defend. (Applause.) And we honor—we honor those ideals by upholding them not when it's easy, but when it is hard.

I have spoken at some length to the question that must weigh on our minds and our hearts as we choose to wage war. But let me now turn to our effort to avoid such tragic choices, and speak of three ways that we can build a just and lasting peace.

First, in dealing with those nations that break rules and laws, I believe that we must develop alternatives to violence that are tough enough to actually change behavior—for if we want a lasting peace, then the words of the international community must mean something. Those regimes that break the rules must be held accountable. Sanctions must exact a real price. Intransigence must be met with increased pressure—and such pressure exists only when the world stands together as one.

One urgent example is the effort to prevent the spread of nuclear weapons, and to seek a world without them. In the middle of the last century, nations agreed to be bound by a treaty whose bargain is clear: All will have access to peaceful nuclear power; those without nuclear weapons will forsake them; and those with nuclear weapons will work towards disarmament. I am committed to upholding this treaty. It is a centerpiece of my foreign policy. And I'm working with President Medvedev to reduce America and Russia's nuclear stockpiles.

But it is also incumbent upon all of us to insist that nations like Iran and North Korea do not game the system. Those who claim to respect international law cannot avert their eyes when those laws are flouted. Those who care for their own security cannot ignore the danger of an arms race in the Middle East or East Asia. Those who seek peace cannot stand idly by as nations arm themselves for nuclear war.

The same principle applies to those who violate international laws by brutalizing their own people. When there is genocide in Darfur, systematic rape in Congo, repression in Burma—there must be consequences. Yes, there will be engagement; yes, there will be diplomacy—but there must be consequences when those things fail. And the closer we stand together, the less likely we will be faced with the choice between armed intervention and complicity in oppression.

This brings me to a second point—the nature of the peace that we seek. For peace is not merely the absence of visible conflict. Only a just peace based on the inherent rights and dignity of every individual can truly be lasting.

It was this insight that drove drafters of the Universal Declaration of Human Rights after the Second World War. In the wake of devastation, they recognized that if human rights are not protected, peace is a hollow promise.

And yet too often, these words are ignored. For some countries, the failure to uphold human rights is excused by the false suggestion that these are somehow Western principles, foreign to local cultures or stages of a nation's development. And within America, there has long been a tension between those who describe themselves as realists or idealists—a tension that suggests a stark choice between the narrow pursuit of interests or an endless campaign to impose our values around the world.

I reject these choices. I believe that peace is unstable where citizens are denied the right to speak freely or worship as they please; choose their own leaders or assemble without fear. Pent-up grievances fester, and the suppression of tribal and religious identity can lead to violence. We also know that the opposite is true. Only when Europe became free did it finally find peace. America has never fought a war against a democracy, and our closest friends are governments that protect the rights of their citizens. No matter how callously defined, neither America's interests—nor the world's—are served by the denial of human aspirations.

So even as we respect the unique culture and traditions of different countries, America will always be a voice for those aspirations that are universal. We will bear witness to the quiet dignity of reformers like Aung Sang Suu Kyi; to the bravery of Zimbabweans who cast their ballots in the face of beatings; to the hundreds of thousands who have marched silently through the streets of Iran. It is telling that the leaders of these governments fear the aspirations of their own people more than the power of any other nation. And it is the responsibility of all free people and free nations to make clear that these movements—these movements of hope and history—they have us on their side.

Let me also say this: The promotion of human rights cannot be about exhortation alone. At times, it must be coupled with painstaking diplomacy. I know that engagement with repressive regimes lacks the satisfying purity of indignation. But I also know that sanctions without outreach—condemnation without discussion—can carry forward only a crippling status quo. No repressive regime can move down a new path unless it has the choice of an open door.

In light of the Cultural Revolution's horrors, Nixon's meeting with Mao appeared inexcusable—and yet it surely helped set China on a path where millions of its citizens have been lifted from poverty and connected to open societies. Pope John Paul's engagement with Poland created space not just for the Catholic Church, but for labor leaders like Lech Walesa. Ronald Reagan's efforts on arms control and embrace of perestroika not only improved relations with the Soviet Union, but empowered dissidents throughout Eastern Europe. There's no simple formula here. But we must try as best we can to balance isolation and engagement, pressure and incentives, so that human rights and dignity are advanced over time.

Third, a just peace includes not only civil and political rights—it must encompass economic security and opportunity. For true peace is not just freedom from fear, but freedom from want.

It is undoubtedly true that development rarely takes root without security; it is also true that security does not exist where human beings do not have access to enough food, or clean water, or the medicine and shelter they need to survive. It does not exist where children can't aspire to a decent education or a job that supports a family. The absence of hope can rot a society from within.

And that's why helping farmers feed their own people—or nations educate their children and care for the sick—is not mere charity. It's also why the world must come together to confront climate change. There is little scientific dispute that if we do nothing, we will face more drought, more famine, more mass displacement—all of which will fuel more conflict for decades. For this reason, it is not merely scientists and environmental activists who call for swift and forceful action—it's military leaders in my own country and others who understand our common security hangs in the balance.

Agreements among nations. Strong institutions. Support for human rights. Investments in development. All these are vital ingredients in bringing about the evolution that President Kennedy spoke about. And yet, I do not believe that we will have the will, the determination, the staying power, to complete this work without something more—and that's the continued expansion of our moral imagination; an insistence that there's something irreducible that we all share.

As the world grows smaller, you might think it would be easier for human beings to recognize how similar we are; to understand that we're all basically seeking the same things; that we all hope for the chance to live out our lives with some measure of happiness and fulfillment for ourselves and our families.

And yet somehow, given the dizzying pace of globalization, the cultural leveling of modernity, it perhaps comes as no surprise that people fear the loss of what they cherish in their particular identities—their race, their tribe, and perhaps most powerfully their religion. In some places, this fear has led to conflict. At times, it even feels like we're moving backwards. We see it in the Middle East, as the conflict between Arabs and Jews seems to harden. We see it in nations that are torn asunder by tribal lines.

And most dangerously, we see it in the way that religion is used to justify the murder of innocents by those who have distorted and defiled the great religion of Islam, and who attacked my country from Afghanistan. These extremists are not the first to kill in the name of God; the cruelties of the Crusades are amply recorded. But they remind us that no Holy War can ever be a just war. For if you truly believe that you are carrying out divine will, then there is no need for restraint—no need to spare the pregnant mother, or the medic, or the Red Cross worker, or even a person of one's own faith. Such a warped view of religion is not just incompatible with the concept of peace, but I believe it's incompatible with the very purpose of faith—for the one rule that lies at the heart of

every major religion is that we do unto others as we would have them do unto us.

Adhering to this law of love has always been the core struggle of human nature. For we are fallible. We make mistakes, and fall victim to the temptations of pride, and power, and sometimes evil. Even those of us with the best of intentions will at times fail to right the wrongs before us.

But we do not have to think that human nature is perfect for us to still believe that the human condition can be perfected. We do not have to live in an idealized world to still reach for those ideals that will make it a better place. The non-violence practiced by men like Gandhi and King may not have been practical or possible in every circumstance, but the love that they preached— their fundamental faith in human progress—that must always be the North Star that guides us on our journey.

For if we lose that faith—if we dismiss it as silly or naive; if we divorce it from the decisions that we make on issues of war and peace—then we lose what's best about humanity. We lose our sense of possibility. We lose our moral compass.

Like generations have before us, we must reject that future. As Dr. King said at this occasion so many years ago, "I refuse to accept despair as the final response to the ambiguities of history. I refuse to accept the idea that the 'isness' of man's present condition makes him morally incapable of reaching up for the eternal 'oughtness' that forever confronts him."

Let us reach for the world that ought to be— that spark of the divine that still stirs within each of our souls. (Applause.)

Somewhere today, in the here and now, in the world as it is, a soldier sees he's outgunned, but stands firm to keep the peace. Somewhere today, in this world, a young protestor awaits the brutality of her government, but has the courage to march on. Somewhere today, a mother facing punishing poverty still takes the time to teach her child, scrapes together what few coins she has to send that child to school—because she believes that a cruel world still has a place for that child's dreams.

Let us live by their example. We can acknowledge that oppression will always be with us, and still strive for justice. We can admit the intractability of depravation, and still strive for dignity. Clear-eyed, we can understand that there will be war, and still strive for peace. We can do that—for that is the story of human progress; that's the hope of all the world; and at this moment of challenge, that must be our work here on Earth.

Thank you very much. (Applause.)
END
2:20 P.M. CET

CPSIA information can be obtained at www.ICGtesting.com
Printed in the USA
LVOW03s2122081213

364268LV00016B/125/P